Cracking the
AP®
SPANISH
Exam

with Audio CD

2013 Edition

The Princeton Review®

Cracking the
AP®
SPANISH
Exam
with Audio CD
2013 Edition

By Mary Leech

PrincetonReview.com

Random House, Inc. New York

The Princeton Review, Inc.
111 Speen Street
Suite 550
Framingham, MA 01701
E-mail: editorialsupport@review.com

Antología de la poesía española del siglo XX (1890–1939). Arturo Ramoneda ed., Alianza Editorial, S.A., Madrid, 1995. Reprinted by permission. Special thanks to Herederos de Juan Ramón Jiménez for permission to reprint.
Thanks also to Drake Turrentino for use of the name Special Olympics.
Every effort has been made to trace and acknowledge copyright material.
The author and publisher would welcome any information from the people who believe they own copyrights to material in this book.

The Princeton Review is not affiliated with Princeton University.

ISBN: 978-0-307-94518-1
ISSN: 1933-1053

Editor: Calvin S. Cato
Production Editor: Stephanie Tantum
Production Coordinator: Deborah A. Silvestrini

Printed in the United States of America on partially recycled paper.

10 9 8 7 6 5 4 3 2

2013 Edition

Editorial
Robert Franek, Senior VP, Publisher
Laura Braswell, Senior Editor
Selena Coppock, Senior Editor
Calvin Cato, Editor
Meave Shelton, Editor

Production
Michael Pavese, Publishing Director
Kathy Carter, Project Editor
Michelle Krapf, Editor
Michael Mazzei, Editor
Michael Breslosky, Associate Editor
Stephanie Tantum, Associate Editor
Kristen Harding, Associate Editor
Vince Bonavoglia, Artist
Danielle Joyce, Graphic Designer

Random House Publishing Team
Tom Russell, Publisher
Nicole Benhabib, Publishing Manager
Ellen L. Reed, Production Manager
Alison Stoltzfus, Managing Editor

ACKNOWLEDGMENTS

I would like to thank Lesly Atlas, Marika Alzadon, Evelin Sanchez-O'Hara, Allegra Viner, Patricia Dublin, Katie O'Neill, Jennifer Arias, Omar Amador, John Moscatiello, and Dan Edmonds for their tireless efforts producing this book. I would also like to thank Daniel Wallance and Chad Singer for their expert technical support. I feel indebted to Josette Amsellem, James P. Godfrey, and William Moore for their guidance and friendship, which greatly enhanced my initiation into the field of teaching. I would like to thank my colleague Margaret Callery, and also Amy Brown and Nelly Rosario, for their expert review of the Spanish portions of the manuscript.

I would also like to thank my parents for encouraging and facilitating my advanced studies of Spanish. Last, but certainly not least, I would like to thank my husband, David, for his continued love and support.

The Princeton Review would like to thank Michael Giammarino for a thorough review of this edition. Special thanks to Kim Howie, Emma Parker, and Meave Shelton.

CONTENTS

INTRODUCTION

WHAT IS THE PRINCETON REVIEW?

The Princeton Review is an international test-preparation company with branches in all major U.S. cities and several cities abroad. In 1981, John Katzman started teaching an SAT course in his parents' living room. Within five years, The Princeton Review had become the largest SAT coaching program in the country.

The Princeton Review's phenomenal success in improving students' scores on standardized tests is the result of a simple, innovative, and radically effective approach: Study the test, not what the test *claims* to test. This approach has led to the development of techniques for taking standardized tests based on the principles the test writers use to write the tests.

The Princeton Review has found that its methods work not only for cracking the SAT, but also for any standardized test. We've successfully applied our system to the GMAT, GRE, LSAT, and MCAT, to name just a few. Although the AP Spanish Literature and Language exams are different than the exams mentioned above, a standardized test is a standardized test.

WHY DO YOU NEED THIS BOOK?

Of course, it is important to know Spanish in order to do well on the Spanish Language and Literature exams, but it is also important to be a shrewd test taker. In this book, you'll find strategies for smart test taking. We offer suggestions to help you scrutinize and maximize your performance on test day. In addition, we will give you some background on the Advanced Placement (AP) program, and provide you with practice tests so that you can perfect your test-taking skills before test day.

1

ABOUT THE ADVANCED PLACEMENT PROGRAM

WHAT IS THE ADVANCED PLACEMENT PROGRAM?

The Advanced Placement program is administered by the College Board, which is the same organization that coordinates college admissions exams. The College Board consists of college educators, administrators, and admissions officers in addition to high school educators, guidance counselors, and administrators. Advanced Placement courses are offered in high schools across the United States in thirty-two disciplines.

As you may know, the Advanced Placement courses offered in high schools are generally the most demanding and therefore the most prestigious courses available. They are considered college-level high school courses.

Students enrolled in AP courses are expected, although not obligated, to take the corresponding AP exam offered in May. Exams are graded on a scale of 1 to 5 with 5 being the highest grade. Depending on the college, the student may earn hours of college credit for a grade of 3 or better. It is important to note that a student does not have to enroll in the AP course offered to take the AP exam in May. This is particularly important information for native speakers of any language. Most native speakers with strong written skills will earn a 5 on the AP Language exam with little or no advanced preparation. In fact, most strong language students or native speakers have nothing but the price of the exam to lose. In fact, the process of taking the test is considered by many educators to be a valuable learning experience.

WHY ENROLL IN AP COURSES? WHY TAKE THE AP EXAMS?

As the name implies, Advanced Placement courses are more demanding than regular high school courses. AP classes require more outside reading and much more writing in the form of weekly essays, textual analyses, tests, and, in some cases, research papers. In addition to the increased workload, students in AP courses will most likely encounter harder grading standards and possibly a lower grade. So, why take AP courses?

- **Admissions officers look favorably upon transcripts that include AP courses.**

  The student with college aspirations will find that the AP program provides several advantages. For one, some admissions officers consider an AP grade equivalent to the next highest grade in the regular course. Thus a B in an AP course would be equivalent to an A in a regular course.

- **AP courses demonstrate that you are committed to a rigorous level of study.**

  A second advantage to AP courses is that they provide a good introduction to college-level courses. In other words, AP courses prepare students best by emphasizing the skills most needed in college, such as extensive outside reading and frequent essay writing. In many cases, students accustomed to AP courses make a very smooth transition to college-level study because these courses teach students to think. Simply stated, students in AP courses are likely to learn more in any educational environment.

- **AP courses can save you time and money.**

  AP courses culminate with the AP exam. If you earn a grade of 3 or higher, you may be awarded college credit. Considering the cost of college credit hours, AP courses may save a considerable amount of money for successful AP exam takers. In some colleges, a student who receives high enough grades on three or more AP exams may be admitted as a sophomore. There is virtually nothing to lose by taking either the AP Spanish Language or Literature Exam, except the cost of the exam.

WHAT ARE THE AP SPANISH LANGUAGE AND LITERATURE EXAMS?

The AP Spanish Language Exam is intended to test the four basic language skills: reading, writing, listening, and speaking. The exam is made up of two main sections that test these skills. Part I is the multiple-choice section, which is divided into listening and reading portions. Part II of the exam is the free-response section, which includes both written and spoken responses.

The AP Spanish Literature Exam is also divided into two main sections. Part I consists of various literary passages followed by multiple-choice questions. This section includes both listening and written passages. Part II is the free-response portion of the exam, which is divided into three essay questions.

Detailed information about both exams will follow in the coming chapters.

HOW TO GET STARTED

If you are interested in taking an AP exam, you should speak to your school guidance counselor. The guidance counselor should direct you to the school's AP coordinator. The AP coordinator is responsible for registering students for the exam, collecting exam fees, and ordering and administering exams. If, for any reason, you are not able to take the AP exam at your own school, arrangements may be made for you to take the test at another school. You may inquire about schools offering the test by calling the College Board's AP Services office at 609-771-7300, or write by March 1 to PO Box 6671, Princeton, New Jersey, 08541-6671.

The fee for each exam is $87. Generally, the school keeps a small amount of that fee for administrative costs. The school may, upon request, refund part or all of this amount to students with financial need. The College Board also offers a fee reduction to students with financial need. If, for some reason, a student needs to take the test at a time different from the scheduled date, an additional fee may be assessed. All fees are to be paid to the school AP coordinator. The College Board will not accept direct payments from students.

RECOMMENDED TIMETABLE FOR STUDENTS

Generally, students take the AP Spanish Literature Exam during senior year, although very advanced students may take it earlier. The AP Spanish Language Exam is generally taken during junior or senior year, although native Spanish speakers could probably take it earlier if necessary.

JANUARY: You should meet with your Spanish teacher to discuss the exam. If you choose to take the exam, you should speak to the appointed AP coordinator to register and submit the fees. If you have any special needs (which we discuss in greater detail later), you should make arrangements at this time. If, for any reason, your school does not offer the AP exam, you should contact the College Board and request the nearest location of a school offering the exam.

MARCH: If you have not expressed your interest in taking the exam, do so ASAP!

Early to mid MAY*: AP Spanish Language Exam is offered in the morning session.

Early to mid MAY*: AP Spanish Literature Exam is offered in the afternoon session.

JUNE: Exams are graded by more than 3,000 college and high school faculty consultants. If you wish to send your scores to colleges other than those listed on the exam registration form, or if you wish to cancel the reporting of the scores, you may submit your request to ETS until June 15.

JULY: Exam grades are sent to students' designated colleges, home high schools, and home addresses.

*Check the most up-to-date exam schedule at http://professionals.collegeboard.com/testing/ap/about/dates

ON EXAM DAY

You will want to bring the following items:

- two No. 2 pencils for the multiple-choice section (make sure you have an eraser)
- a pencil sharpener
- a black or blue pen for the essay questions
- a watch
- photo identification
- your school code

You may NOT bring the following items:

- dictionaries, books, notes, scratch paper
- electronic translators or laptop computers
- cameras or radios
- cell phones or MP3 players

Special Circumstances

Students with special needs, such as disabilities, who require particular testing conditions should have either a signed letter from the appropriate professional (psychologist, doctor, learning specialist, and so on) or a current Individualized Education Program (IEP) on file at the school. The IEP should describe the disability and confirm the need for different testing conditions. Students with valid disabilities have a variety of options. Vision-impaired students, for example, may take large-type or Braille tests, or they may use a reader.

It is very important that students with special needs document their disabilities so that score reports accurately reflect the testing situation as a "Certified Disability." Without the proper documentation, the score report will indicate "Nonstandard Administration," which would be the designation given to students without disabilities who took the exam untimed. Clearly, an untimed exam suggests an unfair advantage if there is no documented disability and reflects poorly on a student's score report. Thus, students with disabilities should contact the AP coordinator as soon as possible (no later than April 1) to stipulate testing conditions. Documentation should be prepared and ready well before the exam date.

Exam-Day Errors

Although they are not very common, errors do occasionally occur on exam day. Occasionally, the College Board writes a lousy question. Once in a blue moon ETS misprints a test question, misprints a page of the exam, or even leaves it blank! It is important to remember that these errors are very infrequent. If, during the test, you believe that one or more of the questions on the test is invalid or unfair, you should contact the College Board as soon as possible after the test. Provide the test title, the question number, and a description of what you think was wrong with the question. Such errors are very unlikely to occur on the Spanish Language or Spanish Literature exams. They generally occur on math or science exams.

It is more likely that an error may occur in the administering of the actual exam, for instance, if the directions are poorly stated. You should have no difficulty with poorly read instructions on exam day because this book will review instructions and the format of the AP exams in great detail. More troublesome, however, is a proctor who times the exam incorrectly. If you find that you've been given too little time to complete the exam, you should contact the school's administration immediately. If you wait too long, you may be forced to retake the exam, or even worse, get stuck with the score you received on the mistimed exam.

That covers what happens when the College Board, ETS, or your proctor messes up. What about when *you* mess up? If you think (or know) that you blew the exam, you have until June 15 to contact the College Board and cancel your score. You should also contact the College Board by June 15 if you wish to change the list of colleges receiving score reports. In most cases, unless you feel you have earned a score of 1 or lower, scores should not be canceled.

The following is a list of things that you should avoid doing at all costs on exam day. Any one of them could get you thrown out of the test (leading to your scores being canceled), or question the validity of your performance on the exam.

- Leafing through the exam booklet before the exam begins

- Working on the wrong section of the exam

- Trying to get answers from or give answers to another student during the exam

- Continuing to work on the exam after you have been instructed to stop

- Tearing a page out of the exam booklet or trying to sneak the exam out of the testing location

- Using notes, textbooks, dictionaries, electronic translators, and so on during the exam

FINALLY...

Much of the information covered in this chapter also appears in a free College Board publication called *Bulletin for AP Students and Parents*. You should be able to get a copy of it from your college counselor. If not, write for your copy to

AP Services
PO Box 6671
Princeton, New Jersey
08541-6671

The College Board website is another good source of information. Please check out
http://apcentral.collegeboard.com

2

GOOD TEST-TAKING STRATEGIES

Very few students stop to think about how to improve their test-taking skills. Most assume that if they study very hard, they will test well; if they don't study, they will do poorly. Most students continue to believe this even after experience teaches them otherwise. Have you ever studied really hard for an exam, then blown it on test day? Or, maybe you aced an exam you barely studied for. If the latter is true, you were probably employing good test-taking strategies without even realizing it.

Make no mistake; studying thoroughly will enhance your performance on the exam. However, in addition to that, this section targets the best test-taking techniques that will help you perform better on the AP Spanish Language and the AP Spanish Literature Exams—and on other exams as well.

TEST ANXIETY

Everyone experiences some kind of nervousness or anxiety before and during an important exam. Some students are able to channel that energy and use it to help them enhance their performance. A little anxiety can actually help students focus more clearly and work more effectively on an exam. However, that is not always the case. In high-stress situations, some students find they are unable to recall any of the information they so painstakingly studied. These students may become increasingly nervous and make poor decisions on the remaining portions of the exam. If you find that you stress out during exams, here are a few preemptive actions you can take.

- **Take a reality check.** Assess your strengths and weaknesses before entering the testing room. If you have in fact studied thoroughly, you should feel satisfied that you've done your best to prepare for the exam. Also, keep in mind that not all students taking the exam will be as prepared as you are, so you already have an advantage. If you didn't study enough, you probably won't ace the test.

- **Don't forget to breathe!** Deep breathing works for almost everybody. Take a few seconds, close your eyes, and take a few slow deep breaths, concentrating on nothing but inhaling and exhaling. This is a basic form of meditation and should help you clear your mind of stress and facilitate good concentration. Learning to relax is the key to a successful performance in almost any situation, especially during standardized tests.

- **Be prepared.** Those Boy Scouts couldn't be more right about this one. The best way to avoid excessive anxiety on test day is to study the subject material and the test itself. By reading this book, you are taking a major step toward a stress-free AP Spanish Exam. Also, make sure you know where the test is, when it starts, what type of questions are going to be asked, and how long the test will take. Of course, you should have with you all the materials you'll need during the exam (see page 5). You don't want to be worrying about any of this on the day of the test.

- **Be realistic about your final score.** Given your background, preparation, and interest level, you should aim to do your own personal best. For native speakers with good written skills, the Language exam should be an easy 5, although you will need to be prepared and focus well on the exam. For excellent nonnative speakers, the Language exam should be challenging, but manageable. For both native and nonnative speakers, the Literature exam should be a significant challenge.

PACING

A large part of scoring well on an exam is working at a consistent pace. The worst mistake made by test takers is that they spend too long on a single question. Rather than skipping a question they can't answer, they panic and stall. Students lose all sense of time when they are trying to answer a question that puzzles them. You want to be sure to get to every question you *do* know something about.

It is very important for you to pace yourself, and to pay close attention to the number of multiple-choice questions per section and the total time allotted for that section. Try not to skip too many of the easy questions, and don't spend an inordinate amount of time pondering the difficult ones. If you draw a complete blank on a few questions, it may be appropriate to skip them and come back to them later. Often, after returning to a question later, you are able to think more clearly and answer the previously puzzling question more easily. Such minor victories often provide a significant boost in morale and help to refuel your energy. However, if you are still unable to answer a couple of difficult questions, you should just skip them.

One important note: If you decide to skip any of the questions and return to them later, you must be certain that you also skip the corresponding oval on the answer sheet. This may seem obvious, but, nonetheless, it can be a costly mistake that would throw off the rest of your answers on the test, resulting in a disastrous score. Make a note next to any skipped questions in your test booklet, not on your answer sheet.

PROCESS OF ELIMINATION (POE)

The usefulness of the Process of Elimination is one of the gifts of multiple-choice questions. The idea is simple: Knowing which answer is right is the same as knowing which answers are wrong, so if you can do either, you can pick up a point. If you can eliminate answers that you know are wrong, you will eventually stumble upon the right answer because it will be the only one left. POE may vary a bit for different types of questions, but the general idea is always the same.

THE WEEKS BEFORE THE EXAM

There are a few things you should start doing some time after January 1 (but certainly before May 1). One of them is to read this book. Here are some others.

- **Ask your teacher for copies of old exams.** The College Board makes available copies of old exams for both the Language and Literature exams. Study them well. Be sure to take into account changes in format if you are taking the Language exam!

- **Practice!** You may also try making your own outline of Spanish grammar and verb forms. For the listening portion of the exam, you may like to listen to language tapes and check your own comprehension. Listening to Spanish radio stations and television programs may also increase listening comprehension.

- **Commit a little time each night to test preparation.** Your teacher can provide you with past Literature exams complete with essay and poetry questions. For each practice test you study, you should briefly review the five authors' biographies and the cultural and historical circumstances of their times. You should also review in greater detail all the works studied, making outlines that include the main characters and major themes of each work. It is very important to examine how the same theme may be treated differently by different authors. Spend time studying literary terminology and poetic devices. You should also practice writing answers to prior essay questions and timing yourself to see that you can complete the essays in 30 to 40 minutes. Later, you should ask your teacher if you may set up a time to review these essays together. Most teachers will be happy to help you out. They would prefer that their own students do as well as possible on the exam because it makes them look good.

Spend time each night reviewing the grammar topics, verb forms, and vocabulary lists for the Language exam. In addition, you should practice speaking about various thematic topics, such as your favorite pastimes, class schedule, and so on. You should also practice reading comprehension passages and questions. A regular short period of study time each night is preferable to cramming the week prior to the exam. By late March, you should ideally spend about 45 minutes four times per week reviewing this book, primary texts, class notes, outlines, and any other class materials.

You may also consider forming study groups in which each member is responsible for a specific portion of the material. In both the Literature and Language exams, you can benefit from explaining your understanding of the material verbally in Spanish.

THE FINAL WEEK BEFORE THE EXAM

- **Maintain your usual routine**. You may have more than one AP exam to take during the month of May. Get plenty of rest the week before and during the week of the exams, but try not to change your sleeping patterns too drastically. You should also avoid drastic changes in diet or exercise.

- **Do a general subject review.** You should focus less on details and more on general issues. For the Language exam, you should do a general grammar review, looking over your own outlines. You should practice speaking and writing about various academic and conversational topics, such as your daily routine, your favorite foods, as well as prominent social issues, such as equal rights for women, or the increasing threat of pollution in the environment.

  For the Literature exam, you should practice writing two essays (with outlines) on thematic questions and one essay on a prior poetry question. Review your own outlines on the authors and literary works studied.

- **Know all the directions for the exam**. Familiarize yourself with the instructions to each portion of the exam by reading them in this book. You should clearly understand all instructions before test day.

THE DAY OF THE EXAM

- **Start the day with a reasonable, but not huge, breakfast.** You'll need energy for the exam. Beware of drinking too much liquid, such as coffee or tea, because it may cause frequent trips to the restroom.

- **Wear comfortable clothing.** Dressing in light layers is a good idea. You don't want to feel too hot or too cold while trying to concentrate on an important exam.

- **Take a snack.** A piece of fruit or a candy bar during the break can give you a much-needed energy boost.

FINALLY

The fewer surprises encountered on test day, the better the chances of your success. If you are holding this book right now, congratulations—you're already ahead of the game.

SUMMARY

- Begin preparing for your exam a few months in advance. Study for at least 45 minutes three to four times per week. Review old copies of prior exams.

- Practice your speaking skills, study vocabulary and grammar, and ask your teacher to review the essays you have written.

- Get plenty of rest, and maintain a regular routine during the week before the exams.

- On test day, you should dress comfortably, eat sensibly, and take the proper materials to the testing site.

- Maintain a consistent pace throughout the exam and avoid spending too much time on any one question.

- Beat test anxiety. Prepare for the test so that there will be few surprises on test day. Don't forget to breathe.

PART ◆ I

AP SPANISH LANGUAGE:
HOW TO CRACK THE SYSTEM

OVERVIEW

The AP Spanish Language Exam consists of the following two sections:

- **Section I** is the multiple-choice section, which tests *listening* and *reading* skills.
- **Section II** is the free-response section, which tests *writing, listening,* and *speaking* skills.

The College Board provides a breakdown of the types of questions covered on the exam. This breakdown will *not* appear in your test booklet: It comes from the preparatory material the College Board publishes. The chart below summarizes exactly what you need to know for the AP Spanish Language Exam.

Multiple-Choice Section I	Description	Number of Questions	Percent of Grade	Time
Part A: Listening	Short and Long Dialogues and Narratives	30–35 questions	20%	30–35 mins.
Part B: Reading Comprehension	Reading Comprehension	35–40 questions	30%	50–60 mins.

Free-Response Section II	Description	Number of Questions	Percent of Grade	Time
Part A: Writing	Interpersonal Writing	1 prompt (10%) 10 minutes	30%	Approx. 65 min.
	Formal Writing	1 prompt (20%) 55 minutes		
Part B: Speaking	Informal Speaking (Simulated Conversation)	5–6 response prompts (10%) 20 seconds to respond to each	20%	Approx. 20 min.
	Formal Oral Presentation (Integrated Skills)	1 prompt (10%) 2 minutes to respond		

Clearly, the composition in the free-response section will be weighted significantly. No need to worry; this book will show you exactly what the AP readers look for in an essay. Also, note the weight of the listening exercises. You should prepare for those sections of the exam as thoroughly as possible. The following chapters examine the various sections of the exam in greater detail.

Let's take a closer look at the question types on the Writing portion of the exam:

- **Interpersonal Writing:** As the name suggests, you'll be asked to write in an informal style and format; for example, the assignment may involve writing a letter or e-mail to a friend or close relative. You'll have only ten minutes for this section, so you shouldn't plan to write more than a couple of paragraphs.

- **Formal Writing:** Formal writing, in the language of the College Board, means writing a clear, well-organized essay. Unlike the old essay question, which allowed you to focus on your own views and experiences, the new essay requires you to synthesize information from a variety of print and audio sources. You'll be given an essay prompt and several minutes to read and listen to the materials before you start writing.

That's it for the Writing portion of the test. Here's what you can expect to find on the Speaking portion:

- **Informal Speaking:** Like the old Oral Cues section, this section requires you to verbally respond to a series of recorded cues. Your responses will be guided by an outline of a short conversation, which will be provided. You will be assigned one side of the conversation, and the recording will supply the other. Your responses will be recorded.

- **Formal Oral Presentation:** For this part of the test, you will be asked to speak for two minutes, as if you were delivering an oral presentation. As in the Formal Writing section, the presentation will involve synthesizing information from print and audio materials. You will be given a prompt, as well as time to read and listen to the materials and to prepare your answer. Once again, your answer will be recorded.

A NOTE ON DIRECTIONS

All directions in the examination booklet will be printed in English and in Spanish. You won't really need to spend much time reading directions on test day because you are using this book and will be very familiar with the test directions already. Nevertheless, choose the language you are more comfortable with and skim only that set of the directions. Don't waste time reading both sets of directions, or worse yet, comparing the translations for accuracy.

3

THE MULTIPLE-CHOICE SECTION:
LISTENING AND READING

THE BASICS

The multiple-choice section (Section I) of the AP Spanish Language Exam tests two major skills: listening and reading. It is made up of two parts, A and B. The listening portion of the exam (Part A) tests your understanding of spoken Spanish. The reading portion of the exam (Part B) tests your knowledge of Spanish vocabulary, as well as structure and comprehension of written passages.

The table on the next page breaks down the multiple-choice section for your reference.

Multiple-Choice Section I	Description	Number of Questions	Percent of Grade	Time
Part A: Listening	Short and Long Dialogues and Narratives	30–35 questions	20%	30–35 mins.
Part B: Reading	Reading Comprehension Passages	35–40 questions	30%	50–60 mins.

The following exercises will give you a pretty good indication of the types of multiple-choice questions you'll see on the actual test.

PART A: LISTENING

The listening portion of the exam is accompanied by a tape recording. In the sample passages and questions that follow, the information that is printed in *italics* is heard only by the student, and *does not* appear printed in the examination booklet. You can listen to these sections on the audio CD included with this book. General directions for the dialogues and narratives appear at the beginning of each new set of exercises, printed in the test booklet in both English and Spanish.

In Part A, you will encounter three different types of spoken exercises: dialogues, short narratives, and then slightly longer narratives, each approximately five minutes in length. For these five-minute narrative exercises, the questions are heard on the master tape, but do not appear printed in the examination booklets; conversely, the answer choices are not spoken on the master tape, but appear printed in the test booklets.

DIALOGUES

You will hear a series of dialogues on various subjects and be asked to choose the correct answer for three to five questions per dialogue.

Remember: Information printed in this text in italics is heard, not read. You can listen to these sections on the audio CD included with this book.

Sample Dialogue

Here are the general directions for the dialogues that you will see printed in your test booklet on test day.

Directions: You will now listen to a series of dialogues. After each one, you will be asked some questions about what you have just heard. Select the best answer to each question from among the four choices printed in your test booklet and fill in the corresponding oval on the answer sheet.

Remember: Information printed here in italics is heard, not read.

AUDIO CD: Track 1

Anita: *Buenos días, Doña Clara, ¿cómo le va?*

Doña Clara: *Pues aquí, fregando el suelo, con los niños pasando continuamente por esta cocina. Siempre me dejan los pies marcados en el suelo.*

Anita: *Perdone, siento que la interrumpa, pero ¿está Elena en casa?*

Doña Clara: *No, no es nada. Sí, Elenita está con su abuela. Están hablando de la boda de su hermana.*

Anita: *¿Dónde están? ¿Están en el salón?*

Doña Clara: *No, están en el jardín.*

1. *¿Dónde tiene lugar esta conversación?*
   (A) En el salón
   (B) En el jardín
   (C) En la cocina
   (D) En la casa de Anita

2. *¿Qué está haciendo Doña Clara?*
   (A) Limpiando
   (B) Interrumpiendo
   (C) Pasando
   (D) Cantando

3. *¿Qué está haciendo Elena?*
   (A) Hablando con su hermana
   (B) Paseando con los niños
   (C) Hablando con su abuela
   (D) Casándose

Here's How to Crack It

In these dialogues, a considerable bit of information is communicated. Remember: You will *hear* these dialogues and the accompanying questions only once; you will not see them in printed form. You will have about twelve seconds to choose the correct answers and blacken the corresponding ovals on your answer sheet. It is important to listen carefully and choose the most obvious answer. Do your best to follow along with the conversations, and do not fall behind answering the numbered questions after the dialogues.

Listening comprehension is what is being tested here, and most answers will not be conceptually difficult. Don't bother trying to write down any notes at this point; simply listen attentively. You will need to remember the context of the conversation to answer the questions accurately.

Answers and Explanations to the Sample Dialogue

Translation

Anita: Good morning, Doña Clara. How are you?

Doña Clara: Well, I'm here, scrubbing the floor, with the children continually passing through this kitchen. They always leave footprints marked on the floor for me!

Anita: Excuse me, I'm sorry to interrupt, but is Elena home?

Doña Clara: No, it's no bother. Yes, Elenita is with her grandmother. They are talking about her sister's wedding.

Anita: Where are they? In the living room?

Doña Clara: No, they are in the garden.

1. Where does this conversation take place?
   (A) In the living room
   (B) In the garden
   (C) In the kitchen
   (D) In Anita's house

The conversation takes place in the kitchen where Doña Clara is cleaning the floor. We know that she is in the kitchen because Doña Clara complains about the children constantly running through *esta cocina*, or "this kitchen." Anita comes into the kitchen and interrupts Doña Clara in her work.

2. What is Doña Clara doing?
   (A) Cleaning
   (B) Interrupting
   (C) Passing through
   (D) Singing

As suggested above, Doña Clara is cleaning. *Fregando* literally means "scrubbing" or "mopping." Thus, of the choices, (A) is the obvious answer.

3. What is Elena doing?
   (A) Talking with her sister
   (B) Walking around with the children
   (C) Talking with her grandmother
   (D) Getting married

Elena, as it turns out, is not present in the dialogue. Her friend Anita comes calling on her. Doña Clara tells Anita that Elenita, her affectionate name for Elena, is talking with her grandmother.

SHORT NARRATIVES

You will also hear a series of two to three short narratives on various topics. You will be asked three to five oral questions on what you have just heard. You must choose among the four answers printed in your test booklet and blacken the corresponding oval on your answer sheet.

Sample Short Narrative

Here are the general directions for the short narratives that you will see printed in your test booklet on test day.

> **Directions:** You will now listen to a series of short narratives. After each one, you will be asked some questions about what you have just heard. Select the best answer to each question from among the four choices printed in your test booklet and fill in the corresponding oval on the answer sheet.

Remember: Information printed here in italics is heard, not read.

> AUDIO CD: Track 2

El mercado hispano en Estados Unidos

El mercado hispano en Estados Unidos es una fuente de oportunidad para muchas compañías grandes. El mercado hispano en EE.UU. es un mercado que está creciendo más día a día. Hay hispanohablantes en casi todas las ciudades grandes del país, sobre todo en Nueva York, Los Angeles, Chicago, Dallas, San Antonio y San Francisco, por mencionar sólo algunas. Todas las grandes compañías han visto el valor del consumidor hispano en el mercado actual. Muchas compañías grandes como los productores de refrescos, los restaurantes de servicio rápido y los productores de zapatillas deportivas gastan mucho dinero en publicidad dirigida al consumidor hispano. El típico consumidor hispano es muy tradicional, le gusta la familia. También le gustan los valores tradicionales. Es un consumidor fiel a las marcas que considera de buena calidad. El consumidor hispano identifica fácilmente las marcas que le gustan. No le importa gastar más dinero en un producto si es un producto de buena calidad.

El mercado hispano seguirá creciendo. Las compañías que ignoran la importancia del mercado hispano lo hacen a su propio riesgo. El consumidor hispano es una fuerza potente en el mercado del futuro.

4. *¿Qué tienen en común las ciudades de Nueva York, Los Angeles, Chicago, Dallas, San Antonio y San Francisco?*
   (A) Tienen una gran población de personas que hablan español.
   (B) Los nombres son de origen hispano.
   (C) Son ciudades crecientes.
   (D) Son ciudades con grandes compañías.

5. *¿Qué están haciendo con respecto al mercado hispano las compañías grandes como los productores de refrescos y zapatillas deportivas?*

   (A) Están comprando más productos.

   (B) Están creciendo más y más.

   (C) Están comprando publicidad para el mercado hispano.

   (D) Están comprando productos hechos por hispanos.

6. *¿Cómo es el típico consumidor hispano?*

   (A) Joven

   (B) Mayor

   (C) Liberal

   (D) Conservador

7. *¿Con cuáles marcas se identifica el consumidor hispano?*

   (A) Marcas hispanas

   (B) Marcas de buena calidad

   (C) Marcas de mala calidad

   (D) Marcas que cuestan menos

Here's How to Crack It

Again, in this portion of the exam it is important to follow along with the narrative, as the oral questions that follow it will be based on the context of the narrative. Try not to fall behind, and don't get stressed out if you hear a few words you don't understand. Try to understand the main ideas and, most important, try to keep pace with the narrative. You shouldn't try to take notes at this point, but listen very attentively. Also listen carefully to the oral questions. In most cases, they are fairly straightforward. If they aren't, remember to try to weed out the wrong answers using POE (Process of Elimination).

Answers and Explanations to the Sample Short Narrative

Translation

The Hispanic Market in the United States

The U.S. Hispanic market is a source of opportunity for many large companies. The U.S. Hispanic market is a market that is growing daily. There are Spanish speakers in almost all of the major U.S. cities, especially in New York, Los Angeles, Chicago, Dallas, San Antonio, and San Francisco, just to name a few. All of the large companies have seen the value of the Hispanic consumer in today's marketplace. Many of these companies, such as beverage producers, quick-service restaurants, and sport-shoe producers, spend a lot of money on advertising directed at the Hispanic consumer. The typical Hispanic consumer is very traditional; he likes the family. He also likes traditional values. The Hispanic consumer is also one who is loyal to the brand names that he considers of good quality. He identifies very easily with the brands that he likes. It doesn't matter to him to spend more money on a product if it is of better quality. The Hispanic market will continue to grow. The companies that ignore the importance of the Hispanic market do so at their own risk. The Hispanic consumer is a strong force in the marketplace of the future.

4. What do the cities New York, Los Angeles, Chicago, San Antonio, and San Francisco have in common?

(A) **They have a large population of Spanish speakers.**

(B) Their names are of Hispanic origin.

(C) They are growing cities.

(D) They are cities with large companies.

Answer choices (B), (C), and (D) may or may not be true, but they have nothing to do with the short narrative. Therefore, the correct answer is (A); each of those cities has a large Spanish-speaking population.

5. What are the large companies, such as the beverage producers and the sport-shoe producers, doing with respect to the Hispanic market?

(A) They are buying more products.

(B) They are growing more and more.

(C) **They are buying advertising for the Hispanic market.**

(D) They are buying products made by Hispanics.

The word for advertising is *publicidad*. The large companies are, in fact, buying advertising directed at the Hispanic market. Notice that incorrect answer choices (A) and (D) also include the verb *comprando* to see if you can be easily fooled; don't fall into this trap.

6. What is the typical Hispanic consumer like?

(A) Young

(B) Old

(C) Liberal

(D) **Conservative**

The typical Hispanic consumer is *tradicional*, which is closest to *conservador*. If this isn't immediately apparent, you may use POE to rule out the other answer choices. The age range (*joven* or *mayor*) of the typical Hispanic consumer is impossible to identify without detailed demographic information, which is not discussed in the short narrative. *Liberal* doesn't really make any sense, so it is an obvious wrong answer.

7. With which brand names does the Hispanic consumer identify?

(A) Hispanic brand names

(B) **Good-quality brand names**

(C) Bad-quality brand names

(D) Economical brand names

Hispanic consumers identify with good-quality brands. In fact, we are told that they do not mind paying more for an item if it is of better quality. Therefore, you should use POE to rule out answer choices (C) and (D). Nothing in the narrative indicates that the Hispanic market identifies with only Hispanic brand names, so you can say *adiós* to (A) as well.

FIVE-MINUTE NARRATIVES

In addition to the dialogues and short narratives, you will hear two oral pieces of about five minutes in length each. These five-minute narratives may be interviews, cultural communications, broadcasts, or anything else deemed appropriate for oral communication. In this portion of the exam, you will be allowed and, in fact, encouraged to take notes. Your notes will not be graded. Remember: Everything printed in italics will be spoken on the master tape but *not* printed in your test booklet.

Note: Unlike the dialogues and short narratives, you will *not* be permitted to see the printed questions while listening to the recording during these five-minute narratives.

Sample Five-Minute Narrative

Here are the general directions for the five-minute narratives that you will see printed in your test booklet on test day.

Directions: You will now listen to a selection of about five minutes in duration. You should take notes in the blank space provided. You will not be graded on these notes. At the end of the selection, you will read a number of questions about what you have heard. Based on the information provided in the selection, select the BEST answer for each question from among the four choices printed in your test booklet and fill in the corresponding oval on the answer sheet.

Remember: Information printed here in italics is heard, not read.

AUDIO CD: Track 3

Interview with Luz Hurtado, Fashion Editor of the magazine *Mujer Moderna*.

(Ahora, vamos a escuchar una entrevista con una persona muy informada en el mundo de la moda, Srta. Luz Hurtado, editora de la revista Mujer Moderna.*)*

MAN: *Luz, para empezar, ¿puedes describirnos a la lectora típica de la revista* Mujer Moderna? *Es decir, ¿a quién va dirigida la revista?*

WOMAN: *Nuestra revista va dirigida a la mujer de hoy, principalmente entre los veinte y treinta y cinco años. Muchas de nuestras lectoras trabajan, pero otras se dedican a la familia y el hogar. Casi todas tienen en común un interés apasionado en la moda. No son necesariamente mujeres que trabajan en la industria de la moda, pero muchas mujeres de la industria también leen nuestra revista. Digamos que nuestra revista lleva el mundo interior de la moda a la mujer contemporánea.*

MAN: *¿Cómo se diferencia* Mujer Moderna *de las otras revistas de moda?*

WOMAN: *Es una pregunta muy importante. Cuando me ofrecieron el puesto de editora de esta revista, me pregunté, '¿quiero de verdad trabajar en otra revista de moda?' Yo había trabajado en el pasado como reportera en otras revistas de moda, y no me interesaba la idea de trabajar en otra revista igual a las demás. Pero* Mujer Moderna *es distinta porque se dirige a la mujer que vive en el mundo real de hoy. No se trata de una revista de muñecas en un mundo protegido, o un mundo de fantasía. Nuestras lectoras viven en el mundo real, trabajan en el mundo real y se ocupan de la familia en el mundo real. No nos dedicamos exclusivamente a la moda, sino al papel de la moda dentro del complicado mundo moderno.*

MAN: *He leído que la revista* Mujer Moderna *está muy metida en varias causas sociales, sobre todo los niños que nacen con el virus del SIDA. ¿Puedes explicarnos la relación entre la moda y esta causa social tan importante?*

WOMAN: *Aunque quizás sea un poco fuera de lo corriente en el mundo de la moda, yo creo que es sumamente importante que ayudemos a los menos afortunados. ¿Hay víctima más inocente que un pobre niño que nace contaminado con el virus del SIDA?* Mujer Moderna *procura cultivar una relación con causas sociales para demostrar a nuestras lectoras que es la responsabilidad de cada una de nosotras contribuir a mejorar la sociedad. Además, hubo otros que crearon relaciones entre la moda y la causa social; por ejemplo, recordemos la figura de la Princesa Diana.*

MAN: *Es cierto, Diana fue símbolo de la moda y la causa social. Era una persona muy admirable, ¿no crees?*

WOMAN: *Claro que fue admirable. Era una persona buenísima. La figura pública era solamente una parte de la persona de Diana. La conocí en varias ocasiones y me impresionaron muchísimo su sinceridad y su interés genuino en la gente que sufre.*

MAN: *Cambiando un poco de tema, ¿tiene valor tu revista para el hombre moderno?*

WOMAN: *Yo creo que hay mucho valor para el hombre moderno que se interese en causas sociales que nos afectan a todos. Claro que también tendrá interés para el hombre que quiere enterarse de la última moda de sus amigas, su novia, su esposa, su madre, su hermana, etcétera. En fin, es una revista dirigida principalmente a la gente interesada en la moda femenina, basándose en una filosofía filantrópica. Por eso, puede interesarle también a muchos hombres. Sin embargo, también tenemos una sección de deportes muy buena. (Ella ríe.)*

MAN: *¿Qué relación hay, si es que hay, entre la moda y el deporte?*

WOMAN: *Claro que hay relación entre ambos. La moda puede ser considerada como una actitud hacia la vida. Se puede ver la moda en cada cosa que hacemos. O las hacemos con o sin estilo. Todo depende de la mentalidad y el nivel de interés del individuo. En los deportes, por ejemplo, hay un mundo de moda que ha evolucionado precisamente alrededor del deporte. El tenis y el golf son dos ejemplos muy claros. Tienen una moda muy concreta que permite expresar el estilo individualista también. Por ejemplo, los tenistas americanos Andre Agassi y las hermanas Williams muestran su individualidad con la ropa poco tradicional que llevan y la forma en el diseño de sus peinados. Gusten o no los estilos que llevan, hay que admirar su estilo individualista.*

MAN: *Claro, los tres son muy originales. Pero dinos, Luz, ¿cómo empezaste en el mundo de la moda?*

WOMAN: *Siempre, desde pequeña me ha interesado la moda de los hombres y las mujeres. Mi padre trabajaba con el cuerpo diplomático español, y nosotros pasamos mucho tiempo en el extranjero. Vivimos en Milán, en París, en Singapur y en Nueva York. Quizás por los cambios que observé entre los estilos de las culturas variadas, me incliné al mundo de la moda. También, sentí desde muy pequeña una responsabilidad por los desafortunados. Mi madre siempre se dedicaba a las causas sociales. Aprendí mucho de ella.*

MAN: *Bueno, Srta. Luz Hurtado, ya se nos acabó el tiempo. Muchas gracias por estar aquí con nosotros.*

(Ha terminado esta selección. No se leerán las preguntas en voz alta, pues las tienes impresas en tu libreta de examen. Ahora pasa a las preguntas. Te quedan cuatro minutos para elegir las respuestas correctas. FIN DE LA GRABACIÓN)

8. *¿A quién va dirigida la revista* Mujer Moderna?

   (A) Las mujeres del mundo interior de moda.

   (B) Las mujeres que trabajan.

   (C) La mujer que se ocupa de la familia y la casa.

   (D) La mujer contemporánea del mundo actual.

9. *¿Cómo se distingue* Mujer Moderna *de las otras revistas de moda?*

   (A) Es una revista de muñecas.

   (B) Es una revista de fantasía.

   (C) Se dedica a cómo la moda forma parte de la vida en el mundo actual.

   (D) Se dedica exclusivamente al mundo interior de la moda.

10. *¿Por qué está metida la revista* Mujer Moderna *en la causa social de los niños que nacen con el virus del SIDA?*

   (A) Quiere dar ejemplo de responsabilidad hacia los desafortunados.

   (B) Quiere ser más contemporánea.

   (C) Era la causa de la Princesa Diana.

   (D) Es la moda ayudar a los menesterosos.

11. *¿Qué hay de interés para el hombre moderno en* Mujer Moderna?

   (A) Puede aprender de la moda para hombres.

   (B) Puede aprender de la moda para su madre, hermana, novia o esposa.

   (C) Puede aprender sobre la Princesa Diana.

   (D) Puede aprender sobre si mismo.

12. *¿Qué relación hay entre la moda y el deporte, según la entrevista?*

   (A) Muchos deportes tienen una moda desarrollada alrededor de ellos.

   (B) Muchos deportistas son modelos.

   (C) Todos los deportistas tienen mucho estilo.

   (D) La moda y el deporte son sinónimos.

Answers and Explanations to the Sample Five-Minute Narrative

Translation

Now we are going to listen to an interview with someone very informed in the world of fashion, Ms. Luz Hurtado, editor of the magazine *Modern Woman*.

MAN: Luz, to begin, can you describe for us the typical reader of *Modern Woman*? In other words, who is your target audience?

WOMAN: Our magazine is directed at the woman of today, primarily between the ages of twenty and thirty-five years of age. Many of our readers work, but others devote themselves to the care of family and the home. Almost all of them have in common a deep interest in fashion.

They are not necessarily those who work in the fashion industry, although many women in the fashion world do read our magazine. Let's say that our magazine brings the insider world of fashion to the contemporary woman.

MAN: How is *Modern Woman* different from other fashion magazines?

WOMAN: That is a very important question. When they offered me the job of editor at this magazine, I asked myself, "Do I really want to work for another fashion magazine?" I had worked in the past as a reporter for other fashion magazines, and I was no longer interested in working for another magazine like all of the others. But *Modern Woman* is different because it is directed at the woman who lives in the real world of today. It is not about silly dolls in a protected world or fantasy world. Our readers live in the real world, they work in the real world, and they care for their families in the real world. We don't devote ourselves exclusively to fashion but rather to the role of fashion in the complicated modern world.

MAN: I have read that *Modern Woman* is very involved in various social causes, above all, children who are born with the AIDS virus. Can you explain to us the relationship between fashion and this very important social cause?

WOMAN: Although it may be a bit out of the ordinary in the world of fashion, I think it is extremely important that we help those who are less fortunate. Is there a more innocent victim than a poor child who has been born contaminated with the AIDS virus? *Modern Woman* tries to foster a relationship with social causes to show our readers that it is the responsibility of each and every one of us to contribute to the improvement of society. Furthermore, there have been others who have cultivated a relationship between fashion and social causes; for example, let's remember the image of Princess Diana.

MAN: That's true. Princess Diana was a symbol of fashion and of dedication to social causes. She was a very admirable person, don't you think so?

WOMAN: Of course she was admirable. She was a very good person. The public figure was only a part of Diana. I met her on various occasions and was impressed by her sincerity and her genuine concern for those who suffer.

MAN: Changing the topic a bit if I may, is your magazine valuable for the modern man?

WOMAN: I think that there is a lot of value for the modern man who is interested in social causes that affect us all. Of course, it will also be interesting to the man who wants to find out about the latest fashion trends of his female friends, his girlfriend, his wife, his mother, or his sister. In short, it is a magazine directed primarily at those interested in feminine fashion, based on a philanthropic philosophy. For that reason, it can also be interesting to many men. However, we also have a very good sports section. (She laughs.)

MAN: What relationship is there, if any, between fashion and sports?

WOMAN: Of course there is a relationship between them. Fashion could be considered an attitude toward life. Fashion can be seen in everything that we do. We either do them with style or without style. It all depends on the mentality and the level of interest of the individual. For example, there is an entire fashion that has evolved precisely around sports. Tennis and golf are two very clear examples. They have a very determined fashion requirement that allows for individual styles as well. For example, the American tennis players Andre Agassi and the Williams sisters show their individuality with the unique clothing that they wear and their hairstyles. Whether or not we care for the styles they wear, we must admire their individualistic styles.

MAN: Of course, all three are very original. But tell us Luz, how did you get started in the world of fashion?

WOMAN: Always, ever since I was young, men's and women's fashions have interested me. My father worked in the Spanish Diplomatic Service, so we spent a lot of time abroad. We lived in Milan, Paris, Singapore, and New York. Perhaps because of the differences I observed between the styles of clothing of the various cultures, I leaned toward the field of fashion. I have also, since I was young, always felt a sense of responsibility for the less fortunate. My mother always dedicated herself to social causes. I learned a great deal from her.

MAN: Well, Ms. Luz Hurtado, we've run out of time. Thank you very much for being here with us.

The short narrative has finished. The questions will not be read out loud because you have them printed in your test booklet. Now you may go on to the questions. You have four minutes to choose the correct answers. End of recording.

Here's How to Crack It

As with the short narratives, it is imperative that you keep up with the pace of the five-minute narrative. Don't worry if there are words that you don't understand. Try to comprehend the major ideas being discussed. Use the space provided to take notes, which should help you maintain focus on the narrative. You may write your notes in any language that you choose, although it may be easier to jot things down in Spanish and later translate your notes into English if necessary. Make sure not to draw from your own opinions or ideas that may not have been voiced in the five-minute narrative. For example, in question 11, you may feel that there is nothing pertinent for the modern man in *Modern Woman*, but that is not what is discussed in the interview. Luz Hurtado tried to identify reasons for the modern man to read her magazine, and that is the basis we have for answering the question. Always remember to use POE to eliminate any ridiculous or obviously wrong answers. The test writers know that it is difficult to retain everything you hear in the five-minute narrative, and they are certain to throw in a few easily eliminated answers to get you on the right track.

8. Who is the target audience of *Modern Woman*?
   (A) Women from the inside world of fashion.
   (B) Women who work.
   (C) Women who care for their homes and families.
   (D) The contemporary women of the real world.

The correct answer is (D). The target audience of the magazine *Modern Woman* is the contemporary woman of today. Luz Hurtado says that the magazine is directed at those women who work and those who stay home and take care of the family. It tries to appeal to as many groups as possible. Use POE to eliminate answer choices (A), (B), and (C).

9. How is the magazine *Modern Woman* different from other fashion magazines?
   (A) It is a magazine about dolls.
   (B) It is a fantasy magazine.
   (C) It is devoted to the role of fashion in the real world today.
   (D) It is devoted exclusively to the inside world of fashion.

Modern Woman is different from other magazines because, according to the interview, it tries to explore the relationship between fashion and life in the modern world of today. It is not a magazine about dolls (A), nor of fantasy (B), nor an insider fashion magazine (D). Answer choices (C) and (D) may seem close, but the word *exclusivamente* in choice (D) should clue you in to the correct answer, choice (C), since you already know that the magazine tries to encompass a wide audience.

10. Why is *Modern Woman* involved with children that are born with the AIDS virus?
    (A) To provide an example of responsibility to the needy.
    (B) To be more contemporary.
    (C) It was Princess Diana's cause.
    (D) It is fashionable to help the needy.

Even if you didn't know that SIDA means AIDS in Spanish, you should be able to identify the one reasonable response among these four choices. If you use POE, you would quickly eliminate (C) and (D): The magazine would not be involved with a social cause just because Princess Diana had been involved without talking in greater detail about her. To say that it is fashionable to help those in need is just plain silly. Choice (B) is more reasonable, but once you compare it with (A), you'll find the correct answer.

11. What is of interest to the modern man in *Modern Woman*?
    (A) He can learn about men's fashions.
    (B) He can learn of the fashion trends affecting his mother, sister, girlfriend, or wife.
    (C) He can learn about Princess Diana.
    (D) He can learn about himself.

Choice (B) is the correct answer. According to the interview, the modern man can learn about the fashion interests of his sister, female friends, mother, girlfriend, or wife by reading *Modern Woman*. Rule out (A) since men's fashion is never discussed in the interview except for a mention of Andre Agassi's individuality on the tennis court. Choices (C) and (D) simply refer to topics mentioned in the interview but not thoroughly discussed.

12. What relationship exists between fashion and sports, according to the interview?
   (A) Many sports have a fashion developed around them.
   (B) Many sports figures are models.
   (C) All sports figures have a lot of style.
   (D) Fashion and sports are synonymous.

According to what is said in the interview, the relationship between sports and fashion is that many sports figures, such as those in golf and tennis, develop their own styles within the sport. Choice (D) is completely wrong; fashion and sports are not synonymous. Choices (B) and (C) may be true but are not discussed in the interview. POE cancels these out right away.

PART B: READING

The reading portion of the exam is designed to test your reading comprehension skills as well as your knowledge of Spanish grammar and vocabulary. In this section, you are asked to read short passages and answer the questions that follow. There are approximately six passages in Part B.

As we mentioned earlier, when you begin the multiple-choice portion of any standardized test, it is up to you to find the easier questions to do first. Reading comprehension passages are no exception. You should skim through the reading comprehension passages to determine the order in which you will work. Leave the most difficult one for last, and start with an easier passage. This is important; if you run out of time, it is better to be working on the passage that is most difficult and where you would potentially miss the most questions anyway.

THE BIG PICTURE (HOW TO READ)

For the reading comprehension passages, you should read through the entire passage once for the general meaning. Next, you should scan the questions that follow the reading, and then go back through the reading and find the answers. Most of the questions will follow very logically from the order of the actual reading. In the first reading, try to identify the main topic of the passage, and get the general idea of the content. If you understand what the overall passage is about, and you can identify the main point in each paragraph, you've read the passage properly. Don't worry about facts or details (such as names, dates, places, or titles). Focus on the whole passage. Don't dwell on a few words that you do not understand or read a sentence over and over again if you don't understand it. Focus on general ideas and main ideas from each paragraph; this way you will know where to find the answers to the questions that do focus on the details.

TYPES OF PASSAGES

The main types of passages are fictional pieces and pieces that discuss current events or cultural topics. Passages can now include web pages or other multimedia materials. Subject matter has nothing to do with the difficulty of a passage. You may feel that if a certain passage is about a topic familiar to you, it will contain vocabulary that you understand. Don't assume anything. Read a few sentences to make sure.

QUESTION ORDER

The questions for each passage are best done in the order in which they appear (although you want to follow the golden rule of skipping any question that looks really difficult). This is because the order of questions usually follows the progression of the passage—early questions come from the beginning of the passage, and subsequent questions come from the middle and end of the passage. Something that you read in the early part of the passage can sometimes help on a later question.

As with the paragraph completion exercises we discussed earlier, there may be a tendency to feel as if you're not done until you've answered every question for each passage. However, if you've done all the questions that you understand and can easily find the answers to, then move on to the next passage and see if you can find some easy questions there.

ANSWERING QUESTIONS

Although some questions ask you about the main idea or the overall content of the passage, most questions ask you about specific details that come from a particular part of the passage. These are the two types of questions: general and specific.

General Questions

After finishing the first reading, you should scan the set of questions and look for those that may be of a general nature. If you looked for the main idea and structure of the reading the first time through, then you will be able to answer these general questions quite easily. Some sample general questions include the following.

¿Quién narra este pasaje?

Who is narrating the passage?

¿De qué se trata este pasaje?

What is this passage about?

Specific Questions

Many of the reading comprehension questions ask you to refer back to the passage to look for details. This is why it is crucial to get a sense of the structure of the passage during the first reading. If you don't, you may waste a good deal of time looking for the specific point in the passage that answers the question. The approach to these questions is as follows:

- Read the question.

- Locate the source of the question by examining key words from the question.

- Carefully read the section in the passage that answers the question.

- Go to the answers and select the choice that best matches the information you read in the passage.

DON'T FORGET THE PROCESS OF ELIMINATION (POE)

One of the biggest problems students have with the reading comprehension section is that they don't like or understand any of the answer choices for some questions. Sometimes the correct answer to a reading comprehension question is so obvious that it will practically leap off the page. Other times, however, it may not be quite so simple. But with POE, even the most difficult questions can be conquered.

SAMPLE READING COMPREHENSION PASSAGE

Directions: Read the following passage carefully for comprehension. The passage is followed by a number of incomplete statements. Select the completion or answer that is best according to the passage and fill in the corresponding oval on the answer sheet.

El siguiente artículo apareció en 1996 en el periódico La Jornada de Lima.

LIMA, PERÚ: "No hubo ningún otro remedio", explicó el presidente peruano Alberto Fujimori al hablar con Eduardo Taboada, corresponsal extranjero de la
Línea *emisora Univisión, durante una entrevista realizada*
5 *en la capital peruana. Fujimori habló pocos minutos después del ataque militar contra el grupo terrorista Tupac Amaru, que se había apoderado de la embajada japonesa hacía 4 meses. El grupo, integrado por 22 guerrilleros y sus cuatro líderes, secuestró a 72 rehenes,*
10 *la mayoría de ellos diplomáticos extranjeros, quienes habían sido cautivos dentro del recinto japonés por 130 días.*

Los soldados peruanos iniciaron el ataque a las tres de la tarde, según el periodista Taboada, quien
15 *presenció el evento tan inesperado. A pesar de que el ataque empleara muchas estrategias, apenas duró cuarenta minutos. Un grupo de soldados se dirigió por la parte delantera de la embajada y otro grupo se abalanzó a la parte posterior. Utilizaron armas con*
20 *láser y rifles que hasta pudieron ubicar a los terroristas adentro, gracias a la ayuda de una computadora especial. Ninguno de los terroristas salió con vida de la residencia, de acuerdo con los informes del noticiero Univisión de Miami. La emisora nacional de Perú, NotiUno,*
25 *interrumpió su programación para transmitir en vivo escenas de la crisis. Pocos detalles fueron divulgados por la censura de la prensa para proteger a los rehenes.*

Fujimori proclamó orgullosamente que habían acabado de una vez con el terrorismo y nunca negociaría con
30 *terroristas, lo cual sigue siendo la política oficial del Perú. Sin embargo, Fujimori se vio obligado a iniciar conversaciones con los rebeldes fuertemente armados después de que varios gobiernos extranjeros, cuyos ciudadanos se encontraban dentro de la embajada,*
35 *presionaron para evitar un ataque militar. Fujimori sí dialogó con los rebeldes, pero al mismo tiempo iba planeando clandestinamente un asalto militar.*

        Mucha gente de la comunidad mundial
opinó que las acciones del gobierno peruano eran
40 *innecesarias. Un sacerdote conocido en el Perú,*
el Padre Xavier Venancio, reiterando la opinión
de la iglesia peruana, pensó que la situación podría
haberse resuelto a través de una manera pacífica.
El presidente Fujimori reafirmó que no había
45 *otra manera de resolver la crisis, ya que "se*
nos acababa el tiempo y nuestro compromiso
principal fue garantizar la seguridad y bienestar de
los rehenes. Esperar más no nos convenía". El
presidente japonés Hashimoto dijo pocos minutos
50 *después de la exitosa liberación de los rehenes que*
"no debe haber nadie que pueda criticar al
presidente". La prensa peruana confirmó esto, a
través de unas encuestas realizadas en todo el
territorio nacional en las cuales el noventa por
55 *ciento (90%) de la población peruana estuvo a*
favor de la acción militar de Fujimori. Con esta
nueva derrota de otro grupo subversivo, Fujimori
ya marca su segunda victoria militar contra el
terrorismo. En 1990, Fujimori arrasó con el grupo
60 *terrorista más temido del mundo, El Sendero Luminoso,*
tras el arresto de su enigmático líder, Aníbal Guzmán.
Con estos gloriosos éxitos, el gobierno peruano
pretende restaurar, según Fujimori, "el progreso,
la paz, y la prosperidad" en la nación andina.

La Jornada de Lima, 1996

15. *¿Por qué Fujimori negoció con los rebeldes?*

(A) Porque era su política oficial.

(B) Porque había sentido presión de otros países.

(C) Porque le daba tiempo para organizar un ataque militar simultáneamente.

(D) Todas las respuestas son correctas.

16. *¿Cuál de las siguientes oraciones no es verdadera sobre el asalto militar a la embajada?*

(A) El ataque había sido planeado detalladamente.

(B) El ataque ocasionó el fallecimiento de muchos terroristas.

(C) El ataque marcó la segunda vez que Fujimori había derrotado a un enemigo del Estado.

(D) Si se hubiera utilizado la tecnología, la crisis habría podido resolverse de una forma más eficaz y pacífica.

17. *Fue difícil publicar información sobre el ataque porque...*

(A) Univisión controló los detalles.

(B) Hubo pocos detalles.

(C) Hubo control estricto sobre la información.

(D) Los rehenes querían protegerse.

18. *Un titular apropiado para este artículo sería...*

(A) Fujimori en un jaque mate con los terroristas

(B) Salvajes invaden embajada, perecen muchos

(C) Fujimori deja que los terroristas lo pisoteen

(D) Negociaciones logran defraudar a los terroristas, militares triunfan

19. *La siguiente oración se puede añadir al texto:*
"Se sabe que la violencia no resuelve nada, y a su vez, perpetúa aún más violencia". ¿Dónde serviría mejor la oración?

(A) Línea 37

(B) Línea 41

(C) Línea 44

(D) Línea 56

20. *La siguiente oración se puede añadir al texto:*
"Sólo una pequeña minoría expresó su desdén ante la solución militar del Presidente". ¿Dónde serviría mejor la oración?

(A) Línea 36

(B) Línea 38

(C) Línea 41

(D) Línea 56

Answers and Explanations to the Sample Reading Comprehension Passage

Translation

The following article appeared in 1996 in the newspaper *La Jornada de Lima*.

LIMA, PERU: "There was no other solution," explained the Peruvian president Alberto Fujimori while speaking with Eduardo Taboada, foreign correspondent for the broadcast station Univisión, during an interview taking place in the Peruvian capital. Fujimori spoke several minutes after the military attack against the terrorist group Tupac Amaru, who had taken control of the Japanese embassy four months earlier. The group, comprised of 22 guerillas and their four leaders, had kidnapped 72 hostages—the majority of whom were foreign diplomats—and who were held captive inside the Japanese residence for 130 days.

The Peruvian soldiers began the attack at 3 P.M., according to the journalist Taboada, who witnessed the unexpected event. Yesterday's attack lasted only 40 minutes in spite of the fact that it involved many strategies. One group of soldiers rushed through the front part of the embassy, while the other group went to the back. They utilized weapons with lasers and rifles that were even able to locate the terrorists inside, thanks to the use of a special computer. None of the terrorists left the residence alive, according to reports from the news station Univisión in Miami. The national broadcast station of Peru, Notiuno, interrupted its programming to transmit live scenes of the crisis. Few details were divulged by the press in order to protect the hostages.

Fujimori proudly proclaimed that he had eliminated terrorism once and for all, and would never negotiate with terrorists, which continues to be the official policy of Peru. However, Fujimori was obliged to begin conversations with the heavily armed rebels, after various foreign governments, whose citizens were inside the embassy, pressured him to avoid a military assault. Fujimori did indeed speak with the rebels, but at the same time was secretly planning a military attack.

Many people of the global community felt that the actions of the Peruvian government were unnecessary. A well-known priest in Peru, Father Xavier Venancio, reiterating the opinion of the Peruvian church, felt that the situation could have been resolved through peaceful means. President Fujimori reaffirmed that there wasn't any other way to resolve the crisis, given that "time was running out for us, and our main goal was to guarantee the safety and well-being of the hostages. To wait any longer wouldn't have been beneficial. The Japanese president Hashimoto said a few minutes after the successful liberation of the hostages that "no one should be criticizing the president." The Peruvian press confirmed this, through interviews carried out throughout the nation in which ninety percent (90%) of Peruvians were in favor of Fujimori's military action. With this recent defeat of yet another subversive group, Fujimori marks his second victory against terrorism. In 1990, Fujimori obliterated the most feared terrorist group in the world, The Shining Path, with the arrest of its enigmatic leader, Anibal Guzman. With these glorious successes, the Peruvian government intends to restore, according to Fujimori, "progress, peace and prosperity" to the Andean nation.

Here's How to Crack It

15. Why did Fujimori negotiate with the rebels?

   (A) Because it was his official policy.

   (B) Because he received pressure from other countries.

   (C) Because it gave him time to organize a military attack at the same time.

   (D) All of these answers are correct.

Choice (B) is the correct answer because the article states that he began to dialogue with the rebels because the foreign governments wanted him to avoid a military attack. While Choice (C) may be correct, the article doesn't state that Fujimori used the negotiations to "buy time." Choice (A) is incorrect, because Fujimori is quoted as saying he would never negotiate with terrorists. As a result, choice (D) is also incorrect.

16. Which of the following phrases is not correct concerning the military assault on the embassy?

    (A) The attack was planned with great detail.

    (B) The attack caused the death of many terrorists.

    (C) The attack marks the second time that Fujimori defeats an enemy of the state.

    (D) If technology had been used, the crisis could have been solved in a more efficient and peaceful manner.

This type of question is sometimes included to trip up the fast reader. Be sure to focus on the qualifying word "no" in the question. Thus, this question is looking for a false statement. The article states that the attack employed many strategies, which would suggest that Answer (A) is a true statement. Likewise, Answer (B) is also true, as the article stated that there were 26 terrorists and that none escaped. Answer (C) is a true statement as the article at the end discusses Fujmori's past successes. Answer (D) is a false statement, as technology (lasers and computers) was indeed used to end the crisis quickly. Thus, (D) is the correct answer.

17. It was difficult to publicize information about the attack because...

    (A) Univisión controlled the details.

    (B) There were few details.

    (C) There was strict control over the information.

    (D) The hostages wanted to protect themselves.

Choice (C) is the correct answer, as the article states that there was strict control over the information. Choice (B) is a trap; although it is a true statement, it is not the cause of the difficulty in publicizing the information. Choice (D) is also a trap, as the hostages never expressed a desire to be protected. Rather, it was a decision of the press to do so. Univisión merely reported the news, and being located outside the area implies that it had no control over the details, so (A) is also incorrect.

18. An appropriate title for this article would be...

    (A) Fujimori in a checkmate with the terrorists.

    (B) Savages invade embassy, many perish.

    (C) Fujimori lets terrorists step all over him.

    (D) Negotiations manage to mislead terrorists, military triumphs.

The best answer is (D), as it captures the overall main idea of the article. While Choice (A) does show that Fujimori has the upper hand, it doesn't give the detail of Choice (D). Choice (B) refers to savages, which would not be used to describe the military in this article. Choice (C) is also incorrect, as it clearly is the opposite of the outcome of the standoff between the president and the terrorists.

19. The following sentence can be added to the text:
    "It is known that violence doesn't resolve anything, and in turn, perpetuates even more violence." Where would this fit best?

    (A) Line 37

    (B) Line 41

    (C) Line 44

    (D) Line 56

The correct answer is (C), as it would be a logical quote by the nonviolent priest mentioned in the article. In this position it advances the flow and meaning of the paragraph. Choice (A), line 37, does reinforce the idea of a nonviolent solution, but as our inserted sentence is an opinion, it wouldn't fit here since the following sentence is about planning a military intervention. Choice (D) is incorrect, as the previous sentence in the article speaks of the nation's overwhelming approval of the attack. While Choice (B) could also accommodate the sentence, a clearly better fit would be Choice (C) given the preceding and subsequent sentences. These types of questions are testing your ability to accommodate sentences in a paragraph where they would have the best flow and impact; be sure to read the surrounding sentences to get a better idea of where to put them.

20. The following sentence can be added to the text:
    "A small minority expressed their disdain towards the President's military solution." Where would this sentence fit best?

    (A) Line 36

    (B) Line 38

    (C) Line 41

    (D) Line 56

Choices (B) and (C) are incorrect as they would contradict the paragraph's topic sentence, which states that many people felt the military actions were unnecessary. Choice (D) is the correct answer as it complements the previous sentence that discusses how the majority of people felt, and thus it would make sense in that position to mention how the remainder felt. Choice (A) would not be a good position for that sentence as "various governments" of the previous sentence would constitute more than a small minority.

READING COMPREHENSION SUMMARY

- Choose the order in which you want to do the passages. Read a couple of sentences to see if the writing style is easy to follow and the vocabulary is manageable. If so, go for it. If not, look ahead for something easier.

- Read the passage for topic and structure only. Don't read for detail, and don't try to memorize the whole thing. The first read is for you to get a sense of the general idea and the overall structure—that's all.

- Go straight to the general questions. Ideally, you should be able to answer any general questions without looking back to the passage. However, very few passages have general questions, so don't expect to find many.

- Now, do the specific questions in order. For these, you're going to let the key words in the question tell you where to look in the passage. Then, read the area that the question comes from slowly and carefully. Find an answer choice that basically says the same thing. Answer choices are often paraphrases from the passage.

- Avoid specific answers on general questions, and on specific questions avoid answers that are reasonable but are not present in the passage.

- Don't be afraid to leave blanks if there are questions that stump you. You're done with a passage whenever you've answered all the questions that you can answer. Instead of wasting time trying to answer the last remaining question on a passage after all other techniques have failed to indicate the correct answer, go on to the next passage.

- Don't pick an answer choice just because you recall hearing the word in the passage. Frequently that is a trick; correct answers will often use synonyms rather than the word originally used in the passage.

4

THE FREE-RESPONSE
SECTION: WRITING
AND SPEAKING

THE BASICS

WHAT IS THE FREE-RESPONSE SECTION?

The free-response section (Section II) of the AP Spanish Language Exam also tests two important skills: writing and speaking. The Writing portion (Part A) consists of two samples of writing: Interpersonal and Presentational. The Speaking portion (Part B) consists of Interpersonal Speaking in the form of a simulated conversation, as well as a Presentational Speaking sample in which an integration of reading and listening skills will yield an oral presentation. On the speaking part, you will be paced and prompted by a master tape for a total of 20 minutes.

Here is the free-response portion of that handy chart we showed you in the beginning of Part I:

Free-Response Section II	Description	Number of Questions	Percent of Grade	Time
Part A: Writing	Interpersonal Writing	1 prompt (10%) 10 minutes	30%	Approx. 65 min.
	Presentational Writing	1 prompt (20%) 55 minutes		
Part B: Speaking	Informal Speaking (Simulated Conversation)	5–6 response prompts (10%) 20 seconds to respond to each	20%	Approx. 20 min.
	Formal Oral Presentation (Integrated Skills)	1 prompt (10%) 2 minutes to respond		

PART A: WRITING

Part A of the free-response section consists of two compositions. The first part is an informal writing task. You will have 10 minutes to read a prompt and reply with your response. Some samples of this could be an e-mail, a postcard, a letter to a friend, or a journal, diary, or blog entry. The second part examines your ability to write formally. Here, you will have 10 minutes to read a few printed sources and listen to an audio prompt. After this, you will have about 5 minutes to formulate your ideas and plan your response. Then, you will have 40 minutes to write your essay for a total time allotment of 55 minutes.

INTERPERSONAL WRITING

Let's take a look at a sample task for the interpersonal writing section. A typical response prompt might look something like this:

Escribe un correo electrónico a un(a) amigo(a) latinoamericano que quiere asistir a una universidad cerca de tu ciudad. Saluda a tu amigo(a) y

- explícale cómo es el proceso de solicitar admisión en las universidades en los EEUU

- expresa tus sentimientos hacia su decisión

- comenta sobre las diferencias entre su cultura y la tuya

When presented with a topic to write about, try to immerse yourself into the situation. Maybe you don't currently have a friend in another country that just happens to want to study at a university close to your home. Graders who look at your essay aren't going to consider the rationale behind a writing assignment. They're going to look at how convincing you are in your writing piece. Lose yourself in the question. Imagine you met this person while traveling abroad with your family or maybe they studied at your high school. Try to make that connection. This section is about informal writing. It will not be convincing if you're starting off a writing piece with "Hola. Me llamo Roberto." Use *tú* and *vosotros* forms when necessary, as this is one of the areas readers consider in their evaluation. Remember, though, that you have only 10 minutes to answer this informal writing section, so make your answers concise and address the prompts listed above. Make it friendly, lively, and real.

Some other good points while you write your informal piece would be to vary your vocabulary and your grammar. Graders don't want to see you use "bueno" and "malo" throughout your writing and they definitely don't want to see you use only the present tense. Think about your speaking pattern in English. You don't speak only in present tense. You use a variety of tenses. Try to use some idiomatic expressions as well to show that you are familiar with the intricacies of the language. Remember to use original ways to open and close your letter. Use appropriate structural indicators and transitional words like *por lo tanto*, *sin embargo*, *en primer lugar*, *para concluir*, *finalmente*, and *adicionalmente*. Also, because this writing sample is so short, do not repeat yourself. Some final tips would be to avoid Anglicism and never, under any circumstance, use English in your writing. If you don't know the word for something, find a way to describe it.

Scoring Guidelines

Writing samples are graded on their degree of task completion, topic development, and use of language. As AP graders are grading large numbers of compositions, make sure yours stands out with creative and memorable vocabulary and content. Scores are awarded on a 1 to 5 scale, just like the overall scores of the AP are given. Here are the rubrics for receiving scores from 5 to 1:

Five: Demonstrates Excellence

For a response to merit a 5, students must fully address and complete the task, and respond completely or almost completely to all the parts/prompts of the writing task. Responses should be thorough, well-organized, and culturally and socially appropriate. Vocabulary and grammar are rich, high level, and virtually error-free. There should be demonstrated command of orthography, sentence structure, paragraphing, and punctuation.

Four: Demonstrates Command

Responses appropriately address and complete the task; it responds fully or almost fully to the parts/prompts of the writing task. Responses are well-developed and generally well-organized, and are generally culturally and socially appropriate. There is use of complex vocabulary and grammar, but there are a few errors. Vocabulary, pronunciation, and overall fluency are very good. Orthography, sentence structure, paragraphing and punctuation are generally correct.

Three: Demonstrates Competence

To achieve this score, students must address the task and adequately answer most parts/prompts of the writing task. Answers are adequately relevant, organized, and generally socially and culturally appropriate. Grammatically, the student shows mastery of simple structures, but struggles with more complex forms. There is good vocabulary, but some English influence may be detected. There may be errors in spelling and structure.

Two: Suggests Lack of Competence

Responses in this category only partially complete or address the task. Some responses to certain parts of the writing prompt may be irrelevant or inappropriate. Parts of the response may have some irrelevancies; answers may lack organization and social and cultural appropriateness. Responses show limited control of the simple grammatical and vocabulary structures: limited breadth of vocabulary, frequent English influence, and frequent grammatical and structural errors.

One: Lack of Competence

Student does not complete the task and does not respond appropriately to most parts of the prompt. Most responses are irrelevant, disorganized, and are not socially and culturally appropriate. There are frequent grammar and vocabulary errors, frequent English influence, and poor comprehension which make understandability difficult.

Zero

Answer is in a language other than Spanish, blank or nearly blank, completely off topic, or simply a restatement of the question.

Sample Question

> *Instrucciones:* Para la siguiente pregunta, escribirás una carta. Tendrás 10 minutos para leer la pregunta y escribir tu respuesta.

Escribe un correo electrónico a un(a) amigo(a) latinoamericano que quiere asistir a una universidad cerca de tu ciudad. Saluda a tu amigo(a) y

- explícale cómo es el proceso de aplicar a las universidades en los EEUU

- expresa tus sentimientos hacia su decisión

- comenta sobre las diferencias entre su cultura y la tuya

Here's How to Crack It

Quickly brainstorm the vocabulary necessary for the task (*aconsejar, incluir, solicitar, solicitud, alegrarse, en cambio, por otra parte,* etc). Also, as it is an informal communication, have some of your generic lines in your back pocket that can be used for the opening and ending parts, for example: *No sabes cuánto me alegro escuchar noticias tuyas* (You don't know how happy I am to hear news from you) and *Espero con ganas escuchar de ti nuevamente* (I hope to hear from you soon). And of course, don't forget all that great grammar: subjunctive, indirect object pronouns, transitional words, variety of tenses, and idiomatic expressions. Try to have several in each category prepared beforehand so you can refer to them and use them quickly. It's almost like having your clothes picked out the night before school; it makes things a lot easier when you are under pressure. Also, don't forget the inverted exclamation points and question marks. Don't overdo commas and semicolons; Spanish uses them much more sparingly than English.

Student Response and Translation

Querido Pablo:

¡No sabes cuánto me alegro escuchar noticias tuyas! ¡Qué bien que hayas decidido estudiar en los Estados Unidos! Yo sé que te encantará. Has tomado una decisión muy importante en cuanto a tu porvenir. Y con lo trabajador que eres, aprovecharás al máximo las oportunidades que te aporte esta nueva experiencia.

Como sabrás el proceso de solicitar admisión a las universidades es diferente del proceso latinoamericano. Primero, necesitarás tomar algunos exámenes estandarizados para demostrar tus habilidades lingüísticas en el inglés. Segundo, te recomiendo que escojas solamente las universidades que realmente te interesen, ya que cuesta hasta 50 dólares por cada solicitud que sometas. Recuerda también que las universidades exigen evidencia de servicio a la comunidad, participación en actividades extra curriculares y recomendaciones de dos profesionales, ya sea profesores u otros adultos.

Es un poco agobiante el proceso, pero sabes que puedes contar conmigo para cualquier ayuda que necesites en el proceso.

Culturalmente encontrarás diferencias entre nuestros países. Notarás algunas diferencias en los dos sistemas universitarios. Primero, en contraste al sistema latinoamericano, en los Estados Unidos casi todos los estudiantes viven en la misma universidad. También hay muchas actividades sociales, deportivas y académicas. Así conocerás a mucha gente de muchas culturas diferentes. Además hay que tener en cuenta que en los Estados Unidos, el ritmo de la vida es más acelerado que en tu país, pero sé que te acostumbrarás. Necesitarás conseguirte un trabajo de tiempo parcial para ganarte un dinero para poder salir y comprar lo que necesites. Sé que en tu país no es normal que los estudiantes trabajen, pero será una buena experiencia para ti. Como puedes ver, habrá muchas oportunidades para aprender dentro y fuera del salón.

Bueno, espero que esta información sea beneficiosa para ti. Se me está acabando el tiempo y me toca despedirme. Espero con ganas tu llegada a los Estados Unidos. Si hay alguna duda que tengas, o si te gustaría que te ayudara con las solicitudes, gustosamente estoy a tus órdenes. ¡Nos vemos pronto!

Te aprecia,

Jennifer

Translation

Dear Pablo:

You can't imagine how happy I am to receive news from you! How nice that you have decided to study in the United States! I know you will love it! You have taken a very important decision in terms of your future. And with your hardworking personality, I know you will take full advantage that this new experience will provide for you.

As you may know, the application process in the United States is different from that of Latin America. First, you will need to take some standardized tests to demonstrate your linguistic abilities in English. Secondly, I recommend that you choose only the universities that truly interest you as it can cost up to 50 dollars for each application you submit. Remember also that the universities require evidence of community service, participation in extra curricular activities and recommendation from two professionals, either professors or other adults.

The process is a little overwhelming, but you know you can rely on me for any help you may need in the process. Culturally, you will find differences between our two countries. You will notice some differences in the two university systems. First, in contrast to the Latin American system, in the United States almost all students live on the college campus. Also, there are many social, sporting and academic activities. This way you will meet many people from different cultures. Also, you should keep in mind that the daily pace is faster than in your country, but I know you will get used to that. You will need to get a part time job to earn some money in order to go out and to buy the things you may need. I know its not normal for students to work in your country, but it will be a good experience for you. As you can see, there will be many learning opportunities for you in and out of the classroom.

Well, I hope this information was helpful for you. I am running out of time, and I must say goodbye. I eagerly await your arrival to the United States. If you have any doubts, or if you would like for me to help you with your applications, I am happily at your service. See you soon!

With fondness,

Jennifer

Evaluation

The opening paragraph of this essay really racked up the points: The first sentence was appropriate and creative, the second one used present perfect subjunctive, the third used the future tense, and the fourth used idiomatic expressions and showed a deep understanding of grammar by using subjunctive in the last part of the sentence! The second paragraph developed the topic and really had strong sentences, grammatically and content wise. The third paragraph wasn't the most cohesive (you could see the student was grabbing a little bit for sentences to try to develop the topic) and did use some slight Anglicisms (*en contraste al*, *tener en cuenta*, *admisión*). But, with the short time allowed, this is to be expected even from the best students. The ending of the second paragraph was strong and tied the previous sentences together, so things worked out nonetheless. The conclusion was strong, used past subjunctive and tied it all together. Notice the student used "Te aprecia," a unique ending, rather than "Tu amiga." That's something very native sounding, and as it was the last thing the graders read, you can be sure it left a very good overall impression. Look for those "native" things in all of the materials you read, and try to incorporate them into your writing. It would be a wonderful idea to get an online pen pal in Spanish or some other way to view familiar letters in Spanish. It might give you some insight on how to write for this section.

PRESENTATIONAL WRITING

The second composition in the free-response section is a formal presentational writing sample. In this section, you will be required to read two sources and hear one audio piece and then respond to a written prompt. All resources will be related and must be referred to when you write your formal composition. You will have 7 minutes to read the scripts and 3 minutes to listen to the audio piece. After you have finished, you will have 5 minutes to organize your thoughts and plan your response. Finally, you will have 40 minutes to write your formal piece for a total of 55 minutes.

Preparation for this section of the exam is much more extensive than the informal section because we naturally have more practice with informal writing through e-mails, diary entries, and other such writing. Unless you expose yourself to formal writing regularly, this could be a challenging section for you. Exposing yourself to certain media before the exam is an absolute must. Think of social and cultural topics that may appear in an exam. There could be questions on poverty, global warming, social unrest, or literary implications across Latin America and Spain, or there could be questions based on music, food, and clothing trends. Making yourself as well rounded as possible and actively seeking Spanish printed and audio material will greatly help your score on this part.

So how do you plan for topics that are apparently limitless? Take the time to read newspapers from different areas of Latin America and Spain. Surely, you know how to use the Internet. Just do searches for *noticias latinoamericanas* or *periódicos chilenos* (*argentinos/españoles/peruanos*, and so on.) and choose an article that is more challenging for you and grasp its message the best you can. It's not expected for you to understand every word in an article, but if you can read the article's title, skim over it, then read through it, you'll certainly be able to deduce its meaning. Read several articles and follow this procedure as you plan for the exam.

In order to train yourself for the audio prompt of this section, you will need to practice with dialects and search for meaning in a message. A fantastic and fun way to practice with dialects would be to turn on a Spanish soap opera (telenovela) or a movie in Spanish, lie back, and just listen. Some students choose an hour to watch television in Spanish and keep a notebook nearby. They jot down words they don't know or even full sentences they would like to include in their repertoire. Another way you can practice for this section is to download some podcasts. Change your Internet browser into Spanish so you can see and read what is happening in the Spanish-speaking world. Listen to Spanish-speaking radio stations; music is an amazing way to learn vocabulary and improve comprehension. Listen to speeches or interviews in Spanish and start somewhere in the middle of the selection and pay close attention to detail. Take notes as you listen. Be sure to get materials from both Spain and Latin America, as the AP loves to include listening passages with a Spanish accent, which can be a little difficult to understand if you are not used to hearing it.

By reading various selections and listening to diverse audio samples, you begin to build a vocabulary and you enhance your ability to make connections to meaning. These are essential tools to write a thorough formal composition. When you write the essay, be sure to make references to all three resources. When making references to the resources, that does not mean to repeat something written or said in the selections; rather, you make an assertion or connection and use the materials to support your point of view. In your introduction you will explain your goal or position in reference to the topic question. In the paragraphs that follow, be sure to have a topic sentence in each to guide your thoughts and support your ideas with information from the sources. In your conclusion, do not repeat what you said in your introduction; rather, let it serve as a summation of your ideas throughout the essay. If you have time, proofread your composition and make sure you place accents when necessary and check your spelling. If you need to change a thought or idea, do not use correction fluid or try to erase what you wrote; just cross it out. You will not be penalized for doing this. Of course, this may sound silly, but try to be as neat as possible, as a well-presented essay is viewed favorably by graders.

Scoring Guidelines

Writing samples are graded on their degree of task completion, topic development, and use of language. As AP graders are grading large numbers of compositions, make sure yours stands out with creative and memorable vocabulary and content. Scores are awarded on a 1 to 5 scale, just like the overall scores of the AP are given. Here are the rubrics for receiving scores from 5 to 1:

Five: Demonstrates Excellence

For a response to merit a 5, students must fully address and complete the task, and must integrate all sources into the essay. Responses should be relevant, thorough, well-organized, and referenced culturally and socially. There should be significant synthesis of the information rather than mere summarizing or citing of the information. Vocabulary and grammar are rich, high level, and virtually error-free. There should be demonstrated command of orthography, sentence structure, paragraphing, and punctuation.

Four: Demonstrates Command

Responses appropriately address and complete the task; it references and integrates all sources into the essay. Responses are well-developed and generally well-organized, and are generally culturally and socially appropriate. The response is accurate and shows more synthesis than citation. There is use of complex vocabulary and grammar, but there are a few errors. Vocabulary, pronunciation, and overall fluency are very good. Orthography, sentence structure, paragraphing, and punctuation are generally correct.

Three: Demonstrates Competence

To achieve this score, students must address the task and refer to most if not all sources in the essay. Answers are adequately relevant, organized, and generally socially and culturally appropriate. There is more summarizing or citation rather than synthesis. Grammatically, the student shows mastery of simple structures, but struggles with more complex forms. There is good vocabulary, but some English influence may be detected. There may be errors in spelling and structure.

Two: Suggests Lack of Competence

Responses in this category only partially complete or address the task. Only some of the sources are referred to in the essay. Parts of the response may have some irrelevancies; answers may lack organization and social and cultural appropriateness. There is very little evidence of synthesis in the response. Responses show limited control of the simple grammatical and vocabulary structures: limited breadth of vocabulary, frequent English influence, and frequent grammatical and structural errors.

One: Lack of Competence

Student does not complete the task and refers poorly to only one or two sources. Most responses are irrelevant, disorganized, and are not socially and culturally appropriate. The information is limited and inaccurate. There are frequent grammar and vocabulary errors, frequent English influence, and poor comprehension which make understandability difficult.

Zero

Answer is in a language other than Spanish, blank or nearly blank, completely off topic, or simply a restatement of the question.

Sample Question

Directions: The following question is based on the accompanying sources 1-3. The sources include both print and audio material. First, you will have 7 minutes to read the printed material. Afterward, you will hear the audio material; you should take notes while you listen. Then, you will have 5 minutes to plan your response and 40 minutes to write your essay. Your essay should be at least 200 words in length.

This question is designed to test your ability to interpret and synthesize different sources. Your essay should use the information from the sources to support your ideas. You should refer to ALL of the sources. As you refer to the sources, identify them appropriately. Avoid simply summarizing the sources individually.

Instrucciones: La pregunta siguiente se basa en las Fuentes 1-3. Las fuentes comprenden material tanto impreso como auditivo. Primero, dispondrás de 7 minutos para leer el material impreso. Después escucharás el material auditivo; debes tomar apuntes mientras escuches. Luego, tendrás 5 minutos para preparar tu respuesta y 40 minutos para escribir tu ensayo. El ensayo debe tener una extensión mínima de 200 palabras.

El objetivo de esta pregunta es medir tu capacidad de interpretar y sintetizar varias fuentes. Tu ensayo debe utilizar información de TODAS las fuentes, citándolas apropiadamente. Evita un simple resumen de cada una de ellas.

¿Por qué nos urge mejorar las condiciones de vivir de los niños latinoamericanos?

Fuente No. 1

Fuente: Este artículo apareció en la revista mexicana Auge en 2009.

A través del continente americano, a pesar de los enormes avances tanto en la tecnología agrícola como en las mismas técnicas de arar la tierra, los niveles de nutrición de varios países siguen estancados a niveles tan reducidos que se ven comprometidas la estatura física, la habilidad de poder trabajar una jornada completa y, peor aún, las capacidades intelectuales de sus ciudadanos. La Organización de Desarrollo y Fomento Internacional reporta que, según cifras de los gobiernos latinoamericanos, el consumo de calorías de la región alcanza un promedio de unas 2680 por día (comparado con unas 3450 en los Estados Unidos), y peor aun en los países centroamericanos apenas sobrepasa las 2250 calorías diarias. En los países de mayor actividad económica, como Argentina, Brasil y México, las diferencias regionales han dejado a ciertas zonas marginadas en condiciones similares. La malnutrición se empeora por la falta de servicios de salud, el desempleo y la alta tasa de enfermedad que resulta de la escasez de debido a los escasos servicios sanitarios adecuados.

Los efectos de la modernización y la caída económica mundial requieren una mano de obra de tiempo completo listo para trabajar horas extensas, y a los niveles de nutrición actuales muchos adultos apenas contarán con la energía necesaria para trabajar las 40 o más horas necesarias semanalmente. Entre el 40% de la población adulta clasificada como "pobre" (con un ingreso diario equivalente a unos $2.50 estadounidenses), la falta de nutrición es un factor constante que les aqueja muy a menudo.

No faltan de los esfuerzos para aliviar el problema, sino que lo que ha variado es la magnitud de su alcance y su eficacia en condiciones sociales y económicas sumamente inhóspitas. Se han registrado victorias en algunas áreas (como el programa Salta de Vitarte en Perú, que se concentró en las personas más pobres y les facilitó 3 servicios básicos) pero el obstáculo más formidable es la irremediable realidad económica en la que vive la población. Los programas de bienestar público intentan repartir certificados a las familias de bajo ingreso—parecido al programa de Cupones de Alimentos en los Estados Unidos— pero no existen ni los recursos ni la infraestructura para sostener el programa a largo plazo. Otros programas tienen como meta enfatizar la educación de salud y nutrición, pero los esfuerzos se hacen en balde ya que los ingresos familiares no generan lo suficiente para sostener dietas mejor balanceadas. Ningún esfuerzo ha logrado tener el impacto necesario para lidiar con el problema en toda su magnitud.

Fuente No. 2

Fuente: Este artículo apareció en "Páginas Escolares", una revista juvenil colombiana.

EL CÍRCULO DE AMOR

Cuando uno piensa en Guatemala, tal vez le llegue a la mente la imagen de un país pobre donde predomina la agricultura, o tal vez recuerde a la famosa Rigoberta Menchú, ganadora del Premio Nobel de La Paz en 1992 y con ella la gran tradición indígena que por siglos ha representado un papel omnipresente en la historia guatemalteca. Pero si conoce a Maria Giammarino, de Mahwah, Nueva Jersey, entonces lo primero que sabrá de Guatemala es sobre El Círculo de Amor.

El Círculo de Amor fue fundado por Giammarino en 2001, pero su interés en los guatemaltecos proviene desde los años 90, cuando visitaba el país por su trabajo de aeromoza en una línea aérea americana. Así nos cuenta su experiencia: "Durante unas cuantas estadías en el país, tuve la oportunidad de recorrer muchas de las zonas rurales más pobres. Una vez hicimos una excursión en canoa cerca de Livingston, que nos llevó a una aldea prácticamente olvidada por el mundo. Vimos una pobreza que me partió el alma. Llegamos a un pueblo retirado, y de repente vi a unas niñas de edad escolar vendiendo caramelos y cigarrillos en el muelle. ¡Les correspondía estar en la escuela! Una me llamó la atención: llevaba su ropita harapienta y andaba pata pelada, pero me ofreció una sonrisa dulce e inocente. Una mirada hacia el pueblo me confirmó lo peor: unas covachas con techo de estaño, y el desagüe en la calle cuyo olor perduraba y perduraba. Ni Dante hubiera vislumbrado un mundo así".

Después de cultivar una amistad, Giammarino empezó por enseñarle a tejer a la niña. Le obsequió el material y pronto la novata creó chompas de algodón no sólo para su familia, sino también para la venta. Giammarino le alquiló un pequeño puesto donde vendían la mercancía. Y así se inició El Círculo de Amor. Su aerolínea también le dio la mano, lanzando el programa "Quédate con el vuelto", que les pide a pasajeros norteamericanos que vuelven a su tierra que donen los quetzales sobrantes de su estudía en a Guatemala. La campaña ha recaudado más de 10.000 dólares desde su inicio. Ahora hay talleres de tejer, los cuales les ayudan a las mujeres a aprender un oficio ya que juegan éstas un papel esencial en la estrategia de la sobrevivencia de las familias. Hay una pequeña cantina que sirve almuerzos a los residentes del pueblo. Y este año, gracias a la bondadosa ayuda de varios auspiciadores, se presenció la apertura de un pequeño consultorio médico que otorga un servicio de salud básico a los 1200 habitantes del pueblo.

El Círculo de Amor tiene como meta principal procurar el bienestar de las niñas guatemaltecas, muchas veces las más explotadas y marginadas de la sociedad. Las contribuciones también se destinan a la educación femenina, porque según Giammarino "a la gente sin acceso a la educación básica se les priva la voz". Por sólo 30 dólares mensuales, un patrocinador puede mandar a una niña a la escuela. El Círculo de Amor pone atención especial en reclutar a las niñas más pequeñas de una familia para que asistan a la escuela, lo cual es un privilegio reservado mayormente para los niños varones. La estrategia de elegir a la niña menor viene de la perspectiva de que mientras más joven sea ella al iniciar los estudios, más probabilidad tendrá de continuarlos en el futuro.

Fuente No. 3: Audio Selection

[While this is normally an audio component, for the purposes of demonstrating the source content, this has been included as a written document only]

El siguiente discurso lo ofreció Alessandra Dávila, decana de la escuela de Economía de la Pontificia Universidad Católica del Perú en La X Asamblea del Pacto Andino, celebrado en Cajamarca, Perú el año pasado. Se titula "Declive de inversiones gubernamentales con la crisis económica andina".

Lo que puedo pronosticar con certeza es que lo único que cambiará en la región latinoamericana es el clima. Nuestra problemática nacional da muchas vueltas, pero al fin y al cabo, termina siendo lo mismo: somos un país pobre y los más marginados se ven cada vez más atrapados en este círculo vicioso que es la pobreza. La realidad que vivimos es que nuestra deuda externa nos sofoca y hasta quita las ganas de querer progresar. Casi el 50% de nuestro Producto Bruto Interno se destina para satisfacer los pagos a nuestros acreedores europeos y norteamericanos. Nuestros problemas sí están fuertemente arraigados en nuestra relación con el exterior. Queda una cantidad mezquina para programas de planificación familiar, educación y vacunas. No nos alcanza el presupuesto nacional para todo, y nuestros niños están sufriendo lo peor.

Las inversiones en el sector educativo han disminuido en un 50%, y varios recintos (ya en decadencia física) ni siquiera pueden abastecer lo mínimo necesario para sus aulas: libros, pizarras, pisos y agua potable. Y cuando se trata de supervivencia, muchos optan por trabajar en vez estudiar. Como resultado, como región tenemos una de las tasas de analfabetismo más altas del continente.

Uno de los problemas más sentidos, por el cual en este momento está atravesando la población en nuestros países en general y específicamente aquellos grupos más marginados, es la fuerte caída de ingresos. En Lima, la canasta familiar (productos de primera necesidad) aguanta menos pero cuesta más. Y ahora La Liga Leche suspenderá las entregas de este valioso alimento a los jardines infantiles debido a los costos desorbitados. Los almuerzos gratuitos son ya una especie en peligro de extinción. Hace 10 años, todos los niños en las provincias andinas recibían vacunas, exámenes dentales y meriendas en sus escuelas. Ahora con suerte recibirán una de las tres. Las cifras indican la triste realidad: en Bolivia, el presupuesto nacional para programas educativos disminuyó en un 33%, aunque la población estudiante aumentó en un 8%. En Chile, la caída de ingresos por las exportaciones resultó en la eliminación de programas de nutrición, planificación familiar, estudios becados y 4 clínicas gratuitas en las zonas más necesitadas. La conclusión que se puede extraer con confiabilidad es que la desigualdad y la pobreza absoluta han aumentado con la crisis económica. Por desgracia, el mundo es ciego frente al problema. El "bail out", un lujo primer mundista, no nos es una opción.

Para el futuro, por lo que se ve actualmente, es probable que el continente sudamericano experimente un crecimiento negativo, tal como la hiperinflación de la década de los 80, lo cual aumentará las deficiencias nutritivas, la productividad, y tristemente, el potencial de crecimiento y desarrollo del futuro.

Sample Student Response and Translation

¿Por qué nos urge mejorar las condiciones de vivir de los niños latinoamericanos?

Es sumamente importante que mejoremos las condiciones de vivir de los niños latinoamericanos, ya que ellos son esenciales para el bienestar del futuro. Hoy en día, se puede decir que la falta de acceso a servicios básicos es uno de los problemas más grandes que confronta a los niños a través del mundo latinoamericano. Como resultado, los niños son atrapados en una problemática sin salida: la pobreza, la cual trae consigo un menor acceso a la educación, la medicina y la vivienda. El trabajo reemplaza la educación como la primera prioridad. Según la fuente #3, algunos niños latinoamericanos carecen de buena nutrición, vacunas y alfabetismo básico. Esto concuerda con otra triste realidad: el hecho preocupante que la inversión financiera en educación, según la fuente número 3, es mucho menor en América Latina, lo cual es claramente paradójico, ya que es donde más se necesita esta clase de inversión (Fuente 2).

Pienso que si las necesidades básicas de la gente se satisficieran, entonces podrían preocuparse de los lujos como la edu-

cación. Como nos explica la fuente #1, la gente hambrienta no puede funcionar en el mundo laboral. Vivir, comer y estar libre de enfermedades son necesidades básicas del hombre. Si esta gente no recibe los servicios básicos, ello puede causar epidemias tal como se presencia en México actualmente. Además, la educación, la planificación familiar, la nutrición y la vivienda adecuadas ayudan a la gente a que contribuyan más a sus países. Y hasta es posible que puedan aportar al futuro de su país al convertirse en políticos o doctores. Se dice que con el apoyo y el deseo todo es posible. El mundo está conectado social, económica y políticamente, entonces es nuestra responsabilidad ayudar a estas personas que, según la fuente 2, "se les priva de voz" en su futuro.

Hemos visto que nuestras acciones sí hacen una diferencia en las vidas de los niños latinoamericanos y, obviamente, se sabe que no hay soluciones rápidas y fáciles. Sin embargo, la señora Giammarino se empeñó en ayudar a una comunidad pequeña guatemalteca, demostrando que los esfuerzos pequeños pueden lograr milagros. Esperamos que otras personas reconozcan la urgencia de ayudar a estas personas necesitadas.

Translation

Why is it urgent for us to help improve the living conditions of children in Latin America?

It is extremely important for us to improve the living conditions of Latin America's children, as they are essential to the well being of the future. Nowadays, it can be said that the lack of access to basic services is one of the formidable problems that confront children throughout the Latin American world. As a result, children are trapped in a problem without solution: poverty that brings with it a reduced access to education, medicine, and shelter. Work replaces education as the first priority. According to source #3, some Latin American children lack good nutrition, vaccinations, and basic literacy. This goes with another sad reality—the frightening fact that the financial investment in education in Latin America is much less—clearly paradoxical as this is precisely where this type of investment is needed. (source #2).

I believe that if the basic needs of the people were satisfied, then they would be able to concern themselves with luxuries such as education. As source #1 explains to us, hungry people cannot function in the workplace. Living, eating and being free of illness are basic necessities of Man. If these people don't receive basic services, it could cause epidemics as we have witnessed recently in Mexico. Also, adequate education, family planning, nutrition and housing help people to contribute more to their respective countries. Maybe they might contribute to the future of their countries by becoming politicians or doctors. It is said that with support and desire that anything is possible. The world is connected socially, economically, and politically and thus is our responsibility to help those people, who, according to source 2 "are denied a voice" in their future.

We have seen that our actions do indeed make a difference in the lives of Latin American children. And obviously, we know there are no quick and easy solutions. However, Mrs. Giammarino gave of herself to help a small Latin American community, demonstrating that the small efforts can produce miracles. We can only hope that other people recognize the urgency of helping these needy persons.

Evaluation

This essay had strong vocabulary, grammar, and organization. One of the challenges with the presentational writing section is to try to refer to all the sources, because the AP often includes sources that don't have a clear correlation to each other. It is your responsibility to try to find connections between them, however minor, in order to include all of them in your analysis, your synthesis, and ultimately, your composition. Mentioning ALL the sources will help you score higher. One weakness in this essay was that it needed a greater incorporation of the sources, and possibly a deeper analysis. The writer did make some connections among the materials, although somewhat predictable, but nonetheless it carried an idea from start to finish and used data to back up the conclusions. Summary was kept to a minimum and affirmations referred to information in the readings, which are things to remember when writing your essay. This essay would probably score in the 4 range.

PART B: SPEAKING

The directions for the speaking part (Part B) will be given to you by the master CD. You will be told when to open the booklet containing the material. You will be asked to respond to different prompts and to record your voice. Most directions will be spoken in English, but you will be asked different types of questions in Spanish in the Directed Response part of the exam. There are two sections in the speaking part: a role play conversation where the student listens to a speaker and responds to prompts, and an oral presentation of two minutes based on reading and listening passages. Together these sections comprise approximately 20 percent of your overall score.

SECTION 1: INFORMAL SPEAKING (SIMULATED CONVERSATION)

This section integrates both listening and speaking skills in a role play conversation. Students will be asked to interact with the recorded conversation. You will be required to answer either five or six times to various prompts. Each response will be 20 seconds long and will be timed by a beep on the CD. Before beginning, you will have the opportunity to read the outline of the simulated conversation and the instructions.

Sample Question

Directions: You will now participate in a simulated conversation. First, you will have 30 seconds to read the outline of the conversation. Then, you will listen to a message and have one minute to read again the outline of the conversation. Afterward, the conversation will begin, following the outline. Each time it is your turn, you will have 20 seconds to respond; a tone will indicate when you should begin and end speaking. You should participate in the conversation as fully and appropriately as possible.

Instrucciones: Ahora participarás en una conversación simulada. Primero, tendrás 30 segundos para leer el esquema de la conversación. Luego, escucharás un mensaje y tendrás un minuto para leer de nuevo el esquema de la conversación. Después, empezará la conversación, siguiendo el esquema. Siempre que te toque un turno, tendrás 20 segundos para responder; una señal te indicará cuando debes empezar y terminar de hablar. Debes participar en la conversación de la manera más completa y apropiada posible.

(A) Imagina que recibes un mensaje del Departamento de Estudios para Extranjeros de una universidad latinoamericana. El director te llama para invitarte a acudir a su oficina para una entrevista sobre tu solicitud de beca.

[You will hear the message on the recording.
Escucharás el mensaje en la grabación.]

(B) La conversación

[The shaded lines reflect what you will hear on the recording.
Las líneas en gris reflejan lo que escucharás en la grabación.]

Entrevistador	Te saluda
Tú	Salúdalo y preséntate
Entrevistador	Te explica por qué te hace la entrevista y te hace una pregunta
Tú	Responde a la pregunta
Entrevistador	Continúa la conversación
Tú	Responde a la pregunta
Entrevistador	Continúa la conversación
Tú	Responde a la pregunta
Entrevistador	Continúa la conversación
Tú	Responde a la pregunta
Entrevistador	Continúa la conversación
Tú	Haz una pregunta

Scoring of Directed Response Speaking

Students' responses will be evaluated using a 5-point scale, similar to the way the overall AP score is generated. The three variables that are evaluated are task completion, topic development, and language use. Here are the criteria for achieving each score:

Five: Demonstrates Excellence

For a response to merit a 5, students must fully address and complete the task, and respond completely or almost completely to all the parts/prompts of the conversation. Responses should be thorough, well-organized, and culturally and socially appropriate. Vocabulary and grammar are rich, high level, and virtually error-free. Pronunciation is excellent as well.

Four: Demonstrates Command

Responses appropriately address and complete the task, and responds fully or almost fully to the parts/prompts of the conversation. Responses are well-developed and generally well-organized, and are generally culturally and socially appropriate. There is use of complex vocabulary and grammar, but there are a few errors. Vocabulary, pronunciation, and overall fluency are very good.

Three: Demonstrates Competence

To achieve this score, students must address the task and adequately answer most parts/prompts of the conversation. Answers are adequately relevant, organized, and generally socially and culturally appropriate. Grammatically, the student shows mastery of simple structures, but struggles with more complex forms. There is good vocabulary, but some English influence may be detected. Fluency and pronunciation are good, with some hesitation and correction of errors.

Two: Suggests Lack of Competence

Responses in this category only partially complete or address the task. Some responses to certain parts of the conversation may be irrelevant or inappropriate. Parts of the conversation may have some irrelevancies; answers may lack organization and social and cultural appropriateness. Responses show limited control of the simple grammatical and vocabulary structures: limited breadth of vocabulary, errors, frequent English influence, and fair pronunciation and minimal overall fluency.

One: Lack of Competence
Student does not complete the task and does not respond appropriately to most parts of the conversation. Most responses are irrelevant, disorganized, and are not socially and culturally appropriate. There are frequent grammar and vocabulary errors, frequent English influence, and poor comprehension which make understandability difficult.

Zero
Answer is in a language other than Spanish, completely off topic, or simply a restatement of the question.

Here's How to Crack It
This section is testing your ability to initiate, sustain and conclude a conversation in a given situation as well as use language that is culturally, semantically, grammatically and socially correct. In other words, are you using the correct *Usted* and *tú* forms? Are you being culturally appropriate in a social setting by using correct markers in your conversation, such as the subjunctive and formal commands, when necessary? Many of these situations involve traveling or studying overseas or applying for jobs, internships, and scholarships. So it would be smart to study up on some of the vocabulary involved in job applications, college courses, scholarships, internships, and so on.

Remember that you have only 20 seconds to respond to each prompt. Do not restate the question in your answer, as it wastes valuable time. Speak clearly and slowly. Don't worry if you get cut off in mid-sentence by the tone. Make it your goal to provide interesting and high level answers that address the question or situation with correct grammar and pronunciation. Try to incorporate certain phrases that can help you introduce your answers: *Me es importante, Quisiera, Si fuera posible*, for example. The higher level structure and vocabulary you use, the higher your score will be. Also, try not to use the simple way to say things, use the higher order vocabulary. For example use, *dirigirse* or *acudir* instead of *ir*. Try to use all 20 seconds as it will enable you to give two solid, high-level sentences. Remember that if you are using the *Usted* form, which is probably more often than not, you need to have all of the verbs, possessive pronouns and especially the object pronouns in the corresponding forms. Pay attention to the Student Answers on the sample script with Student Response as these are the kinds of answers that will get your high scores.

Sample Script with Student Response and translation

Narrador:	Imagina que recibes un mensaje telefónico de parte del director del Departamento de Estudios para Extranjeros de una universidad latino-americana. El director te llama para invitarte a acudir a su oficina para una entrevista sobre tu solicitud de beca.
	Imagine that you receive a phone message from the director of the Department of Foreign Student Studies at a Latin American university. The director calls you to invite you to his office for an interview about your scholarship application.
MA:	[Answering machine] [Beep] Buenos días, le habla el señor Guillermo Butrón director del programa de Estudios para Extranjeros. Quisiera que pasara por mi oficina mañana para una entrevista sobre

la solicitud que usted nos envió. Tengo algunas preguntas que quisiera hacerle.

Good morning, this is Mr. Guillermo Butrón, director of the Foreign Student Studies program. I would like you to pass by my office tomorrow for an interview concerning the application you submitted. I have a few questions I would like to ask you.

Narrador: Ahora tienes un minuto para leer el esquema de la conversación

Now you have one minute to read the conversation outline.

Ahora imagina que te encuentres en la oficina del señor Butrón para realizar una entrevista.

Now imagine that you are in Mr. Butrón's office for an interview.

Entre: Buenos días. Me es muy grato conocerle en persona. Soy Guillermo Butrón, director del programa de Estudios para Extranjeros y de becas en la región latinoamericana. Por favor, pase y siéntese.

Good morning. It is a pleasure to meet you in person. I am Guillermo Butrón, director of the Foreign Student Studies program and scholarships in Latin America. Please, come in and sit down.

Tú: Es un verdadero gusto conocerle también, Señor Butrón. Soy Michael Randello de Nueva York.

It is real pleasure to meet you also, Mr. Butrón. I am Michael Randello, from New York.

Entre: Tengo su solicitud para una beca de estudios y necesito hacerle algunas preguntas para saber un poco más sobre usted. ¿Por qué le interesa estudiar en Latinoamérica?

I have your scholarship study application and I need to ask you some questions to find out a little more about you. Why are you interested in studying in Latin America?

Tú: Siempre me han llamado la atención la cultura y el idioma de esa región. Como quisiera trabajar en un empleo relacionado con América Latina, necesito hablar mejor el español y entender más a fondo su cultura y costumbres.

I have always been interested in both the culture and language of that region. Since I would like to work in a position that relates to Latin America, I need to speak Spanish better and understand in depth its culture and customs.

Entre: Ah, muy interesante. Se nota que tiene un verdadero interés en estudiar en el extranjero. ¿Dónde en Latinoamérica le gustaría estudiar y vivir, y por qué?

Ah, very interesting. I see that you have a real interest in studying abroad.
Where in Latin America would you like to study and live, and why?

Tú: Definitivamente me interesaría estar en Argentina. Encuentro tanto la
        historia como la cultura fascinante. Además, ahí podría perfeccionar el
        español.

        I would definitely like to be in Argentina. I find both the history and culture
        fascinating. In addition, there I would be able to perfect my Spanish.

Entre: Si fuera a recibir la beca, ¿qué le gustaría estudiar y por qué?

        If you were to receive the scholarship, what would you like to study and why?

Tú: Bueno, obviamente necesitaría estudiar el español, pero como quisiera
        trabajar en negocios internacionales, sería buena idea que estudiara
        comercio, relaciones internacionales, e historia.

        Well, obviously I would need to study Spanish, but as I would like to work in
        international business, it would be a good idea that I study commerce, inter-
        national relations, and history.

Entre: Además de sus responsabilidades académicas, los estudiantes que
        reciben becas deben participar en actividades culturales. ¿Qué aspectos
        de la cultura del país que visitará le interesan?

        In addition to their academic responsibilities, the students who receive schol-
        arships must participate in cultural activities. What aspects of the culture
        interest you in your country of choice?

Tú: Siempre me ha fascinado el tango. La historia y el significado del tango
        me son muy interesantes. Siempre soñé con aprender a bailar el tango,
        así que tomaré clases.

        The tango has always fascinated me. The history and meaning of the tango are
        very interesting. I always dreamed about learning to dance the Tango, so I will
        take classes.

Entre: ¡Qué bien! Y para terminar, ¿qué preguntas tiene sobre la beca o sobre
        nuestro programa en general?

        How nice. And to conclude, what questions do you have about the scholarship
        or about our program in general?

Tú   Por favor, dígame: ¿Cuándo empezará el programa? ¿Viviré con una
        familia o en una residencia estudiantil? ¿Cuándo me informarán sobre
        la beca?

        Please tell me: When does the program begin? Will I live with a family or in a
        student residence? When will I be informed about the scholarship?

The responses by the student were rich, varied, and complete; he used excellent grammatical and vocabulary structures: conditional, subjunctive, and future tenses. The student also fulfilled the requirement of being socially appropriate by using the *Usted* command "*Dígame*" in the last response. Be sure to get one example of that in your response. The responses enriched and advanced the conversation; notice how the topics were addressed and developed with creative and interesting answers: the student showed an understanding of university courses, culture, and studying overseas. You should be sure to have an understanding of several Spanish speaking countries as you may need to discuss their culture in one of these types of questions. This response would certainly score in the 4 or 5 level.

Section II: Formal Oral Presentation (integrated skills)

This section will provide you with a reading comprehension passage of one page, and then a listening selection related in some way to the topic of the reading. You will then be asked to use both sources to provide a 2 minute oral presentation. You should take and use notes, but do that in the target language; DO NOT translate as this wastes precious time.

Sample Question

> **Directions:** The following question is based on the accompanying printed article and audio selection. First, you will have 5 minutes to read the printed article. Afterward, you will hear the audio selection; you should take notes while you listen. Then, you will have 2 minutes to plan your response and 2 minutes to record your answer.

> *Instrucciones:* La pregunta siguiente se basa en el artículo impreso y la selección auditiva a continuación. Primero, tendrás 5 minutos para leer el artículo. Después, escucharás la selección auditiva; debes tomar apuntes mientras escuches. Luego, tendrás 2 minutos para preparar tu respuesta y 2 minutos para grabarla.

Tienes que dar una presentación en tu clase de español sobre el siguiente tema:

En abril de 2006, la junta legislativa del estado de Florida tuvo unas mesas redondas sobre la posibilidad de aumentar la edad mínima para sacar el permiso de aprendiz de conducir de 15 a 16 años, y la edad mínima para licencia completa de 17 a 18 años. El primer artículo es una presentación de parte de Lorena Pérez, abogada y presidente de la organización, Salvando la Juventud. La segunda selección es un informe de radio que presenta las ideas de varios jóvenes estadounidenses sobre esta propuesta. En una presentación oral compara y contrasta las opiniones de los jóvenes con las de la abogada.

Texto impreso

Fuente: Discurso, Lorena Pérez, ante la Junta Legislativa Hispana, Tallahassee, Florida, presentado en mayo de 2008.

Los conductores adolescentes: No hay prisa

"Estimados compañeros: Pueden imaginar la angustia que abarca a un padre al recibir esa llamada telefónica informándole que ha fallecido su único hijo en un accidente automovilístico. Muchas veces es más que alguien se encuentre en el lugar equivocado en el momento inoportuno. Más bien, se trata de que a nuestros adolescentes les carecen la madurez y la experiencia como chóferes. Accidentarse hoy en día es demasiado fácil. No tienen por qué estar recorriendo las carreteras y calles a su temprana edad, y menos con otros amigos en el coche. Los riesgos a la vida sobrepasan cualquier beneficio otorgado por tener la licencia a muy temprana edad.

Según las cifras del gobierno, mueren más de 42.000 personas anualmente en accidentes automovilísticos. Esto sobrepasa las cifras de todas las guerras en las cuales ha luchado nuestra nación. Y de esas muertes, los chóferes adolescentes entre las edades de 16 y 19 comprenden más del 40% del total. Es de esperarse que mientras los chóferes vayan aumentando de edad, conseguirán más años de experiencia, más madurez, y como resultado, las cifras empezarán a bajar.

En muchos estados, la legislación reciente tiene como meta reducir esos números a través de programas de adiestramiento y estándares para licenciamiento por edad. Es mejor que repartamos los derechos de manejar gradualmente. De esa manera los chóferes jóvenes poseerían licencias restringidas, y poco a poco irían mejorando y adquiriendo entrenamiento obligatorio. Cada año recibiría mayores derechos siempre y cuando hayan cumplido con las horas de entrenamiento ya sean de cursos prácticos o de aprendizaje formal. Así aumentamos en etapas su nivel de experiencia.

No es una idea nueva; muchos estados están examinando la posibilidad de adoptar ese plan, y muchos que lo apoyan proponen que ese umbral sea de 18 años. Muchos países europeos ya tienen como edad mínima los dieciocho años para otorgar las licencias de manejar. Otros países han impuesto limitaciones en cuanto a los límites de velocidad, los horarios, el uso de las carreteras y hasta identificación expuesta en el vehículo para identificar chóferes juveniles.

Muchos adolescentes opinarán que con estas leyes pretendamos negarles su independencia o sus derechos. Al contrario, tenemos la obligación de proteger a nuestros ciudadanos más vulnerables. Algunos científicos mantienen que existen diferencias de madurez entre los 16 y los 18 años, y se sabe que en cuanto al desarrollo el ser humano no alcanza niveles de madurez en decisiones ejecutivos hasta el final de los años adolescentes o hasta que se llegue a los 20 años. Les exhorto que consideren esta importante oportunidad para salvarles la vida a nuestros jóvenes".

AUDIO CD: Track 4

Informe de radio

Fuente: Las opiniones de estos jóvenes aparecieron en un grupo focal sobre el tema de conductores adolescentes en Miami.

[A continuación escucharás las opiniones de varios jóvenes sobre la posibilidad de elevar las edades mínimas para manejar.

Amanda Estévez, 18 años

"Yo veo el problema de otra forma. Si es importante recibir más entrenamiento, y mis padres están completamente a favor de que yo consiga cuanta experiencia pueda. Pero hay que tomar en cuenta que muchos estudiantes de 16 y 17 años necesitan transportación a actividades escolares, a la práctica de deportes, y para socializar o estudiar en la biblioteca. Si los jóvenes no pueden guiar hasta los 18 años, entonces sus padres lo tendrán que compensar".

Felicia Badillo, 16 años

"Tal vez sería mejor subir la edad mínima porque los adolescentes mayores son más maduros".

John Grant, 17 años

¿Cómo llegaré a mi trabajo? Trabajo después de la escuela y ambos padres trabajan. No hay recursos para tomar taxi todos los días, y no existen líneas de transportación pública confiables. Mi ingreso es una parte importante de los gastos familiares. Esto es otro ejemplo de una generación de adultos quienes temen y limitan a las oportunidades de los jóvenes. Primero limitaron los cigarrillos, censuraron las películas, y ahora se meten con la edad para manejar. No terminará con esto nomás, te lo aseguro".

Barri Marlowe, 16 años

"La economía también se afectaría si los jóvenes no pudieran manejar, similarmente como lo pasaría si los inmigrantes ilegales se deportaran. No habrá gente para ocupar esos trabajos vacantes. Es más, los jóvenes ganarían menos plata y por lo tanto habría menos consumo de su parte de productos y servicios, y la economía del país sufriría mucho. Aportamos mucho como consumidores a la economía nacional".

Alex Nestle, 16 años

"Se dice que más de un cuarto de jóvenes de 16 años trabajan fuera de la casa durante el año escolar, y más de un tercio durante el verano cuando no está en sesión la escuela. Los negocios sufrirían mucho si sus trabajadores no pudieran llegar a sus negocios".

Cielo Ramírez, 18 años

"Tal vez no es imprescindible que cambiemos la edad mínima. Si todos los estados fueran a tener como requisito clases obligatorias empezando a la edad de 15, estaríamos más diestros en el manejar, y contaríamos con esa experiencia adicional antes de embarcarnos en las carreteras".

Andre Cruz, 16 años

"No es la edad que cuenta sino la personalidad. Habrá jóvenes que pueden manejar responsablemente y otros, aunque tengan 35 años, nunca podrán respetar las reglas del tráfico ni usar el sentido común. La edad es simplemente un número, es la persona en sí que figura más en el manejar".]

Scoring of Oral Presentation

Students' responses will be evaluated using a 5-point scale, similar to the way the overall AP score is generated. The three variables that are evaluated are task completion, topic development, and language use. Here are the criteria for achieving each score:

Five: Demonstrates Excellence

For a response to merit a 5, students must fully address and complete the task, and utilize and fully integrate both sources into the response. The response is well-organized, accurate, and does much more comparing and contrasting than simple summarizing or quoting from the passages. It refers to the sources socially and culturally when appropriate. Vocabulary and grammar are rich, high level, and virtually error-free. Pronunciation is excellent as well.

Four: Demonstrates Command

Responses appropriately address and complete the task. Student refers to and integrates both sources into the response. Responses are well-developed and generally well-organized, and are generally culturally and socially appropriate. There is more comparing and contrasting of the sources than mere summarizing or quoting of the sources. There is use of complex vocabulary and grammar, but there are a few errors. Vocabulary, pronunciation, and overall fluency are very good.

Three: Demonstrates Competence

To achieve this score, students address the task and manage to integrate one source into the presentation but manage only some or little reference to the other. The presentation is relevant, organized, and generally socially and culturally appropriate. There may be some inaccuracies. Summary and quotations outweigh the comparing and contrasting. Grammatically, the student shows mastery of simple structures, but struggles with more complex forms. There is good vocabulary, but some English influence may be detected. Fluency and pronunciation are good, with some hesitation and correction of errors.

Two: Suggests Lack of Competence

Responses in this category only partially complete or address the task; only one source may be utilized in the presentation. Certain parts of the presentation conversation may be irrelevant, unorganized, or inaccurate. Parts of the conversation may have some irrelevancies; answers may lack organization and social and cultural appropriateness. There is little comparing and contrasting. The response shows limited control of the simple grammatical and vocabulary structures: limited breadth of vocabulary, errors, frequent English influence, and only fair pronunciation with minimal overall fluency.

One: Lack of Competence

Student does not complete the task and refers poorly to only one source in the presentation. The response is irrelevant, disorganized, and is not socially and culturally appropriate. There is no comparing and contrasting done in the presentation. There are frequent grammar and vocabulary errors, frequent English influence, and poor comprehension which make understandability difficult.

Zero

Answer is in a language other than Spanish, nearly blank or blank, completely off topic, or simply a restatement of the question.

Here's How to Crack It

This section is testing your ability to describe, narrate, and present information and/or persuasive arguments on certain topics with strong grammar and pronunciation. The graders also want to see you use these authentic materials adeptly. You should be able to navigate your way through a newspaper article, web broadcast, blog, speech, and so on. Good ways to practice for this would be reading online articles or listening to news broadcasts and then summarizing and analyzing. Key words to keep in mind are IDENTIFY, SYNTHESIZE, INFER, and PREDICT. These are all higher-order thinking skills which, when demonstrated, greatly increase your score. In addition, whenever possible, show a recognition and understanding of cultural elements. Often you will be asked to compare and contrast sources, so practice doing that on your own by looking for similarities and differences when reading and comparing articles or other media. Use the specific vocabulary to voice similarities and differences: *por otra parte, se parecen, se diferencian, vale mencionar que mientras una fuente ..., la otra fuente....,* and so on.

In your answer you may summarize briefly and identify key issues, but remember to show similarities or contrasting viewpoints. Explain the advantages/merits versus the disadvantages/weaknesses of both points presented if necessary. Use various points from the article to support your inference or opinion. And of course, organize your answer with an outline to help you stay organized and use transition words (*aunque, como resultado, por otra parte, vemos que,* etc) so you are clear and not repetitive.

Sample Student Answer and Translation

El tema de modificar la edad mínima para manejar es uno que ha despertado sentimientos contradictorios entre las diferentes generaciones. Vemos que la autora del discurso apoya con mucho empeño la decisión de elevar la edad mínima de manejar. Pero por otra parte, creen los menores de fuente #2 que tal vez las preocupaciones se motiven por la necesidad de controlar la generación menor y limitar sus derechos, expresado por el espíritu independiente del joven John Grant en fuente #2. El se pregunta si ese movimiento tal vez sea uno de censurar y negarles a los jóvenes el proceso democrático.

Otros jóvenes están en desacuerdo con la opción de aumentar la edad por razones económicos. Como indican en la fuente #2, 25% de jóvenes mayores de 16 años trabajan después de la escuela. Sus ingresos, explica otro joven, contribuyen a la economía familiar. Negarles esta oportunidad de trabajar al quitarles el derecho de manejar a los 16 años podría traer graves efectos económicos. Hay que recordar que los EEUU no cuenta con un sistema de transportación pública desarrollada como los de otros países; y como hoy en día ambos padres suelen trabajar fuera de la casa, los jóvenes no tienen muchas opciones si no pueden manejar ellos mismos.

La abogada Pérez en la fuente #1 usa la datos para presentar un argumento fuerte, ya que las cifras no mienten. Se dice que los adolescentes representan más de 40 % de los 42.000 fallecimientos automovilísticos anuales. Además, cita prueba científica que muestra que los niveles de desarrollo cerebral no alcanzan el máximo nivel de madurez hasta que la gente llegue a los 20 años o más.

Tal vez una buena solución sería combinar los dos puntos de vista y proponer una ley que tenga lo que los dos buscan: exigirles a los jóvenes adiestramiento formal con unas horas de práctica requeridas, y solo permitirles manejar de noche a los 17 años y 6 meses. Además, con los adelantos tecnológicos, hay maneras de vigilar su manera de conducir, y estos también pueden enseñarles a ser mejores conductores. Es una cuestión de encontrar un balance entre la seguridad y la libertad, para proteger, como explica Pérez, "nuestros ciudadanos más vulnerables".

Translation

The issue of changing the minimum driving age is one that has awakened contradictory feelings among different generations. We see that the author of the speech greatly supports the decision to raise the minimum driving age. But on the other hand, the young people in source #2 question that perhaps her concerns are motivated by the need to control the younger generations and limit their rights, which is expressed by the independent spirit of John Grant in source #2. He questions that perhaps the concerns are motivated by a need to control the younger generation and limit their rights. He wonders if that movement is perhaps one of censoring and denying the young the democratic process.

Other young people disagree with the option of raising the driving age for economic reasons. As source #2 indicates, 25% of young people work after school. Their income, explains another teenager, contributes to the family budget. To deny them this opportunity to drive at 16 years old could bring grave economic effects. We must remember that the United States does not have a developed public transportation system like those of other countries, and since nowadays both parents tend to work outside the home, teenagers don't have many options if they can't drive themselves.

In source #1, the lawyer Pérez uses data to present a strong argument, given that statistics don't lie. It is said that teenagers represent 40% of the 42,000 annual automotive deaths. In addition, she cites scientific evidence that shows that the brain development levels do not reach full maturity until people reach their twenties.

Perhaps a good solution would be to combine the two perspectives and propose a law that offers what both groups want: require young people to have formal training with required practice hours and allow them to drive at night only at 17 years and six months old. In addition, with technological advances, there are ways to monitor their driving; these also can teach them to be better drivers. It is a question of finding a balance between safety and freedom, to protect, as Pérez explains, "our most vulnerable citizens."

Explanation

This response did a good job in fulfilling all the requirements. The solution offered in the conclusion shows great synthesis of the material. There is visible comparing and contrasting throughout the presentation. A good way to help yourself do that is to write *"en cambio / por otra parte,"* which introduces contrasting ideas. This will force you to compare and contrast and fulfill a requirement. This response shows strong use of the language, it completes the task by referring to both sources, and has excellent topic development. As a result, it would score a 5.

5

REVIEW OF SPANISH VERB AND GRAMMAR FORMS

Time does not permit us to review every grammar topic covered on the AP Spanish Language Exam. Your best bet is to assume that you need to know all the grammar that you have studied. In the following pages, we will highlight the topics you should have mastered by test day. We strongly urge you to study your textbook and class notes for a more comprehensive review of grammar. If there is a topic that you don't fully understand and is not covered here, be sure to go through your textbook and ask your teacher about it well before test day. This is intended as a brief grammatical overview. It is *not* a comprehensive review. Keep in mind, however, that while there may be many grammar details to keep track of, they are not all complex or difficult topics. In other words, if you review the verb forms and grammar rules carefully and thoroughly, it can translate into higher quality responses on the exam.

BASIC TERMS

Although you won't see the following terms on the test, they are important because they will come up later in the chapter. Knowing these terms will allow you to understand the rules of grammar that you're about to review.

Noun: a person, place, or thing

EXAMPLES: Abraham Lincoln, New Jersey, a taco

Pronoun: a word that replaces a noun

EXAMPLES: Abraham Lincoln would be replaced by "he," New Jersey by "it," and a taco by "it." You'll see more about pronouns later.

Adjective: a word that describes a noun

EXAMPLES: cold, soft, colorful

Verb: an action—a word that describes what is being done in a sentence

EXAMPLE: Ron *ate* the huge breakfast.

Infinitive: the original, unconjugated form of a verb

EXAMPLES: to eat, to run, to laugh

Auxiliary Verb: the verb that precedes the past participle in the perfect tense

EXAMPLE: He *had* eaten his lunch.

Past Participle: the appropriate form of a verb when it is used with the auxiliary verb

EXAMPLE: They have *gone* to work.

Adverb: word that describes a verb, adjective, or another adverb, just like an adjective describes a noun

EXAMPLES: slowly, quickly, happily (In English, adverbs often, but don't always, end in -ly.)

Subject: the person or thing (noun) in a sentence that is performing the action

EXAMPLE: *John* wrote the song.

Compound Subject: a subject that's made up of two or more subjects or nouns

EXAMPLES: *John and Paul* wrote the song together.

Object: the person or thing (noun or pronoun) in the sentence that the action is happening to, either directly or indirectly

EXAMPLES: Mary bought *the shirt*. Joe hit *him*. Mary gave a gift to *Tim*.

Direct Object: the thing that receives the action of the verb

EXAMPLE: I see *the wall*. (The wall "receives" the action of seeing.)

Indirect Object: the person who receives the direct object

EXAMPLE: I wrote *her* a letter. (She receives a letter.)

Preposition: a word that marks the relationship (in space or time) between two other words

EXAMPLES: He received the letter *from* her. The book is *below* the chair.

Article: a word (usually a very small word) that precedes a noun

EXAMPLES: *a* watch, *the* room

That wasn't so bad, was it? Now let's put all those terms together in a few examples.

Dominic	spent	the	entire	night	here.
subject	verb	article	adjective	dir. obj.	adverb

Margaret	often	gives	me	money.
subject	adverb	verb	indir. obj. pronoun	dir. obj.

Alison and Rob	have	a	gorgeous	child.
compound subject	verb	article	adjective	dir. obj.

PRONOUNS

You already learned that a pronoun is a word that takes the place of a noun. Now you'll review what pronouns look like in Spanish. There are three basic types.

SUBJECT PRONOUNS

These are the most basic pronouns and probably the first ones you learned. Just take a moment to look them over to make sure you haven't forgotten them. Then spend some time looking over the examples that follow until you are comfortable using them.

yo	me	**nosotros/as**	us
tú	you (singular)	**vosotros/as**	you (plural)
él, ella, Ud.	him, her, you (singular)	**ellos, ellas, Uds.**	them, you (plural)

When to Use Subject Pronouns

A subject pronoun (like any other pronoun) replaces the noun that is the subject of the sentence.

Marco no pudo comprar el helado.

Marco couldn't buy the ice cream.

Who performs the action of this sentence? Marco, so he is the subject. If we wanted to use a subject pronoun in this case, we'd replace "Marco" with **"él."**

Él no pudo comprar el helado.

He couldn't buy the ice cream.

DIRECT OBJECT PRONOUNS

Direct object pronouns replace (you guessed it) the direct object in a sentence.

me	me	**nos**	us
te	you (*tú* form)	**os**	you (*vosotros* form)
lo/la	him, it (masc.)/you (*Ud.* form)/ her, it (fem.)	**los/las**	them (masc./fem.)/ you (*Uds.* form)

When to Use Direct Object Pronouns

Now let's see what it looks like when we replace the direct object with a pronoun in a sentence.

> *Marco no pudo comprar el helado.*

What couldn't Marco buy? Ice cream. Since ice cream is what's receiving the action, it's the direct object. To use the direct object pronoun, you'd replace **helado** with **lo:**

> *Marco no pudo comprar**lo.***   or   *Marco no **lo** pudo comprar.*

When the direct object pronoun is used with the infinitive of a verb, it can either be tacked on to the end of the verb (the first example), or it can come before the conjugated verb in the sentence (the second example). Here is another example.

> *Voy a ver**lo.***   I'm going to see it.
>
> ***Lo** voy a ver.*   (Both sentences mean the same thing.)

The direct object pronoun also follows the verb in an affirmative command, for example.

> *¡Cóme**lo**!*   Eat it!
>
> *¡Escúcha**me**!*   Listen to me!

INDIRECT OBJECT PRONOUNS

These pronouns replace the indirect object in a sentence. Keep in mind that in Spanish, when the object is indirect, the preposition is often implied, not explicitly stated. So how can you tell the difference? In general, the indirect object is the person who receives the direct object.

me	me	**nos**	us
te	you (*tú* form)	**os**	you
le	him, her, you (*Ud.* form)	**les**	them, you (*Ud.* form)

When to Use Indirect Object Pronouns

This may seem a bit strange, but in Spanish the indirect object pronoun is often present in a sentence that contains the indirect object noun.

> *Juan **le** da el abrigo al viejo.*
>
> Juan gives the old man the coat.

Notice that the sentence contains the indirect object noun (**viejo**) and the indirect object pronoun (**le**). This is often necessary to clarify the identity of the indirect object pronoun, or to emphasize that identity. Typically, an expression of clarification is used with the pronouns **le** and **les** and **se** (see below), but is not used with other pronouns.

*María **nos** ayudó.*	María helped us.
*Juan **me** trae el suéter.*	Juan brings me the sweater.

The identity of the indirect object is obvious with the choice of pronoun in these examples and so is not necessary for clarification. It may be used, however, to emphasize the identity of the indirect object.

*No **me** lo trajeron a mí; **te** lo trajeron a ti.*
They didn't bring it to **me**; they brought it to **you.**

We would change our intonation to emphasize these words in English. This doesn't happen in Spanish; the expressions **a mí** and **a ti** serve the same function.

Se is used in place of **le** and **les** whenever the pronoun that follows begins with **l**.

*¿**Le** cuentas la noticia a María?*	Are you telling Maria the news?
*Sí, **se** la cuento **a María.***	Yes, I'm telling it to her.
*¿**Les** prestas los guantes a los estudiantes?*	Do you lend gloves to the students?
*No, no **se** los presto **a ellos.***	No, I don't lend them to them.

Notice that **le** changes to **se** in the first example and **les** to **se** in the second because the direct object pronoun that follows begins with an **l**. Notice also the inclusion of **a María** and **a ellos** to clarify the identity of **se** in each example.

Prepositional Pronouns

As we mentioned earlier, there are some pronouns that take an explicitly stated preposition, and they're different from the indirect object pronouns. The prepositional pronouns are as follows.

mí	me	**nosotros/nosotras**	us
ti/Ud.	you (*tú* form-*Ud.* form)	**vosotros/vosotras/Uds.**	you (plural)
él/ella/Ud.	him/her	**ellos/ellas/Uds.**	them

When to Use Prepositional Pronouns

Consider the following examples:

1. *Cómprale un regalo de cumpleaños.*	Buy him a birthday present.
2. *Vamos al teatro sin él.*	We're going to the theater **without** him.

Notice that in the first example, "him" is translated as **le,** whereas in the second, "him" is translated as **él.** What exactly is the deal with that?! Why isn't it the same word in Spanish as in English? In Spanish, the different pronouns distinguish the different functions of the word within the sentence.

In the first example, "him" is the indirect object of the verb "to buy" (Buy the gift for whom? For him—"him" receives the direct object), so we use the indirect object pronoun **le.** In the second example, however, "him" is the object of the preposition "without," so we use the prepositional pronoun **"él."** Here are some more examples that involve the prepositional pronouns. Notice that they all have explicitly stated prepositions.

*Las flores son **para** ti.*	The flowers are **for** you.
*Estamos enojados **con** él.*	We are angry **with** him.
*Quieren ir de vacaciones **sin** Uds.*	They want to go on vacation **without** you.

In two special cases, when the preposition is **con** and the object of the preposition is **mí** or **ti,** the preposition and the pronoun are combined to form **conmigo** (with me) and **contigo** (with you).

*¿Quieres ir al concierto **conmigo**?*	Do you want to go to the concert **with me?**
*No, no puedo ir **contigo**.*	No, I can't go **with you.**

When the subject is **él, ella, ellos, ellas, Ud.,** or **Uds.,** and the object of the preposition is the **same** as the subject, the prepositional pronoun is **sí,** and is usually accompanied by **mismo/a** or **mismos/as:**

*Alejandro es muy egoísta. Siempre habla de **sí mismo**.*

Alejandro is very egotistical. He always talks about **himself.**

*Ellos compran ropa para **sí mismos** cuando van de compras.*

They buy clothes for **themselves** when they go shopping.

POSSESSIVE ADJECTIVES AND PRONOUNS

Possessive adjectives and pronouns are used to indicate ownership. When you want to let someone know what's yours, use the following pronouns or adjectives:

STRESSED POSSESSIVE ADJECTIVES

mío/mía	mine	**nuestro/nuestra**	ours
tuyo/tuya	yours (fam.)	**vuestro/vuestra**	yours
suyo/suya	his, hers, yours (for *Ud.*)	**suyo/suya**	theirs, yours (for *Uds.*)

UNSTRESSED POSSESSIVE ADJECTIVES

mi	my	**nuestro/nuestra**	our
tu	your (fam.)	**vuestro/vuestra**	yours
su	his/her/your (for *Ud.*)	**su**	their, your (for *Uds.*)

When to Use Possessive Adjectives

The first question is, "When do you use an unstressed adjective, and when do you use a stressed adjective?" Check out these examples, and then we'll see what the rule is.

*Ésta es **mi** casa.*	*Esta casa es **mía**.*
This is **my** house.	This house is **mine**.
*Aquí está **tu** cartera.*	*Esta cartera es **tuya**.*
Here is **your** wallet.	This wallet is **yours**.

The difference between stressed and unstressed possessive adjectives is emphasis, as opposed to meaning. Saying "This is my house" puts emphasis on the house, while saying "This house is mine," takes the focus off of the house and stresses the identity of its owner—me. To avoid getting confused, just remember that unstressed is the Spanish equivalent of "my" and stressed is the Spanish equivalent of "mine."

In terms of structure, there is an important difference between the two types of adjectives, but it's an easy one to remember: Stressed adjectives come after the verb, but unstressed adjectives come before the noun. Notice that neither type agrees with the possessor; they agree with the thing possessed.

If it's not clear to you why these are adjectives when they look so much like pronouns, consider their function. When you say "my house," the noun "house" is being described by "my." Any word that describes a noun is an adjective, even if that word looks a lot like a pronoun. The key is how it's being used in the sentence.

POSSESSIVE PRONOUNS

Possessive pronouns look like stressed possessive adjectives, but they mean something different. Possessive pronouns *replace* nouns; they don't *describe* them.

When to Use Possessive Pronouns

This type of pronoun is formed by combining the article of the noun that's being replaced with the appropriate stressed possessive adjective. Just like stressed possessive adjectives, possessive pronouns must agree in gender and number with the nouns they replace.

Mi bicicleta es azul.	*La mía es azul.*
My bicycle is blue.	**Mine** is blue.

Notice how the pronoun not only shows possession, but also replaces the noun. Here are some more examples.

Mis zapatos son caros.	*Los míos son caros.*
My shoes are expensive.	**Mine** are expensive.
Tu automóvil es rápido.	*El tuyo es rápido.*
Your car is fast.	**Yours** is fast.
No me gustaban los discos que ellos trajeron.	*No me gustaban los suyos.*
I didn't like the records they brought.	I didn't like **theirs.**

REFLEXIVE PRONOUNS

Remember those reflexive verbs you learned about in class (**ponerse, hacerse,** and so on)? Those all have a common characteristic, which is that they indicate the action is being done to or for oneself. When those verbs are conjugated, the reflexive pronoun (which is always **se** in the infinitive) changes according to the subject.

me	myself	**nos**	ourselves
te	yourself (fam.)	**os**	yourselves (fam.)
se	him/herself/yourself (for *Ud.*)	**se**	themselves/yourselves (for *Uds.*)

Reflexive pronouns are used when the subject and indirect object of the sentence are the same. This may sound kind of strange, but after you see some examples it ought to make more sense.

> *Alicia se pone el **maquillaje.***
>
> **Alicia** puts on makeup.
>
> What does she put on? **Makeup**—direct object.
>
> Who receives the makeup? **Alicia**—she's also the subject.

The action is thus *reflected* back upon itself: Alicia does the action and then receives it. No outside influences are involved.

Another meaning for reflexive verbs is literally that the person does something directly to or for him/herself.

> *Rosa **se cortó** con el cuchillo.*
>
> Rosa **cut herself** with the knife.
>
> *Roberto tiene que **comprarse** una libreta nueva.*
>
> Roberto has to **buy himself** a new notebook.

THE RELATIVE PRONOUNS (QUE, QUIEN, AND QUIENES)

Relative pronouns connect a noun or pronoun to a clause that describes the noun or pronoun. They may represent people or things or ideas, and they may function as subjects, direct or indirect objects, or as objects of prepositions. Unlike English, the relative pronouns cannot be omitted in Spanish.

Let's look at some examples with relative pronouns in their various functions.

Remember that **que** is used to refer to people and things. **Quien(es)** is used to refer only to people.

1. As a subject:	*Busco el libro que estaba en mi mochila.*
	I am looking for the book that was in my bookbag.
2. As a direct object:	*Hicimos la tarea que la profesora nos asignó.*
	We did the assignment that the professor gave us.
3. As an indirect object:	*No conozco a la prima a quien le mandé la invitación.*
	I don't know the cousin to whom I sent the invitation.
4. As an object of a preposition:	*Ud. no conoce a los alumnos de quienes hablo.*
	You don't know the students who I am talking about.

The relative pronoun **cuyo** acts as an adjective and agrees with the noun it introduces, not the possessor.

> *El alumno, cuyas notas son excelentes, es un chico muy simpático.*
>
> The student, whose grades are excellent, is a very nice boy.

INTERROGATIVE WORDS

You probably know most of your interrogative words in Spanish by this time, but it wouldn't hurt for you to review them. Remember that they all have an accent when used as part of a question. Let's look briefly at one common student mistake: **Cuál** (meaning *which* or *what*) is used when a choice is involved. It's used in place of **que** before the verb **ser**, and it has only two forms: singular (**cuál**) and plural (**cuáles**). Both **cuál** and the verb **ser** must agree in number with the thing(s) being asked about.

> *¿**Cuál** es tu ciudad favorita?*   **What** is your favorite city?
>
> *¿**Cuáles** son nuestros regalos?*   **Which** presents are ours?

ADJECTIVES

Demonstrative pronouns have an accent on the first **"e."** The adjectives don't. First, learn the construction and meaning.

este/esta	this (one)	**estos/estas**	these
ese/esa	that (one)	**esos/esas**	those
aquel/aquella	that (one over there)	**aquellos/aquellas**	those (over there)

Adjective or Pronoun—Which Is It?

If the demonstrative word comes before a noun, then it is an adjective.

> ***Este** plato de arroz con pollo es mío.*   **This** plate of chicken and rice is mine.
>
> ***Ese** edificio es de mi hermano.*   **That** building is my brother's.

If the demonstrative word takes the place of a noun, then it's a pronoun.

> *Dije que **éste** es mío.*   I said that this one is mine.
>
> *Sabemos que **ése** es de mi hermano.*   We know **that one** is my brother's.

When used as adjectives, these words mean *this*, *that*, and so on. When used as pronouns, they mean *this one*, *that one*, and so on.

PRONOUN SUMMARY

You should know the following types of pronouns: subject, object (direct and indirect), possessive, prepositional, reflexive, and demonstrative.

- Don't just memorize what the different pronouns look like! Recognizing them is important, but it's just as important that you understand how and when to use them.

- When selecting your final answer choices, don't forget about POE. Something simple (like the gender of a pronoun) is easy to overlook if you're not on your toes. Before you start thinking about grammar, cancel answers that are wrong based on flagrant stuff like gender, singular versus plural, and so on.

- If all else fails, your ear can sometimes be your guide. In learning Spanish, you probably spoke and heard the language on a pretty regular basis, and so you have a clue as to what correct Spanish sounds like. You don't want to use your ear if you can eliminate answers based on the rules of grammar, but if you've exhausted the rules and you're down to two answers, one of which sounds a lot better than the other, choose the correct-sounding one. The fact is many grammatical rules were born out of a desire to make the language sound good.

HOW WELL DO YOU KNOW YOUR PRONOUNS?

1. *Si él puede hacerlo solo, yo no _____ tengo que ayudar.*
   - (A) la
   - (B) lo
   - (C) le
   - (D) los

2. *Pedimos asientos cerca de una ventanilla, pero _____ dieron éstos.*
   - (A) nos
   - (B) les
   - (C) nuestros
   - (D) me

3. *Cuando sus estudiantes se portan mal, la profesora _____ castiga.*
   - (A) las
   - (B) los
   - (C) les
   - (D) le

4. *¿Son _____ aquellos guantes que están sobre la butaca?*
   - (A) mío
   - (B) mía
   - (C) míos
   - (D) mías

5. *Para tus cumpleaños _____ daré un caballo nuevo.*
   (A) le
   (B) te
   (C) a ti
   (D) me

6. *¿ _____ es tu cantante favorito?*
   (A) Quién
   (B) Cuál
   (C) Quiénes
   (D) Qué

7. *¿ _____ prefieres? ¿El azul o el rojo?*
   (A) Qué
   (B) Cuál
   (C) Cuáles
   (D) Ese

ANSWERS AND EXPLANATIONS

1. If he can do it alone, I don't have to help _____ .
   (A) her
   (B) him (direct object)
   (C) him (indirect object)
   (D) them

Whom do I have to help? **Him,** which is the direct object, therefore (B) is the answer.

2. We asked for window seats, but they gave _____ these.
   (A) us
   (B) them (indirect object)
   (C) ours
   (D) me

Pedimos tells you that the subject of the sentence is **nosotros.** Since you are trying to say, "they gave us these," the correct pronoun is **nos.**

3. When her students misbehave, the professor punishes _____ .
   (A) them (f., direct object)
   (B) them (m., direct object)
   (C) to them (indirect object)
   (D) to him (indirect object)

Estudiantes is masculine and plural, so choices (A) and (D) are incorrect. (Remember that in Spanish the masculine pronoun is used whenever the gender of a group is mixed, even if the majority of the group is female. Also, when the gender of the people in the group is unknown [like in this question] the male pronoun is used.) Whom does the professor punish? **Them,** which is the direct object; therefore (B) is the answer.

4. Are those gloves that are on the armchair _____ ?
    (A) mine (m., sing.)
    (B) mine (f., sing.)
    (C) mine (m., pl.)
    (D) mine (f., pl.)

Guantes is a masculine plural word, so the correct form of the possessive adjective is **míos,** which is choice (C).

5. For your birthday, I'll give _____ a new horse.
    (A) him (indirect object)
    (B) you
    (C) to you
    (D) me

The person whose birthday it is in the sentence is **tú,** so **te** is the correct indirect object pronoun. It is indirect in this case because it receives the direct object "horse." Choice (C) is incorrect because it is an expression of emphasis that complements an indirect object pronoun. However, there is no indirect object pronoun to complement, so it can't be right. The indirect object pronoun itself is necessary, so (B) is the best answer.

6. _____ is your favorite singer?
    (A) Who
    (B) Which
    (C) Who (pl.)
    (D) What

Since the question refers to a single person (**el cantante**), **quién** is the correct pronoun.

7. _____ do you prefer? The blue one or the red one?
    (A) What
    (B) Which
    (C) Which (pl.)
    (D) That one

In this question a choice is being given, so **cuál** is used instead of **qué. Cuáles** is incorrect because the choice is between two singular things.

VERBS

You probably learned what felt like a zillion different verbs and tenses in Spanish class. For the purposes of the AP Spanish Language Exam, you should focus on recognizing clues in the sentences that suggest certain tenses, and then finding the answer in the appropriate tense. Even if you don't know which answer is in the tense that corresponds to the sentence, you can still cancel answers that definitely aren't correct. Use POE! A brief review of the tenses that show up on the test is probably a good place to begin, so let's get right to it.

THE PRESENT TENSE (A.K.A. THE PRESENT INDICATIVE)

The present tense is the easiest, and probably the first, tense that you ever learned. It is used when the action is happening in the present, as in the following example:

> *Yo **hablo** con mis amigos cada día.*
>
> I **speak** with my friends each day.

You should know the present tense inside and out if you are enrolled in an AP Spanish class, but take a quick glance at the following verb conjugations just to refresh your memory:

	trabajar	vender	escribir
yo	trabajo	vendo	escribo
tú (fam.)	trabajas	vendes	escribes
él/ella/Ud.	trabaja	vende	escribe
nosotros/nosotras	trabajamos	vendemos	escribimos
vosotros/vosotras (fam.)	trabajáis	vendéis	escribís
ellos/ellas/Uds.	trabajan	venden	escriben

THE PAST TENSE (A.K.A. THE PRETERITE)

> *Ayer yo **hablé** con mis amigos.*
>
> Yesterday I **spoke** with my friends. (The action began and ended.)

There are many different tenses that are considered past tenses—all of which describe actions that took place at various points in the past. There are, for example, different tenses for saying "I spoke," "I was speaking," "I have spoken," and so on. Let's start by reviewing the most basic of these: the plain past tense.

	trabajar	vender	escribir
yo	trabajé	vendí	escribí
tú (fam.)	trabajaste	vendiste	escribiste
él/ella/Ud.	trabajó	vendió	escribió
nosotros/nosotras	trabajamos	vendimos	escribimos
vosotros/vosotras	trabajasteis	vendisteis	escribisteis
ellos/ellas/Uds.	trabajaron	vendieron	escribieron

The easiest forms to spot are the first and third person singular (**yo** and **él/ella/Ud.** forms) because of the accent.

THE FUTURE TENSE

The future tense is used to describe things that will *definitely* happen in the future. The reason we stress definitely is that there is a different verbal mode (the dreaded subjunctive) used to describe things that *may* happen in the future. In Spanish, just as in English, there is a difference between being certain ("I will go") and being uncertain ("I may go"), and different forms are used for the different degrees of certainty. You'll see the fancier stuff later. First take a look at the regular future tense.

*Mañana yo **hablaré** con mis amigos.*

Tomorrow I **will speak** with my friends.

Notice that what takes two words to say in English (**will speak**) takes only one word to say in Spanish (**hablaré**). The future is a nice, simple tense (no auxiliary verb, only one word), which is easy to spot thanks to the accents and the structure. The future is formed by tacking on the appropriate ending to the infinitive of the verb *without dropping the -ar, -er, or -ir.*

	trabajar	vender	escribir
yo	trabajaré	venderé	escribiré
tú (fam.)	trabajarás	venderás	escribirás
él/ella/Ud.	trabajará	venderá	escribirá
nosotros/nosotras	trabajaremos	venderemos	escribiremos
vosotros/vosotras	trabajaréis	venderéis	escribiréis
ellos/ellas/Uds.	trabajarán	venderán	escribirán

THE PRESENT PERFECT

The present perfect is used to refer to an action that began in the past and is continuing into the present (and possibly beyond). It is also used to describe actions that were completed very close to the present. Compare these sentences.

1. *Ayer **hablé** con mis amigos.*
   Yesterday **I spoke** with my friends.

   ***Decidiste** no ir al cine.*
   You decided not to go to the movies.

2. ***He hablado** mucho con mis amigos recientemente.*
   I have spoken a lot with my friends lately.

   ***Has decidido** hacerte abogado.*
   You have decided (recently) to become a lawyer.

The first examples are just the plain past tense: You started and finished talking with your friends yesterday, and you completed the process of deciding not to go to the movies. In the second examples, the use of the present perfect tense moves the action to the very recent past, instead of leaving it in the more distant past. The present perfect, then, is essentially a more precise verb form of the past, used when the speaker wants to indicate that an action happened very recently in the past.

Spotting the perfect tenses is rather easy. This is a compound tense, meaning that it is formed by combining two verbs: a tense of the auxiliary (or helping) verb **haber** (present, imperfect, future, conditional) and the past participle of the main verb.

	trabajar	vender	escribir
yo	**he** trabaj**ado**	**he** vend**ido**	**he** escrito
tú (fam.)	**has** trabaj**ado**	**has** vend**ido**	**has** escrito
él/ella/Ud.	**ha** trabaj**ado**	**ha** vend**ido**	**ha** escrito
nosotros/nosotras	**hemos** trabaj**ado**	**hemos** vend**ido**	**hemos** escrito
vosotros/vosotras	**habéis** trabaj**ado**	**habéis** vend**ido**	**habéis** escrito
ellos/ellas/Uds.	**han** trabaj**ado**	**han** vend**ido**	**han** escrito

Most past participles are formed by dropping the last two letters from the infinitive and adding **-ido** (for **-er** and **-ir** verbs) or **-ado** (for **-ar** verbs). **Escribir** has an irregular past participle, as do some other verbs, but don't worry about it. This is no problem, since the irregulars still look and sound like the regulars, and, with respect to this tense, you still know it's the present perfect because of **haber.**

THE IMPERFECT

The imperfect is yet another past tense. It is used to describe actions that occurred continuously in the past and exhibited no definitive end at that time. This is different from the preterite, which describes "one-time" actions that began and ended at the moment in the past that is being described. Look at the two together, and the difference between them will become clearer.

*Ayer **yo hablé** con mis amigos y luego **me fui**.*

Yesterday **I spoke** with my friends and then left.

(The act of speaking obviously ended, because I left afterward.)

*Yo **hablaba** con mis amigos mientras **caminábamos**.*

I spoke with my friends while we walked.

(The act of speaking was **in progress** at that moment, along with walking.)

The imperfect is also used to describe conditions or circumstances in the past, since these are obviously ongoing occurrences.

Era una noche oscura y tormentosa.

It was a dark and stormy night.

*Cuando **tenía** diez años…*

When **I was** ten years old…

In the first example, it didn't just start or just stop being a stormy night, did it? Was the dark and stormy night already a past event at that point? No. The dark and stormy night was **in progress** at that moment, so the imperfect is used, not the preterite.

In the second example, did I start or stop being ten years old at that point? Neither. Was being ten already a past event at the moment I am describing? No. I was simply in the process of being ten years old at that moment in the past, so the imperfect is the more precise tense to use.

Make sense? Good; now check out the conjugation.

	trabajar	vender	escribir
yo	trabaj**aba**	vend**ía**	escrib**ía**
tú (fam.)	trabaj**abas**	vend**ías**	escrib**ías**
él/ella/Ud.	trabaj**aba**	vend**ía**	escrib**ía**
nosotros/nosotras	trabaj**ábamos**	vend**íamos**	escrib**íamos**
vosotros/vosotras	trabaj**abais**	vend**íais**	escrib**íais**
ellos/ellas/Uds.	trabaj**aban**	vend**ían**	escrib**ían**

Although the imperfect is similar to the other past tenses you've seen (e.g., the preterite and the present perfect), because it speaks of past actions, it looks quite different. That's the key since half of your job is just to know what the different tenses look like. The toughest part will be distinguishing the preterite from the imperfect.

BACK TO THE FUTURE: THE CONDITIONAL

Remember the future tense? (It's the one that is used to describe actions that are *definitely* going to happen in the future.) Well, now you will learn the other future tense you need to know; the one that is used to describe things that *may* happen in the future.

The conditional describes what could, would, or may happen in the future.

> *Me **gustaría** hablar con mis amigos cada día.*
>
> I **would like** to talk to my friends each day.
>
> *Con más tiempo, **podría** hablar con ellos el día entero.*
>
> With more time, I **could** speak with them all day long.
>
> *Si gastara cinco pesos, solamente me **quedarían** tres.*
>
> If I spent (were to spend) five dollars, I **would have** only three left.

It can also be used to make a request in a more polite way.

*¿**Puedes** prestar atención?*	*¿**Podrías** prestar atención?*
Can you pay attention?	**Could you** pay attention?

The conditional is formed by taking the future stem of the verb (which is the infinitive) and adding the conditional ending.

	trabajar	vender	escribir
yo	trabajar**ía**	vender**ía**	escribir**ía**
tú (fam.)	trabajar**ías**	vender**ías**	escribir**ías**
él/ella/Ud.	trabajar**ía**	vender**ía**	escribir**ía**
nosotros/nosotras	trabajar**íamos**	vender**íamos**	escribir**íamos**
vosotros/vosotras	trabajar**íais**	vender**íais**	escribir**íais**
ellos/ellas/Uds.	trabajar**ían**	vender**ían**	escribir**ían**

To avoid confusing the conditional with the future, concentrate on the conditional endings. The big difference is the accented **í**, which is in the conditional, but not in the future.

FUTURE	CONDITIONAL
trabajaré	trabajaría
venderán	venderían
escribiremos	escribiríamos

THE SUBJUNCTIVE

Don't give up now! Just two more verb modes (not tenses—the subjunctive is a different *manner* of speaking) and you'll be done with all this verb business (give or take a couple of special topics).

The Present Subjunctive

The present subjunctive is used in sentences that have *two distinct subjects* in *two different clauses*, generally (on this test, at least) in four situations.

1. When a *desire* or *wish* is involved.
   *Quiero que **comas** los vegetales.*
   I want you **to eat** the vegetables.
   *Ordenamos que Uds. nos **sigan**.*
   We order you (pl.) **to follow** us.

2. When *emotion* is involved.
   *Me alegro que **haga** buen tiempo hoy.*
   I am happy that the weather **is** nice today.
   *Te enoja que tu novio nunca te **escuche**.*
   It makes you angry that your boyfriend never **listens** to you.

3. When *doubt* is involved.
   *Ellos no creen que **digamos** la verdad.*
   They don't believe that **we are telling** the truth.
   *Jorge duda que su equipo **vaya** a ganar el campeonato.*
   Jorge doubts that his team **is going** to win the championship.

4. When an *impersonal expression* or *subjective commentary* is made.
   *Es ridículo que no **pueda** encontrar mis llaves.*
   It's ridiculous that I **can't** find my keys.
   *Es importante que los estudiantes **estudien** mucho.*
   It's important that students **study** a lot.

The subjunctive is formed by taking the **yo** form of the present tense, dropping the **-o**, and adding the appropriate ending.

	trabajar	vender	escribir
yo	trabaj**e**	vend**a**	escrib**a**
tú (fam.)	trabaj**es**	vend**as**	escrib**as**
él/ella/Ud.	trabaj**e**	vend**a**	escrib**a**
nosotros/nosotras	trabaj**emos**	vend**amos**	escrib**amos**
vosotros/vosotras	trabaj**éis**	vend**áis**	escrib**áis**
ellos/ellas/Uds.	trabaj**en**	vend**an**	escrib**an**

Commands are very similar to the present subjunctive form, perhaps because they are an obvious attempt to tell someone what to do. Let's look briefly at the formation of the regular commands.

	hablar	comer	subir
tú (fam.)	habla, no hables	come, no comas	sube, no subas
él/ella/Ud.	hable	coma	suba
nosotros/nosotras	hablemos	comamos	subamos
vosotros/vosotras	hablad, no habléis	comed, no comáis	subid, no subáis
ellos/ellas/Uds.	hablen	coman	suban

Remember: The affirmative **tú** (accent) form derives from the third person present singular tense, except for the verbs that are irregular in the **tú** (accent) form. The affirmative **vosotros** form comes from the infinitive, so the '**r**' is dropped and the '**d**' is added. All other command forms come from the subjunctive. ¡*Muy fácil*!

¡**Trabaja** con tu padre!	¡**Vende** el coche!	¡**Escribe** la carta!
Work with your father!	**Sell** the car!	**Write** the letter!

The Imperfect Subjunctive

This version of the subjunctive is used with the same expressions as the present subjunctive (wish or desire, emotion, doubt, impersonal commentaries), but it's used in the *past tense*.

> *Quería que comieras los vegetales.*
>
> I wanted you **to eat** the vegetables.
>
> *Me alegré que hiciera buen tiempo ayer.*
>
> I was happy that the weather **was** nice yesterday.
>
> *No creían que dijéramos la verdad.*
>
> They didn't believe that **we told** the truth.
>
> *Era ridículo que no pudiera encontrar mis llaves.*
>
> It was ridiculous that **I couldn't** find my keys.

One very important thing to notice in the examples above is that because the *expression* is in the past, you use the imperfect subjunctive. If you're looking at a sentence that you know takes the subjunctive, but you're not sure whether it's present or imperfect, focus on the expression. If the expression is in the present, use the present subjunctive. If the expression is in the past, use the imperfect subjunctive.

The imperfect subjunctive is also always used after the expression **como si,** which means "as if." This expression is used to describe hypothetical situations.

> *Él habla como si supiera todo.*
>
> He speaks as if **he knew** it all.
>
> *Gastamos dinero como si fuéramos millonarios.*
>
> We spend money as if **we were** millionaires.

The imperfect subjunctive is formed by taking the **ellos/ellas/Uds.** form of the preterite (which you already know, right?) and adding the correct ending.

	trabajar	vender	escribir
yo	trabajara	vendiera	escribiera
tú (fam.)	trabajaras	vendieras	escribieras
él/ella/Uds.	trabajara	vendiera	escribiera
nosotros/nosotras	trabajáramos	vendiéramos	escribiéramos
vosotros/vosotras	trabajarais	vendierais	escribierais
ellos/ellas/Uds.	trabajaran	vendieran	escribieran

Verbs that are in the imperfect subjunctive shouldn't be too tough to spot when they show up in the answer choices. The imperfect subjunctive has completely different endings from the preterite. It's not a compound tense, so you won't confuse it with the present perfect. The stems are different from the present subjunctive, so distinguishing between those two shouldn't be a problem.

SPECIAL TOPICS

Ser versus *Estar*

The verbs **ser** and **estar** both mean "to be" when translated into English. You may wonder, "Why is it necessary to have two verbs that mean exactly the same thing?" Good question. The answer is that in Spanish, unlike in English, there is a distinction between temporary states of being (e.g., "I am hungry") and fixed, or permanent states of being (e.g., "I am Cuban"). Although this difference seems pretty simple and easy to follow, there are some cases when it isn't so clear. Consider the following examples:

   El señor González _____ mi doctor.

   Cynthia _____ mi novia.

Would you use **ser** or **estar** in these two sentences? After all, Cynthia may or may not be your girlfriend forever, and the same goes for Mr. González's status as your doctor. You may get rid of both of them tomorrow (or one of them may get rid of you)! So which verb do you use?

In both cases, the answer is **ser**, because in both cases there is no *foreseeable* end to the relationships described. In other words, even though they may change, nothing in either sentence gives any reason to think they will. So whether you and Cynthia go on to marry or she dumps you tomorrow, you would be correct if you used **ser**. When in doubt, ask yourself, "does this action/condition have a definite end in the near or immediate future?" If so, use **estar.** Otherwise, use **ser.** Try the following drill:

Fill in the blank with the correct form of **ser** or **estar.**

1. Pablo _____ muy cansado.

2. El automóvil _____ descompuesto.

3. No puedo salir de casa esta noche porque _____ castigado.

4. Mi hermano _____ muy gracioso.

5. Mis profesores _____ demasiado serios.

6. Ayer salí sin abrigo, y hoy _____ enfermo.

7. Los tacos que mi madre cocina _____ ricos.

8. ¡No podemos empezar! Todavía no _____ listos.

Answers: 1) está 2) está 3) estoy 4) es 5) son 6) estoy 7) son 8) estamos

Don't assume that certain adjectives (like **enfermo**, for example) necessarily take **estar**. If you're saying someone is sick as in "ill," then **estar** is appropriate. If you're saying that someone is sick, as in, "a sickly person," then **ser** is correct.

Unfortunately, usage is not the only tough thing about **ser** and **estar**. They are both irregular verbs. Spend a little time reviewing the conjugations of **ser** and **estar** before you move on.

> **estar**
>
> **present:** estoy, estás, está, estamos, estáis, están
>
> **preterite:** estuve, estuviste, estuvo, estuvimos, estuvistéis, estuvieron
>
> **pres. subj.:** esté, estés, esté, estemos, estéis, estén
>
> **imp. subj.:** estuviera, estuvieras, estuviera, estuviéramos, estuvierais, estuvieran

The other tenses of **estar** follow the regular patterns for **-ar** verbs.

> **ser**
>
> **present:** soy, eres, es, somos, sois, son
>
> **imperfect:** era, eras, era, éramos, erais, eran
>
> **preterite:** fui, fuiste, fue, fuimos, fuistéis, fueron
>
> **pres. subj.:** sea, seas, sea, seamos, seáis, sean
>
> **imp. subj.:** fuera, fueras, fuera, fuéramos, fuerais, fueran

The other tenses of **ser** follow the regular patterns for **-er** verbs.

Conocer versus Saber

As you probably remember from Spanish I, there is another pair of verbs that have the same English translation but are used differently in Spanish. However, don't worry; these two have (for the most part) regular conjugations, and knowing when to use them is really very straightforward.

The words **conocer** and **saber** both mean "to know." In Spanish, knowing a person or a thing (basically, a noun) is different from knowing a piece of information. Compare the uses of **conocer** and **saber** in these sentences.

> *¿**Sabes** cuánto cuesta la camisa?*
>
> **Do you know** how much the shirt costs?
>
> *¿**Conoces** a mi primo?*
>
> **Do you know** my cousin?
>
> ***Sabemos** que Pelé era un gran futbolista.*
>
> **We know** that Pelé was a great soccer player.
>
> ***Conocemos** a Pelé.*
>
> **We know** Pelé.

When what's known is a person, place, or thing, use **conocer.** It's like the English, "acquainted with." When what's known is a fact, use **saber.** The same basic rule holds for questions.

¿Sabe a qué hora llega el presidente?

Do you know at what time the president arrives?

¿Conoce al presidente?

Do you know the president?

Now that you know how they're used, take a look at their conjugations.

conocer

present: conozco, conoces, conoce, conocemos, conocéis, conocen

pres. subj.: conozca, conozcas, conozca, conozcamos, conozcáis, conozcan

The other tenses of **conocer** follow the regular **-er** pattern.

saber

present: sé, sabes, sabe, sabemos, sabéis, saben

preterite: supe, supiste, supo, supimos, supistéis, supieron

future: sabré, sabrás, sabrá, sabremos, sabréis, sabrán

conditional: sabría, sabrías, sabría, sabríamos, sabríais, sabrían

pres. subj.: sepa, sepas, sepa, sepamos, sepáis, sepan

imp. subj.: supiera, supieras, supiera, supiéramos, supieráis, supieran

In the following drill, fill in the blanks with the correct form of **conocer** or **saber:**

1. ¡Él _____ cocinar muy bien!

2. ¿_____ el libro que ganó el premio? (tú)

3. Las mujeres _____ bailar como si fueran profesionales.

4. ¿Es verdad que _____ a Michael Jackson? (ustedes)

5. Es importante _____ nadar.

6. No _____ cómo voy a ganar la carrera.

7. ¿Cómo puede ser que tú no _____ la casa donde viviste?

8. Los dos abogados no se _____ el uno al otro porque nunca han trabajado juntos.

9. _____ que vamos a divertirnos en el circo esta noche. (yo)

Answers: 1) sabe 2) Conoces 3) saben 4) conocen 5) saber 6) sé 7) conoces 8) conocen 9) Sé

VERB SUMMARY

The tenses you need to know are the present, past, future, and perfect tenses; both subjunctive forms; and the command forms. You also need to know the subjunctive mode (both present and imperfect as well as the commands). In terms of memorizing and reviewing them, we think the best approach is to lump them together in the following way:

Present Tenses	Past Tenses	Future Tenses	Subjunctive	Commands
Present	Preterite	Future	Present	
	Imperfect	Conditional	Imperfect	
	Present perfect			

By thinking in terms of these groupings, you'll find that eliminating answers is a snap once you've determined the tense of the sentence. That is your first step on a question that tests your knowledge of verb tenses: Determine the tense of the sentence (or at least whether it's a past, present, or future tense), and cancel.

When memorizing the uses of the different tenses, focus on clues that point to one tense or another.

- There are certain expressions (wish or desire, emotion, doubt, and impersonal commentaries) that tell you to use the subjunctive, and whether the expression is in the present or the past will tell you which subjunctive form to use.

- To distinguish between future and conditional, focus on the certainty of the event's occurrence.

- The three past tenses are differentiated by the end (or lack thereof) of the action and when that end occurred (if it occurred at all). If the action had a clear beginning and ending in the past, use the regular past. If the action was a continuous action in the past, use the imperfect. If the action began in the past and is continuing into the present, or ended very close to the present, use the present perfect.

- Recognizing the different tenses shouldn't be too tough if you focus on superficial characteristics.

- Certain tenses have accents, while others do not.

- Review all the verb forms by studying your textbook.

How Well Do You Know Your Verbs?

1. *Cuando tenga dinero, te _____ un automóvil de lujo.*
   - (A) compraré
   - (B) compré
   - (C) compraría
   - (D) compraste

2. *Quiero que _____ la tarea antes de acostarte.*
   - (A) hiciste
   - (B) hace
   - (C) haga
   - (D) hagas

3. *El año pasado nosotros _____ a México para las vacaciones.*
   - (A) iremos
   - (B) fuimos
   - (C) iríamos
   - (D) vamos

4. *Si tuvieran tiempo, ellos _____ el tiempo relajándose.*
   - (A) pasan
   - (B) pasaban
   - (C) pasen
   - (D) pasarían

5. *Esperaba que Uds. _____ a construir el barco.*
   - (A) ayudarían
   - (B) ayudaran
   - (C) ayudaron
   - (D) ayudan

6. *Carlos _____ mucho tiempo estudiando la biología últimamente.*
   - (A) pasó
   - (B) pasaría
   - (C) pasaba
   - (D) ha pasado

Answers and Explanations to Verb Questions

1. When I have money, I _____ you a luxury car.
   (A) **will buy (future)**
   (B) bought (past, *yo* form)
   (C) would buy (conditional)
   (D) bought (past, *tú* form)

The sentence refers to something that will happen in the future. It is an example of the present subjunctive (**tenga**) used with the future tense to express an action that will happen if another action is fulfilled. In this case, the intent to buy the car is certain (I will buy you a luxury car). Therefore, the future, or choice (A), is correct.

2. I want you to _____ the homework before going to bed.
   (A) did (past, *tú* form)
   (B) does (present, *él* form)
   (C) do (present subjunctive, *él* form)
   (D) **do (present subjunctive, *tú* form)**

Quiero que is one of those expressions that tells you to use the subjunctive. In this case, the expression is in the present tense, so the present subjunctive is correct. If the expression were in the past (**quería que**), you'd use the imperfect subjunctive. The reason (D) is correct is that **te** is the reflexive pronoun in the sentence that tells you to use the **tú** form of the verb.

3. Last year we _____ to Mexico for vacation.
   (A) will go (future)
   (B) **went (past)**
   (C) would go (conditional)
   (D) go (present)

El año pasado (last year) is a big hint that the answer will be in one of the past tenses. There is only one answer choice with the past tense, choice (B).

4. If they had (were to have) time, they _____ the time relaxing.
   (A) spend (present)
   (B) spent (imperfect)
   (C) spend (present subjunctive)
   (D) **would spend (conditional)**

Si tuvieran tells you to use the conditional. In fact, **si** + the imperfect subjunctive often precedes the use of the conditional because it introduces a condition that doesn't currently exist. The only answer that's in the conditional is (D), **pasarían.**

5. I hoped that you _____ build the boat.

    (A) would help (conditional)

    (B) would help (imperfect subjunctive)

    (C) helped (past)

    (D) help (present)

Esperaba que is another one of those expressions of desire that tells you to use the subjunctive, but this time the expression is in the past, so the correct tense is the imperfect subjunctive. The tense of the expression is what tells you whether to use the present or the imperfect subjunctive.

6. Carlos _____ much time studying biology lately.

    (A) spent (past)

    (B) would spend (conditional)

    (C) spent (imperfect)

    (D) has spent (present perfect)

"Lately" suggests the past tense, but a more recent past tense. Answers (A) and (C) place the action too far in the past, while (B) is not a past tense. Therefore, (D) is the answer.

PREPOSITIONS

Prepositions are those little words that show the relationship between two other words. In English, they're words such as to, from, at, for, about, and so on. In Spanish, they're words like *a*, *de*, *sobre*, and so on.

Part of what you need to know about prepositions is what the different ones mean. That's the easy part. The other thing you need to know is how and when to use them. You need to know which verbs and expressions take prepositions and which prepositions they take. This isn't too difficult to learn, but it can be tricky.

COMMON PREPOSITIONS AND THEIR USES

- **a:** to; at

  ¿Vamos a la obra de teatro esta noche?

  Are we going to the play tonight?

  Llegamos a las cinco.

  We arrived at 5:00.

- **de:** of; from

  Son las gafas de mi hermano.

  Those are my brother's glasses.
  (Literally, the glasses of my brother.)

  Soy de la Argentina.

  I am from Argentina.

- **con:** with

  Me gusta mucho el arroz con pollo.

  I like chicken with rice a lot.

- **sobre:** on; about; over

  La chaqueta está sobre la mesa.

  The jacket is on the table.

  La conferencia es sobre la prevención del SIDA.

  The conference is about AIDS prevention.

  Los Yankees triunfaron sobre los Braves en la serie mundial.

  The Yankees triumphed over the Braves in the World Series.

- **antes de:** before

  Antes de salir quiero ponerme un sombrero.

  Before leaving I want to put on a hat.

- **después de:** after

  Después de la cena me gusta caminar un poco.

  After dinner I like to walk a little.

- **en:** in

  Regresan en una hora.

  They'll be back in an hour.

  Alguien está en el baño.

  Someone is in the bathroom.

- **entre:** between

  La carnicería está entre la pescadería y el cine.

  The butcher shop is between the fish store and the cinema.

  La conferencia duró entre dos y tres horas.

  The conference lasted between two and three hours.

- **durante:** during; for

  Durante el verano me gusta nadar cada día.

  During the summer I like to swim each day.

  Trabajé con mi amigo durante quince años.

  I worked with my friend for fifteen years.

- **desde:** since; from

  He tomado vitaminas desde mi juventud.

  I've been taking vitamins since childhood.

  Se pueden ver las montañas desde aquí.

  The mountains can be seen from here.

Para versus *Por*

The prepositions **para** and **por** both mean "for" (as well as other things, depending on context), but they are used for different situations, and so they tend to cause a bit of confusion. Luckily, there are some pretty clear-cut rules as to when you use **para** and when you use **por** because they both tend to sound fine even when they're being used incorrectly. Try to avoid using your ear when choosing between these two.

When to Use *Para*

The following are examples of the most common situations in which **para** is used. Instead of memorizing some stuffy rule, we suggest that you get a feel for what types of situations imply the use of **para,** so that when you see those situations come up on your AP Spanish Language Exam, you'll recognize them.

The preposition **para,** in very general terms, expresses the idea of *destination*, but in a very broad sense.

- **Destination in time**
  *El helado es **para** mañana.*
  The ice cream is for tomorrow. (Tomorrow is the ice cream's destination.)

- **Destination in space**
  *Me voy **para** el mercado.*
  I'm leaving for the market. (The market is my destination.)

- **Destination of purpose**
  *Compraste un regalo **para** Luis.*
  You bought a gift for Luis. (Luis is the destination of your purchase.)
  *Estudiamos **para** sacar buenas notas.*
  We study to get good grades. (Good grades are the destination of our studies.)

- **Destination of work**
  *Trabajo **para** IBM.*
  I work for IBM. (IBM is the destination of my work.)

Two uses of **para** do not indicate a sense of destination.

- **To express opinion**
  Para mí, el lunes es el día más largo de la semana.
  For me, Monday is the longest day of the week.

- **To qualify or offer a point of reference**
  Para un muchacho joven, tiene muchísimo talento.
  For a young boy, he has a lot of talent.

When to Use *Por*

Chances are, if you're not discussing destination in any way, shape, or form, or the other two uses of **para,** then you'll need to use **por.** If this general rule isn't enough for you, however, study the following possibilities and you should have all the bases covered.

- **To express how you got somewhere (by)**

  Fuimos a Italia por barco.

  We went to Italy by boat.

  Pasamos por esa tienda ayer cuando salimos del pueblo.

  We passed by that store yesterday when we left the town.

- **To describe a trade (in exchange for)**

  Te cambiaré mi automóvil por el tuyo este fin de semana.

  I'll trade you my car for yours this weekend.

- **To lay blame or identify cause (by)**

  Todos los barcos fueron destruidos por la tormenta.

  All the boats were destroyed by the storm.

- **To identify gain or motive (for; as a substitute for)**

  Ella hace todo lo posible por su hermana.

  She does everything possible for her sister.

  Cuando Arsenio está enfermo, su madre trabaja por él.

  When Arsenio is ill, his mother works (as a substitute) for him.

IR A AND *ACABAR DE*

Ir a is used to describe what the future will bring, or, in other words, what is going to happen. The expression is formed by combining the appropriate form of **ir** in the present tense (subject and verb must agree) with the preposition **a.**

Mañana vamos a comprar el árbol de Navidad.

Tomorrow we are going to buy the Christmas tree.

¿Vas a ir a la escuela aun si te sientes mal?

You're going to go to school even if you feel ill?

Acabar de is the Spanish equivalent of "to have just," and is used to talk about what has just happened. It is formed just like **ir a**, with the appropriate form of **acabar** in the present tense followed by **de**.

Acabo de terminar de cocinar el pavo.

I have just finished cooking the turkey.

Ellos acaban de regresar del mercado.

They have just returned from the supermarket.

OTHER PREPOSITIONS TO REMEMBER

Other prepositions and prepositional phrases you should know follow. Notice that many of these are merely adverbs with **a** or **de** tacked on to the end to make them prepositions.

hacia	toward
enfrente de	in front of
frente a	in front of
dentro de	inside of
fuera de	outside of
a la derecha de	to the right of
a la izquierda de	to the left of
debajo de	underneath
encima de	above, on top of
alrededor de	around, surrounding
en medio de	in the middle of
hasta	until
tras	behind
cerca de	near
lejos de	far from
detrás de	behind
(a) delante de	in front of
al lado de	next to

PREPOSITION SUMMARY

- Much of your work with prepositions boils down to memorization: which expressions and verbs go with which prepositions, and so on.

- You should concentrate on the boldfaced examples at the beginning of the preposition section since those are the most common. Once you're comfortable with them, the subsequent list should be a snap because many of those expressions are merely adverbs with **a** or **de** after them.

- Some verbs take prepositions all the time, some never do, and others sometimes do. This isn't as confusing as it may sound, however, because prepositions (or lack thereof) change the meaning of verbs. Consider the following:

Voy a tratar _____ despertarme más temprano.

(A) a

(B) de

(C) con

(D) sin

Which one of these goes with **tratar**? Actually, each of them does, depending on what you are trying to say. In this case you want to say "try to," so **de** is the appropriate preposition. **Tratar con** means "to deal with," and **tratar sin** means "to try/treat without," while **tratar a** doesn't mean anything unless a person is mentioned afterward; in which case it means "to treat." None of them makes sense in this sentence. The moral of the story is don't try to memorize which verbs go with which prepositions; concentrate on meaning.

HOW WELL DO YOU KNOW YOUR PREPOSITIONS?

1. Quiero llegar a la fiesta _____ María.

   (A) antes de

   (B) antes de que

   (C) a

   (D) sin que

2. Todos mis alumnos estuvieron _____ acuerdo conmigo.

   (A) entre

   (B) en

   (C) con

   (D) de

3. Estamos apurados, y por eso tenemos que viajar _____ el camino más corto.

   (A) dentro de

   (B) por

   (C) alrededor de

   (D) para

4. Los paraguas se usan _____ evitar la lluvia.

   (A) en medio de

   (B) hacia

   (C) para

   (D) por

5. La próxima semana ellos van _____ tocar aquí.

   (A) a

   (B) de

   (C) con

   (D) por

6. No me gusta ver las películas de horror _____ la noche.

   (A) tras de

   (B) sobre

   (C) en

   (D) durante

7. Salieron hace un rato, así que deben regresar _____ unos cinco minutos.

   (A) alrededor de

   (B) en vez de

   (C) en

   (D) después de que

ANSWERS AND EXPLANATIONS TO PREPOSITION QUESTIONS

1. I want to arrive at the party _____ María.

   (A) before

   (B) before (preceding a verb)

   (C) at, to

   (D) without (preceding a verb)

Answer choice (C) makes no sense in the context, so you can eliminate it right away. Because choices (B) and (D) both include a **que,** they imply another conjugated verb in the second part of the sentence, which is not there. Thus the correct answer is (A), **antes de.**

2. All of my students were _____ agreement with me.

   (A) between

   (B) in

   (C) with

   (D) in

This is a tough question, especially if you haven't seen the expression **estar de acuerdo.** In English we say that two people are "in agreement" with each other, but unfortunately the Spanish translation isn't the literal equivalent of the English expression. In Spanish two people **están de acuerdo.** (We know this isn't on your list, but that list is only a start: If you find new expressions that you don't know, add them to your list!)

3. We're in a rush, so we must travel _____ the shortest route.

   (A) inside of

   (B) by

   (C) around

   (D) for

This is the old **para** versus **por** trap, which is definitely tricky. In this case you want to say "travel by," and **por** is the preposition that sometimes means "by." **Para** is never used to mean "by."

4. Umbrellas are used _____ avoid the rain.
   (A) in the middle of
   (B) towards
   (C) in order to
   (D) for

Here it is again: **para** versus **por**. The other choices are pretty clearly wrong based on meaning, which leaves us with (C) and (D). In what sense are we saying "for" in this sentence? Is it "for the purpose of" (which would tell you to use **para**) or "for," as in a period of time or cause of action (which would tell you to use **por**)? In this case, "for the purpose of," or "in order to," fits pretty neatly, and so **para** is correct.

5. Next week they are going _____ play here.
   (A) to
   (B) of
   (C) with
   (D) for

Nice and easy, no tricks or traps, and it translates straight from English. This is an example of the use of **ir a**. Notice that **ir** is conjugated to agree with the subject of the sentence (**ellos**).

6. I don't like to see horror films _____ the night.
   (A) behind
   (B) on
   (C) in
   (D) during

Pretty tough call between (C) and (D) because both sound fine in the blank, but one of them makes a little more sense than the other if you think carefully about the difference in meaning between the two. Do you see films in (as in, "inside") the night, or during the night? They're sort of close, and the exact English would be "at night," but "during" makes a bit more sense.

7. They left a while ago, so they should return _____ about five minutes.
   (A) around
   (B) instead of
   (C) in
   (D) after

Basically what you're trying to say is that they'll be back soon, and "in five minutes" says that. "Around" would be fine if it were preceded by "in," or if "from now" were tacked on to the end of the sentence, but neither is the case here. Choice (B) doesn't really make sense. For choice (D), "que" eliminates the possibility of being a correct answer since it suggests verb usage after its use.

PART ◆ **II**

THE PRINCETON REVIEW
AP SPANISH LANGUAGE
PRACTICE TEST

6

LANGUAGE
PRACTICE TEST

Note to Reader

Following are the track numbers on the audio CD for all the dialogues, narratives, and selections you will be tested on in Section 1 of this practice test:

- Dialogue 1—Track 5

- Dialogue 2—Track 6

- Dialogue 3—Track 7

- Narrative number 1—Track 8

- Narrative number 2—Track 9

- Selection number 1—Track 10

- Selection number 2—Track 11

Good luck!

AP® Spanish Exam

SECTION I: Multiple-Choice Questions

DO NOT OPEN THIS BOOKLET UNTIL YOU ARE TOLD TO DO SO.

Instructions

Section I of this examination contains 69 multiple-choice questions. Fill in only the ovals for numbers 1 through 69 on your answer sheet.

Indicate all of your answers to the multiple-choice questions on the answer sheet. No credit will be given for anything written in this exam booklet, but you may use the booklet for notes or scratch work. After you have decided which of the suggested answers is best, completely fill in the corresponding oval on the answer sheet. Give only one answer to each question. If you change an answer, be sure that the previous mark is erased completely. Here is a sample question and answer.

At a Glance	
Total Time	
1 hour	
Number of Questions	
69	
Percent of Total Grade	
50%	
Writing Instrument	
Pencil required	

Sample Question   Sample Answer

Chicago is a   Ⓐ ● Ⓒ Ⓓ Ⓔ
(A) state
(B) city
(C) country
(D) continent
(E) village

Use your time effectively, working as quickly as you can without losing accuracy. Do not spend too much time on any one question. Go on to other questions and come back to the ones you have not answered if you have time. It is not expected that everyone will know the answers to all the multiple-choice questions.

About Guessing

Many candidates wonder whether or not to guess the answers to questions about which they are not certain. Multiple choice scores are based on the number of questions answered correctly. Points are not deducted for incorrect answers, and no points are awarded for unanswered questions. Because points are not deducted for incorrect answer, you are encouraged to answer all multiple-choice questions. On any questions you do not know the answer to, you should eliminate as many choices as you can, and then select the best answer among the remaining choices.

This page intentionally left blank.

NOW HERE IS THE FIRST DIALOGUE.

Dialogue number 1
AUDIO CD: Track 5

1. (A) el parque
   (B) el café
   (C) la estación de tren
   (D) la cocina

2. (A) Quiere tomar una merienda.
   (B) Quiere sentarse en el salón.
   (C) Quiere tomar el sol.
   (D) Quiere leer el periódico.

3. (A) la tarta de manzana
   (B) la tarta de chocolate
   (C) chocolate con churros
   (D) bizcochuelos

4. (A) Hace frío.
   (B) Llueve.
   (C) Está nublado.
   (D) Hace calor.

Dialogue number 2
AUDIO CD: Track 6

5. (A) Es la línea aérea.
   (B) Es la compañía de abogados.
   (C) Es el nombre del aeropuerto.
   (D) Es el nombre de la señora.

6. (A) Es azafata.
   (B) Trabaja en el mostrador de la línea aérea.
   (C) Es abogada.
   (D) Es la jefa de administración.

7. (A) Viaja a Londres.
   (B) Viaja a Barcelona.
   (C) Viaja a Burgos.
   (D) Viaja al mostrador de la línea aérea.

Dialogue number 3
AUDIO CD: Track 7

8. (A) Porque se murió su esposo.
   (B) Porque se murió su madre.
   (C) Porque se murió su tío.
   (D) Porque se murió su hermana.

9. (A) viajar
   (B) estudiar
   (C) trabajar
   (D) ir al cine

10. (A) Van al cine y después van a cenar.
    (B) Van a casa.
    (C) Van a una fiesta.
    (D) Van a trabajar.

GO ON TO THE NEXT PAGE.

Directions: You will now listen to two narratives. After each one, you will be asked some questions about what you have heard. Choose the best answer to each question from among the four choices printed in your test booklet and darken the corresponding oval on your answer sheet.

Instrucciones: Ahora oirás dos narraciones breves. Después de cada narración oirás varias preguntas sobre lo que acabas de oír. Elige la mejor respuesta de las cuatro posibles respuestas impresas en tu libreta de examen y rellena el óvalo correspondiente en la hoja de respuestas.

NOW GET READY FOR THE FIRST NARRATIVE.

> Narrative number 1
> AUDIO CD: Track 8

> Narrative number 2
> AUDIO CD: Track 9

11. (A) nuevo y moderno
    (B) pintoresco
    (C) histórico y prestigioso
    (D) innovador

12. (A) Hacía un tiempo agradable.
    (B) Hacía calor.
    (C) Nevaba.
    (D) Hacía un tiempo tempestuoso.

13. (A) Se sintió frustrado.
    (B) Se sintió muy a gusto.
    (C) Se sintió nostálgico.
    (D) Se sintió triste.

14. (A) Jugaba golf con su padre.
    (B) Acompañaba a su abuelo en el campo de golf.
    (C) Jugaba golf con su hermana.
    (D) Jugaba golf con su abuela.

15. (A) a la innovación de la construcción
    (B) a los elefantes y las jirafas
    (C) a la recaudación de dinero
    (D) a la preservación de los animales

16. (A) Costó diez millones de dólares.
    (B) Es muy grande y contiene aspectos de su hábitat natural.
    (C) Es muy limpio.
    (D) Ofrece cursos para la educación.

17. (A) Director del parque y naturalista.
    (B) El veterinario principal.
    (C) El agente de publicidad.
    (D) El gobernador de Virginia.

GO ON TO THE NEXT PAGE.

Directions: You will now hear two selections of about five minutes in length. You should take notes in the blank space provided, though your notes will not be graded. At the end of the narration, you will read a number of questions about what you have heard. Based on the content of the narration, choose the BEST answer for each question from among the four choices printed in your test booklet and darken the corresponding oval on the answer sheet.

Instrucciones: Ahora oirás dos selecciones de unos cinco minutos. Se debe tomar apuntes en el espacio en blanco de esta hoja. Estos apuntes no serán calificados. Al final de la narración, leerás unas cuantas preguntas sobre lo que acabas de oír. Basándote en el contenido de la narración, elige la MEJOR respuesta de las cuatro posibles respuestas a cada pregunta impresa en tu libreta de examen y rellena el óvalo correspondiente en la hoja de respuestas.

Write your notes on this page.

GO ON TO THE NEXT PAGE.

Selection number 1
AUDIO CD: Track 10

18. ¿Cómo interpretan algunos el movimiento feminista en España?

(A) Una lucha política

(B) Una cuestión artística

(C) Una competencia entre iguales

(D) Un concurso de belleza

19. ¿Cuál característica de la cultura española se puede considerar como el opuesto del movimiento feminista?

(A) El marianismo

(B) La honra

(C) La dignidad

(D) El machismo

20. Según la conferencia, ¿cúal es el objetivo ideológico del movimiento feminista?

(A) El triunfo de la mujer sobre el hombre

(B) La aceptación del marianismo en todo el mundo

(C) Una identidad individual para la mujer

(D) La apreciación de la cultura tradicional

21. Según la conferencia, ¿qué pensamiento surgió en la época de Franco?

(A) Un pensamiento radical

(B) Un pensamiento tradicional

(C) Un pensamiento progresivo

(D) Un pensamiento feminista

22. Según la conferencia, ¿qué debemos guardar de la sociedad tradicional machista?

(A) El papel de la mujer como madre

(B) El marianismo

(C) El papel de la mujer subordinada al hombre

(D) El machismo

GO ON TO THE NEXT PAGE.

Selection number 2
AUDIO CD: Track 11

23. ¿Cómo se interesó Alejandro Martínez en los juegos olímpicos especiales?

(A) Siempre había participado en los juegos especiales.

(B) Su hermano participaba en los juegos especiales.

(C) Su hijo respondió favorablemente a los deportes.

(D) Su esposa está muy metida en los juegos especiales.

24. ¿Cuándo se dedica Alejandro completamente a los juegos especiales?

(A) Los fines de semana

(B) Durante las vacaciones escolares

(C) En invierno

(D) En verano

25. Según la entrevista, ¿por qué no trabaja exclusivamente con los juegos especiales?

(A) Porque no gana suficiente dinero

(B) Porque es maestro de matemáticas

(C) Porque su hija le ocupa mucho tiempo

(D) Porque no podría soportarlo

26. ¿Por qué le gusta a Alejandro trabajar con los niños?

(A) Porque son jóvenes

(B) Porque son honestos

(C) Porque tienen mucho interés

(D) Porque tienen más habilidad

27. Según la entrevista, ¿por qué es terapéutico el ejercicio físico?

(A) Porque practican ejercicios especiales

(B) Porque los entrenadores tienen educación en terapia física

(C) Porque es divertido

(D) Porque les hace sentir mejor a los niños mentalmente y físicamente

28. ¿Cómo se caracteriza el espíritu colectivo de los niños?

(A) No saben colaborar con el grupo.

(B) Entienden instintivamente cómo colaborar.

(C) No saben funcionar físicamente.

(D) Hay mucha competencia entre los grupos.

29. Según la entrevista, ¿cuál característica describe mejor a los niños que participan en los juegos olímpicos especiales?

(A) Son muy delgados.

(B) Son muy delicados.

(C) Son muy dedicados.

(D) Son delegados a los juegos especiales.

30. ¿Qué recomienda Alejandro a las familias que no quieren participar en los juegos?

(A) Que se enteren de los eventos planeados

(B) Que sigan su corazón

(C) Que organicen sus propios juegos con los juegos especiales

(D) Que no participen

GO ON TO THE NEXT PAGE.

Directions: Read the following selections carefully for comprehension. Each selection is followed by a series of questions. Choose the BEST answer based on the passage and fill in the corresponding oval the answer sheet. There is no sample for this part.

Instrucciones: Lee con cuidado cada una de las selecciones siguientes. Cada selección va seguida de una serie de preguntas. Elige la MEJOR respuesta según la selección y rellena el óvalo correspondiente en la hoja de respuestas. No hay ejemplo en esta parte.

Nosotros llegamos al aeropuerto Charles de Gaulle a las seis de la mañana del viernes. Llevábamos mucho tiempo de viaje y estábamos rendidos de cansancio. La
Línea combinación de los asientos incómodos, el aire reciclado
5 y la comida genérica nos dejó en un estado de sueño nebuloso e irreal. Nos sentíamos sucios y malolientes. Después de esperar dos horas más (y ¿qué son dos horas más después de casi diez horas de viaje?) en el reclamo de equipaje, por fin supimos que nuestro equipaje se
10 había perdido. Bueno, en realidad el equipaje no se había perdido. Solamente optó por otra ruta y estaba a punto de llegar al aeropuerto Heathrow, en Londres. De acuerdo, el equipaje tenía que pasar primero por Londres. Estaría en el primer avión que sale para Charles de Gaulle. No tenía
15 sentido enfadarnos con los empleados. Ellos no entendían el estado soporífero en que nos encontrábamos. Tampoco les importaba mucho nuestra crisis. Ellos pudieron ducharse esta mañana. Seguramente tomaron su café habitual de las mañanas y su desayuno. Quizás llegaron al
20 trabajo sin ningún atasco ni otro problema de tráfico. Pero para nosotros la vida esta mañana no era tan fácil. ¡Con lo que nos encanta viajar! Decidimos irnos del aeropuerto y buscar el hotel. Luego un mozo nos llevaría el equipaje al hotel. ¡Qué servicial! Nos daba miedo pensar en la
25 propina que estaríamos obligados a regalarle. De todos modos, salimos del aeropuerto en busca de un taxi. Todo el mundo nos miraba de una forma rara. Seguramente querían saber dónde estaba nuestro equipaje. Por fin econtramos la parada de taxis. El señor que nos tocó era
30 mayor, pero con una cara muy amable. "Vamos al hotel Washington, por favor", declaró mi marido casualmente en su mejor francés. El taxista nos miró en el espejo como un lobo cuándo ve una manada de ovejas a través de las ramas de un árbol. Asintió con la cabeza y emprendió el
35 viaje a París.

31. ¿De qué se trata esta selección?
   (A) Las dificultades de unos viajeros
   (B) La vida de un piloto y su esposa
   (C) El aeropuerto Charles de Gaulle en París
   (D) El mejor equipaje para viajes cortos

32. ¿Cuál es el punto de vista de esta selección?
   (A) El punto de vista del piloto
   (B) El punto de vista de la azafata
   (C) El punto de vista de la esposa
   (D) El punto de vista del taxista

33. ¿Por qué se sentían sucios y malolientes?
   (A) No se ducharon antes de subir al avión.
   (B) Hacía mucho calor.
   (C) Había aire reciclado en la cabina del avión y comida mala.
   (D) Porque llevaban mucho tiempo esperando.

GO ON TO THE NEXT PAGE.

34. ¿Qué pasó con el equipaje?

    (A) Algunas maletas llegaron rotas.

    (B) No llevaban equipaje.

    (C) Se perdió.

    (D) No había ningún problema con el equipaje.

35. ¿Por qué no se enfadaron con los empleados?

    (A) Porque todos son amigos

    (B) Porque los empleados son unos imbéciles

    (C) Porque los empleados no están

    (D) Porque a los empleados no les importa su problema

36. ¿A qué se refiere el "estado soporífero" de la línea 16?

    (A) El no poder respirar bien

    (B) El sentirse sucios

    (C) El cansancio

    (D) El estado de crisis

37. ¿Cómo imagina el narrador la vida de los empleados?

    (A) Siguen su rutina diaria sin problemas.

    (B) Tienen mucha tensión en la vida.

    (C) Se desayunan gratis en el aeropuerto.

    (D) Se interesan mucho en la vida de los que pasan por el aeropuerto.

38. La siguiente oración se puede añadir al texto: "Nos tratará de estafar seguramente". ¿Dónde serviría mejor la oración?

    (A) Posición A   (línea 12)

    (B) Posición B   (línea 24)

    (C) Posición C   (línea 30)

    (D) Posición D   (línea 34)

Mi abuela tendría entonces unos doce años. Vino con su madre. Las dos habían abandonado para siempre su país natal y la familia, o lo que quedaba de la familia, después de empezar la guerra. Vinieron a vivir a Estados Unidos. Era su primera vez en Estados Unidos y su primera vez en Nueva York. Mi abuela quedó muy impresionada con la muchedumbre apurada. Todos parecían marchar al ritmo de un reloj secreto que ella no entendía. Pero no era una impresión negativa. No se sentía ofendida por los trajes grises que se le adelantaban en la acera de la avenida Park. Más bien se sentía como una hormiguita curiosa que acaba de descubrir un almuerzo completo abandonado al lado de un arroyo apacible. Tenía todo el tiempo que necesitaba para explorar el universo de Nueva York. De hecho, pasaría su vida entera explorando las esquinas y agujeros de esa ciudad famosa en todo el mundo. Su madre trabajaba como costurera en un almacén grande y famoso. Mi abuela se pasaba las mañanas en el piso y las tardes en el parque cuidando de niños ajenos. Su madre había conocido a una señora rica que tenía dos niños pequeños y quien siempre quería que mi abuela fuera a su casa para jugar con ellos, llevarlos al parque o a alguna excursión especial. Pagaba bien para lo que era entonces, unos cincuenta centavos por hora. Lo mejor era que siempre llevaba a mi abuela a los museos, al teatro, a las tiendas y a los mejores restaurantes. Mi abuela sólo tenía que ocuparse de los niños y asegurar que se portaran bien. La señora rica le compraba vestidos bonitos, zapatos nuevos y siempre pagaba las entradas en los museos, al teatro y las comidas en los restaurantes. Mi abuela era como la hija mayor de la familia. Y los niños la adoraban. Los dos siguen en contacto con ella y la tratan como a una tía querida.

39. ¿Por qué vino la abuela a Estados Unidos?

    (A) Vino de vacaciones.

    (B) Huía de la guerra en su país natal.

    (C) Se murieron sus hermanos.

    (D) Vino para estudiar.

40. ¿Cuál era la impresión de la abuela de Nueva York?

    (A) Tenía una impresión negativa.

    (B) Se asustaba con la cantidad de gente en Nueva York.

    (C) Se sentía cómo un insecto pequeño.

    (D) Veia muchas oportunidades y cosas nuevas que le interesaban.

GO ON TO THE NEXT PAGE.

110 ■ CRACKING THE AP SPANISH EXAM

41. ¿De qué vivían la abuela y su madre?

    (A) Vivían en las esquinas y agujeros.

    (B) La abuela cuidaba niños y su madre trabajaba en un almacén.

    (C) Vivían en la avenida Park.

    (D) Vivían en la pobreza.

42. ¿Cómo pasaba la abuela su tiempo en Nueva York?

    (A) Pasaba las tardes en el parque con los niños que cuidaba.

    (B) Trabajaba en el almacén.

    (C) Estudiaba en el colegio.

    (D) Trabajaba en la avenida Park.

43. ¿Qué se puede inferir de la abuela?

    (A) Que no era muy culta antes de conocer a la señora rica.

    (B) Que de día ayudaba a su mamá en el trabajo.

    (C) Que no asistió a la escuela.

    (D) Que su sueldo fue una gran ayuda a la familia.

44. ¿Por qué iba la abuela al teatro, las tiendas, los museos y los mejores restaurantes?

    (A) Porque la señora rica la invitaba para acompañar a los niños

    (B) Porque buscaba trabajo

    (C) Porque tenía mucho interés

    (D) Porque su madre quería que fuera

45. ¿Que relación tenía la abuela al final con los niños de la señora rica?

    (A) La odiaban mucho.

    (B) La trataban muy mal.

    (C) La ignoraban.

    (D) La amaban mucho.

No me podía dormir. Estaba tan obsesionado con la idea de la inauguración del nuevo restaurante el próximo sábado que millones de ideas pasaban por mi cabeza.
Línea
5 ¿Había invitado a todos los amigos del club deportivo? ¿Había invitado a todos los hermanos y primos de Eliza? No quería ofender a nadie, ni mucho menos a la familia de mi esposa. Escuchaba el ritmo lento de la respiración tranquila de ella. Era tan hermosa y me encantaba verla dormir. Parecía tan serena, como un
10 lirio blanco. En comparación, yo me sentía al punto de un ataque cardíaco. Había tantos detalles y yo estaba seguro de que se me olvidaba algo importante. Había llamado a los críticos de la prensa local. Había hablado con los cocineros y los camareros. Pedí toda la comida
15 para el bufé. ¿Reviso otra vez el menú? Para empezar, tendremos calamares, mejillones, ostras, jamón serrano, canapés, albóndigas suecas y espárragos bañados en crema y caviar. Luego tendremos un cordero asado y un salmón escalfado. También tendremos ensalada y patatas
20 asadas. De postre, tendremos varios sorbetes, una tarta de manzana exquisita y unos chocolates de trufa. La música, ah, la música. ¡Eso sí que se me olvidaba! Se me olvidó llamar al conjunto clásico para confirmar la hora. Los llamo ahora mismo. ¿Qué hora es? Ah, son las tres de
25 la madrugada. No pasa nada, los puedo llamar mañana.

46. ¿Por qué no puede dormir el narrador?

    (A) Está enfermo.

    (B) No tiene sueño.

    (C) Está nervioso.

    (D) Está triste.

47. ¿Por qué se siente así el narrador?

    (A) Va a abrir un nuevo restaurante.

    (B) Va a hablar en público.

    (C) Va a tocar música.

    (D) Va a cocinar.

48. ¿Cómo describe a su mujer?

    (A) Como una persona dormida

    (B) Como una madre ejemplar

    (C) Como una flor

    (D) Como una sirena

GO ON TO THE NEXT PAGE.

49. ¿Qué significa en la líneas 10–11 cuando dice que se siente "al punto de un ataque cardíaco"?

(A) Va a morir.

(B) Está deprimido.

(C) Está ansioso.

(D) Está enfermo.

50. Todas las siguientes comidas son mariscos MENOS:

(A) calamares

(B) mejillones

(C) ostras

(D) albóndigas

51. ¿Qué carne va a servir de plato principal?

(A) Jamón serrano

(B) Canapés

(C) Salmón

(D) Cordero

52. ¿Qué había olvidado el narrador?

(A) Poner el despertador

(B) Llamar al conjunto musical

(C) Poner la mesa

(D) Llamar a la prensa

53. La siguiente oración se puede añadir al texto: "¿Y cómo podría olvidarme de los damascos y arándanos para la macedonia?" ¿Dónde serviría mejor la oración?

(A) Posición A   (línea 16)

(B) Posición B   (línea 19)

(C) Posición C   (línea 21)

(D) Posición D   (línea 22)

54. ¿Qué va a hacer el narrador mañana?

(A) Dormir la siesta

(B) Comer mucho

(C) Llamar a los músicos

(D) Llamar a los críticos

Cuando el tren número 65 se detuvo en la pequeña estación situada entre los kilómetros 171 y 172, casi todos los viajeros de segunda y tercera clase se quedaron durmiendo dentro de los coches, porque el frío penetrante de la madrugada no les permitió a pasear por el desamparado andén. El único viajero de primera clase que venía en el tren bajó apresuradamente, y dirigiéndose a los empleados, les preguntó si aquella era la estación de Villahorrenda.

—En Villahorrenda estamos—repuso el conductor, cuya voz se confundió con el cacarear de las gallinas que en aquel momento estaban debajo del furgón—. Creo que ahí le esperan a usted con los caballos.

—¡Pero hace aquí un frío de tres mil demonios!—dijo el viajero envolviéndose en su manta—. ¿No hay en la estación algún sitio donde descansar y reponerse antes de emprender un viaje a caballo por este país de hielo?

No había terminado de hablar, cuando el conductor, llamado por las apremiantes obligaciones de su oficio, se marchó, dejando a nuestro desconocido caballero con la palabra en la boca. Vio éste que se acercaba otro empleado con un farol pendiente de la mano derecha, el cual se movía al compás de la marcha.

—¿Hay fonda o dormitorio en la estación de Villahorrenda?—preguntó el viajero al del farol.

—Aquí no hay nada—respondió éste secamente.

—Lo mejor será salir de aquí a toda prisa—dijo el caballero para su capote—. El conductor me anunció que ahí estaban los caballos. El hombre salió con la manta en las manos.

Línea

5

10

15

20

25

30

55. ¿De qué se trata esta selección?

(A) Las ventajas de viajar por tren.

(B) Las desventajas de viajar por tren.

(C) Dos amigos viajando por tren con animales.

(D) El viaje de un hombre descontento.

56. ¿Qué busca el caballero en la estación Villahorrenda?

(A) Un lugar para descansar

(B) Sus amigos y sus animales

(C) Un trabajo y un hogar

(D) Los empleados del tren

GO ON TO THE NEXT PAGE.

57. Según las conversaciones entre el caballero y el conductor, ¿qué adjetivo caracteriza mejor la actitud del conductor?

(A) Amable

(B) Desencantado

(C) Ocupado

(D) Dudoso

58. El narrador describe Villahorrenda como un lugar:

(A) desamparado

(B) peligroso

(C) tranquilo

(D) El narrador no describe Villahorrenda.

59. ¿A quién se dirige el caballero cuando dice, "Lo mejor será salir de aquí a toda prisa"? (27)

(A) A las gallinas

(B) Al conductor

(C) A sí mismo

(D) Al otro empleado

60. ¿Quiénes son los que esperan con los caballos?

(A) Los empleados

(B) Las mujeres de Villahorrenda

(C) Los hombres de Villahorrenda

(D) Las personas desconocidas

61. ¿Por qué se envuelve el viajero con su manta?

(A) Porque está muy frío.

(B) Porque necesita dar la manta a los empleados del tren.

(C) Porque cacarean las gallinas debajo del tren.

(D) Porque tiene miedo de los demonios.

62. La siguiente oración se puede añadir al texto: "No le apetecía la idea de una cabalgata de 2 días por sierras ajenas con sus ráfagas, chaparrones y nevadas". ¿Dónde serviría mejor la oración?

(A) Posición A (línea 6)

(B) Posición B (línea 17)

(C) Posición C (línea 21)

(D) Posición D (línea 31)

Mamá, Ana y la chiquitina fueron a visitar al abuelo, pero el pobre papá no pudo ir porque tuvo que quedarse en casa para trabajar.

Línea
5
—¿Qué haré yo sin ti?—dijo él.

—Te escribiré cartas, tres cartas,—contestó Ana—. Te diré lo que estemos haciendo aquí sin ti.

—¿Sabes escribir una carta?—preguntó papá.

—¡Oh sí, la puedo escribir!—dijo Ana—. Ya tengo siete años. Verás que puedo escribir una carta.

10
Ana se divirtió mucho. Un día dijo:

—Abuelita, ¿puedo tomar una pluma? Quiero escribir a Papá.

—Sí—dijo su abuela—, en el escritorio hay plumas.

Ana corrió al escritorio de su abuelo.

15
—¡Oh, Abuelita! aquí hay una pluma muy rara.

—Ésta es una pluma de ave—dijo la abuela—. Tu abuelo la cortó para mí. Es una pluma de ganso; en tiempos pasados todo el mundo escribía con plumas de ave.

20
—Me parece muy bonita—dijo Ana—. No creo que pueda escribir con ella.

Tomó otra pluma y se fue. Al poco tiempo, volvió al escritorio. Y allí vio que la chiquitina había tomado la pluma de ave y había escrito con ella a su papá. ¡Y

25
qué carta había escrito! Ana se dio cuenta de que había derramado la tinta sobre el escritorio.

—¡Oh, chiquitina, chiquitina! ¿por qué has hecho esto?

Mamá envió la carta de la chiquitina a su papá y él dijo que se alegraba de recibir las dos cartas.

30
CARTA DE ANA A SU PADRE.

Aracataca, 12 de julio de 1917.

Mi querido Papá:

Nos estamos divirtiendo mucho. Mi abuelito tiene un gran caballo oscuro. Algunas veces me monta en el caballo. ¡Es tan

35
divertido! Juego mucho en el prado. Mi abuelito me deja pasear sobre los montones de hierba y recojo moras para mi abuelita. Nos dan queso con el café. Quisiera que estuvieses aquí con nosotros. La chiquitina te ha escrito una carta. Tomó la pluma de ave de nuestra abuela, y derramó la tinta. ¿Puedes leer su

40
carta? Dice que ha escrito: "¿Cómo estás, papá? Te quiero mucho."

Tu hijita,
Ana

63. ¿Cómo se puede entender de qué se trata la carta de la chiquitina?

(A) Según la carta misma

(B) Según la carta de Ana

(C) Según lo que dice la abuela al padre

(D) Según el narrador

GO ON TO THE NEXT PAGE.

64. ¿Quién duda que Ana pueda escribir la carta?

(A) La abuela

(B) El padre

(C) El abuelo

(D) La chiquitina

65. Según la selección ¿por qué escribe Ana "¿Puedes leer su carta?" a su padre?

(A) Porque sabe que su padre tiene la vista débil.

(B) Porque sabe que la carta ha llegado.

(C) Porque cree que no puede leer la carta de la chiquitina.

(D) Porque sabe que en tiempos pasados todo el mundo escribía con plumas de ave.

66. La siguiente oración se puede añadir al texto: "Captada por la novedad, la manoseaba por un rato, luego la retornó a su recinto." ¿Dónde serviría mejor la oración?

(A) Posición A (línea 14)

(B) Posición B (línea 19)

(C) Posición C (línea 29)

(D) Posición D (línea 38)

67. ¿Quién es la "ella" (24) con que la chiquitina escribió la carta?

(A) La abuela

(B) La pluma

(C) Ana

(D) La madre

68. ¿Por qué busca una pluma Ana?

(A) Porque quiere escribir tres cartas.

(B) Porque quiere escribir un libro.

(C) Porque quiere derramar la tinta.

(D) Porque necesita a su padre.

69. ¿Quién manda la carta a Papá?

(A) La abuela

(B) Ana

(C) La chiquitina

(D) La madre

END OF SECTION I

IF YOU FINISH BEFORE TIME IS CALLED, YOU MAY CHECK YOUR WORK ON THIS SECTION

SPANISH LANGUAGE

SECTION II

Total Time—100 minutes

50% of total grade

Part A

Time—80 minutes

ENSAYOS CORTOS

Instrucciones: Para la siguiente pregunta, escribirás una carta. Tendrás 10 minutos para leer la pregunta y escribir tu respuesta

Escribe un correo electrónico a un amigo indicándole que te mudarás a su pueblo. Debes incluir en tu carta:

- Un saludo apropiado

- La razón por la cual te mudas

- Cómo te sientes sobre los cambios que experimentarás

- Tus esperanzas al tener que cambiar de recinto y de escuela

- Tu deseo de verse pronto

- Un despido apropiado

GO ON TO THE NEXT PAGE.

Directions: The following question is based on the accompanying sources 1-3. The sources include both print and audio material. First, you will have 7 minutes to read the printed material. Afterward, you will hear the audio material; you should take notes while you listen. Then, you will have 5 minutes to plan your response and 40 minutes to write your essay. Your essay should be at least 200 words in length.

This question is designed to test your ability to interpret and synthesize different sources. Your essay should use the information from the sources to support your ideas. You should refer to ALL of the sources. As you refer to the sources, identify them appropriately. Avoid simply summarizing the sources individually.

Instrucciones: La pregunta siguiente se basa en las Fuentes 1-3. Las fuentes comprenden material tanto impreso como auditivo. Primero, dispondrás de 7 minutos para leer el material impreso. Después escucharás el material auditivo; debes tomar apuntes mientras escuches. Luego, tendrás 5 minutos para preparar tu respuesta y 40 minutos para escribir tu ensayo. El ensayo debe tener una extensión mínima de 200 palabras.

El objetivo de esta pregunta es medir tu capacidad de interpretar y sintetizar varias fuentes. Tu ensayo debe utilizar información de TODAS las fuentes, citándolas apropiadamente. Evita un simple resumen de cada una de ellas.

¿Cómo nos afecta la vida el calentamiento global?

GO ON TO THE NEXT PAGE.

Fuente No. 1

Fuente: Este artículo apareció en un sitio de Internet de España en mayo de 2008.

Las consecuencias del calentamiento global asociadas con un aumento en el nivel de mar

Con la destrucción de la capa de ozono, observamos una mayor penetración de rayos solares al planeta. Estos, a su vez, contribuyen a una expansión térmica de los océanos y el derretimiento de grandes números de montañas glaciares y de los casquetes de hielo ubicados en las partes orientales de las Tierras Antárticas y Groenlandia. Ya con estos niveles elevados del mar, se pronosticarán graves cambios para el porvenir del planeta.

El nivel del mar ya aumentó en entre 4 y 8 pulgadas en el siglo pasado. Se predice que los niveles del mar podrían aumentar en desde 10 hasta 23 pulgadas para el año 2100. Lamentablemente los niveles vienen creciendo más de lo previsto—la capa de hielo de Groenlandia ha disminuido en la última década. Este declive contribuye aproximadamente una centésima de pulgada anualmente al aumento del nivel del mar. La cifra parece ser mínima a primera vista, pero hay que tener en cuenta que Groenlandia cuenta con alrededor de 10% de la masa total del hielo mundial. Si el hielo de Groenlandia fuera a derretirse, los niveles del mar mundiales podrían aumentar en hasta 21 pies. Este año, por primera vez, los barcos pudieron pasar por las aguas árticas sin la ayuda de un barco rompehielos. O sea, que las predicciones de los científicos que el hielo empezaría a derretirse han acontecido 25 años por adelantado. Esto también significará graves consecuencia para el planeta. Ya se pronostica que el oso polar, los lobos marinos y ciertas especies de pingüinos estarán al borde de la extinción en pocos años.

Con la destrucción de los glaciares y casquetes del hielo, más agua dulce entra al mar, y así aumentando los niveles actuales. Estos derretimientos provocarán inundaciones severas en áreas costeñas. Si el nivel de mar subiera apenas 6 metros, arrasaría con lugares como Miami, Florida y San Francisco, California en los Estados Unidos; en China dejaría hundidas a ciudades como Shangai y Beijing, y en India, la ciudad de Calcuta estaría bajo agua. Estos últimos tres centros urbanos figuran entre las ciudades más pobladas del mundo.

GO ON TO THE NEXT PAGE.

Fuente: Este artículo apareció en la prensa argentina en julio de 2008.

Advertencia: El calentamiento global traerá consigo graves consecuencias sobre la vida y la salud humana

"No es ninguna especulación – es una realidad. Los días del planeta están contados. Ya es hora de actuar y poner en marcha programas de planificación y contingencia,"comentó Francisco García, director general de la Organización de Preservación Mundial, en rueda de prensa durante la undécima convocatoria general de La Semana del Planeta celebrada en Buenos Aires, Argentina. Representantes de más de 35 países se reunieron en la capital argentina para discutir, analizar data, y formular planes de acción para que las organizaciones internacionales y nacionales entendieran con mayor profundidad las consecuencias del calentamiento global. Es su esperanza, que una vez armados con esta información los países adopten programas para evitar un desastre que, según García, "está al acecho".

Una de las charlas más alarmantes dio a conocer las cifras actuales sobre enfermedades y desastres por el mundo. El doctor alemán Martin Teuscher, profesor de la Universidad de Tübingen, explicó que el ser humano ya ha sido expuesto a varias enfermedades causadas por cambios o exageraciones del clima. "Es una realidad que hemos estado viviendo durante este siglo. Pero fíjense que con el cambio climático, las bajas serán aún mayores. Intensificarán el balance delicado entre el desastre y la prosperidad, entre tener hogar y ser desamparado, y finalmente, entre la vida y la muerte." Señaló, en concreto, que mundialmente mueren más de 4 millones de personas por la malnutrición, más de 2 millones por enfermedades diarreicas, y 1,2 millones por enfermedades como la malaria. Indudablemente, estas cifras aumentarán con el cambio del clima mundial. Dijo Teuscher que no estaría fuera de lo posible que esas cifras triplicaran en apenas 5 ó 10 años.

Los descensos no pararán ahí. Con las temperaturas más cálidas, los insectos y otros organismos maléficos tendrán más oportunidad de desarrollarse y contagiar a los seres humanos como resultado. Se espera que ocurrirán más brotes de dengue y epidemias de malaria. Ambas enfermedades se trasmiten por la picadura de mosquitos. El calentamiento global favorece a estos insectos portadores de enfermedades. Otro resultado del calentamiento global son las inundaciones, las cuales proveen el ambiente ideal para la cría de mosquitos y las temidas pandémicas de cólera. Los recientes estudios realizados por los científicos ilustran la gravedad del problema del calentamiento global. En apenas 15 años, el número de personas en el continente de África expuesta a la malaria podrá llegar a las 100 millones. Globalmente, el dengue podrá amenazar a casi unos 2.000 millones de personas.

El calentamiento global ha traído trastornos en los climas mundiales, y cada año se manifiestan cambios y matices climáticos jamás vistos anteriormente. Por ejemplo, las olas de calor en Europa y los Estados Unidos significan miles de muertos cada año y los huracanes cada vez se vuelvan más devastadores y potentes. "El huracán Katrina de 2005 y El Huracán Mitch de en 1998 destrozaron grandes partes del territorio americano", puntualizó Felipe Fonseca, meteorólogo mexicano que habló sobre los cambios sufridos en el Golfo de México por el calentamiento global. "Estos efectos sociales, económicos, y políticos, aún se sienten. En 50 años podríamos encontrar partes del América del Norte bajo agua".

Las emisiones ocasionadas por los automóviles, camiones, y aviones envenenan el aire que respiramos. Esa contaminación del aire causa casi un millón de muertes al año. Según los estimados citados por los expertos, por cada grado centígrado que aumente la temperatura global, habrá casi 30.000 muertos anuales adicionales por enfermedades cardiorrespiratorias. Con los recientes aumentos de precio de los combustibles, la demanda no ha disminuido lo suficiente para reducir la contaminación del aire. Muchos temen que con el crecimiento de las economías emergentes de Asia, más el gran número de chóferes que tendrán acceso a automóviles, el daño ambiental continúe perjudicando cualquier intento de conservar el medioambiente.

GO ON TO THE NEXT PAGE.

"El individuo sí tiene el poder para hacer una diferencia", explica Rachel Johnson, estudiante alemana y miembro de GreenWatch, un movimiento estudiantil que educa a jóvenes sobre la conservación y el reciclaje. "Esa bolsa plástica que arrojas a la basura sin pensarlo tardará un centenar en descomponerse. La gasolina y el petroleo influencian casi todos los aspector de nuestra vida, y al mismo tiempo perjudican al nuestro bienestar y el del planeta. Tenemos que cambiar nuestra manera de pensar y actuar ahora. En mi país hay un dicho que dice: *Macht es jetzt! Warte nicht auf bessere Zeiten*. ¡Hazlo ahora! No esperes mejores momentos). Si no hacemos el esfuerzo ahora, nuestras futuras generaciones se condenarán a una vida sin vida".

GO ON TO THE NEXT PAGE.

Fuente No. 3: Audio Selection

Este informe, que se titula "Los expertos señalan mayores riesgos de salud por el calentamiento global" se emitió por la emisora hispanoamericana Enteramérica en julio de 2005.

AUDIO CD: Track 12

END OF PART A

IF YOU FINISH BEFORE TIME IS CALLED, YOU MAY CHECK YOUR WORK ON PART A.

SPANISH LANGUAGE

SECTION II

Part B

Approximate Time—20 minutes

Directions: You will now participate in a simulated conversation. First, you will have 30 seconds to read the outline of the conversation. Then, you will listen to a message and have one minute to read the outline of the conversation again. Afterward, the conversation will begin, following the outline. Each time it is your turn, you will have 20 seconds to respond; a tone will indicate when you should begin and end speaking. You should participate in the conversation as fully and appropriately as possible.

Instrucciones: Ahora participarás en una conversación simulada. Primero, tendrás 30 segundos para leer el esquema de la conversación. Luego, escucharás un mensaje y tendrás un minuto para leer de nuevo el esquema de la conversación. Después, empezará la conversación, siguiendo el esquema. Siempre que te toque un turno, tendrás 20 segundos para responder; una señal te indicará cuando debes empezar y terminar de hablar. Debes participar en la conversación de la manera más completa y apropiada posible.

(A) Has solicitado una posición de aprendiz en una empresa multinacional latinoamericana. Imagina que recibes una llamada telefónica del director del Departamento de Recursos Humanos para hablar sobre la posición que has solicitado.

(B) La conversación

[The shaded lines reflect what you will hear on the recording.
Las líneas en gris reflejan lo que escucharás en la grabación.]

GO ON TO THE NEXT PAGE.

Entrevistador	Te saluda
Tú	Contesta la pregunta
Entrevistador	Te hace una pregunta
Tú	Responde a la pregunta
Entrevistador	Continúa la conversación
Tú	Responde a la pregunta
Entrevistador	Continúa la conversación
Tú	Contesta que no es posible y ofrece una alternativa
Entrevistador	Continúa la conversación
Tú	Responde a la pregunta
Entrevistador	Continúa la conversación
Tú	Despídete

GO ON TO THE NEXT PAGE.

Texto impreso

Compara y contrasta las diferentes opiniones sobre la opción de reducir la semana escolar de 5 a 4 días.

Fuente 1: El siguiente artículo se creó en la Junta Directiva de Educación del Distrito #242 de Los Ángeles sobre la posibilidad de ofrecerles a padres la opción de reducir la semana escolar de 5 a 4 días.

Tema: Cambiando la rutina: Reducir la semana escolar de 5 a 4 días

Estimados padres:

Entiendo cómo la inflación reciente y el aumento en el costo de la vida han afectado a ustedes y sus familias. Es un tiempo difícil para todos. Ya sufriendo del aumento en el costo de combustible para los buses, de calentar y enfriar los edificios, de alimentar a los estudiantes y de casi todos los materiales, los distritos escolares alrededor del país están considerando la idea de reducir la semana escolar de 5 a 4 días. Es una opción que debemos considerar seriamente.

Más de 150 escuelas a través del país ya han adoptado esta opción y por lo visto están contentos con los resultados. Un distrito en Topeka, Kansas ha adoptado un horario de martes a viernes y terminó ahorrando $248.000 de un presupuesto de $8,7 millones. Ese dinero se utilizó en reembolsos a los residentes del distrito. También reportaron mejoras de asistencia estudiantil y mejores resultados en los exámenes estandardizados.

Existen otros beneficios. Un fin de semana de tres días proveerá más tiempo familiar, algo que falta en la sociedad de hoy. Además, los estudiantes podrían dedicarles más tiempo a las asignaturas escolares sin la presión de una semana escolar de 5 días.

Los gastos asociados con el mantenimiento de nuestros edificios y la transportación de nuestros estudiantes son agobiantes. Como nos confronta un futuro inseguro de precios de combustible, tenemos que actuar ahora. Obviamente, la reducción de gastos es la respuesta, y agregar 1,5 horas al cada día escolar y así eliminar un día completo representa ahorros económicos significativos sin la necesidad de sacrificar trabajos, instrucción académica ni programas estudiantiles. Sin estos ahorros, los estudiantes que viven a menos de 2 millas de sus escuelas perderán el beneficio de la transportación gratuita proveída por el distrito.

Les invito a que asistan al foro público que se celebrará en la Escuela Fleetwood el 23 de julio de 2008 a las 7 de la noche. Ahí podemos dialogar más sobre este asunto.

Atentamente,
Luis Maldonado
Superintendente, Distrito 242

GO ON TO THE NEXT PAGE.

Fuente 2: Reunion de padres, Junta Directiva Educativa, Fleetwood School

STOP

END OF THE LANGUAGE PRACTICE TEST

7

Language Practice Test: Answers and Explanations

LANGUAGE PRACTICE TEST
ANSWER KEY

SECTION I: PART A

1.	B	11.	C	21.	B
2.	A	12.	D	22.	A
3.	A	13.	A	23.	C
4.	D	14.	B	24.	D
5.	A	15.	D	25.	B
6.	C	16.	B	26.	B
7.	B	17.	A	27.	D
8.	A	18.	A	28.	B
9.	C	19.	D	29.	C
10.	A	20.	C	30.	A

SECTION I: PART B

31.	A	44.	A	57.	C
32.	C	45.	D	58.	D
33.	C	46.	C	59.	C
34.	C	47.	A	60.	D
35.	D	48.	C	61.	A
36.	C	49.	C	62.	B
37.	A	50.	D	63.	B
38.	D	51.	D	64.	B
39.	B	52.	B	65.	C
40.	D	53.	C	66.	B
41.	B	54.	C	67.	B
42.	A	55.	D	68.	A
43.	C	56.	A	69.	D

SECTION II

See explanations beginning on page 153.

SECTION I: PART A

DIALOGUES

Translation of Dialogue 1 Found on Page 103

(NARRATOR) In a café

(WOMAN) Good afternoon. I would like to have a bite to eat. Is there seating on the terrace?

(MAN) Yes, madam. What would you like to have? We have hot chocolate with churros, coffee, tea, iced lemon slush, ice creams, cakes, soaked sponge cakes.

(WOMAN) I would like to have a coffee with something sweet. What type of cakes have you got?

(MAN) Well, I have rich, homemade apple pie. I also have lemon cake, cheesecake, and chocolate cake.

(WOMAN) A piece of apple pie, please.

(MAN) Okay, and how would you like your coffee?

(WOMAN) I would like a black iced coffee, please. It's so hot I feel as though I will melt.

(MAN) Yes, it is dreadfully hot. So, a piece of apple pie and a black iced coffee, correct?

(WOMAN) Yes, thank you.

Translated Questions and Answers for Dialogue 1

1. Where does this conversation take place?
   - (A) In the park
   - **(B) In the café**
   - (C) In the train station
   - (D) The kitchen

The narrator clearly states at the beginning of the dialogue that the conversation takes place in a café. If you missed that, you may have been tempted to pick choice (D) because of the many references to food. You should, however, have picked up enough to know that choice (B) is the correct answer.

2. What does the woman want?
   - **(A) She wants to have a bite to eat.**
   - (B) She wants to sit in the reception area.
   - (C) She wants to sit in the sun.
   - (D) She wants to read the newspaper.

The correct answer is choice (A): She wants to have a bite to eat. The woman does ask to be seated on the terrace, but that doesn't necessarily mean that she'll be sitting in the sun. Nothing about newspapers or a reception area is mentioned in the narrative.

3. What does the waiter suggest?

(A) Apple pie

(B) Chocolate cake

(C) Hot chocolate with churros

(D) Sponge cakes

The correct answer is choice (A). The waiter says that the homemade apple pie is rich and homemade. He simply states that they also have chocolate cake, hot chocolate with churros, and sponge cakes.

4. What is the weather like?

(A) It is cold.

(B) It is raining.

(C) It is cloudy.

(D) It is hot.

The correct answer is choice (D). It is so hot, the woman feels as if she will melt.

Translation of Dialogue 2 Found on Page 103

(NARRATOR) In the airport

(MAN) Excuse me madam, but would you know where the ticket counter for AeroEspaña is?

(WOMAN) Where are you going?

(MAN) I am going to Barcelona, and I am in a big hurry because I believe the plane leaves within twenty minutes.

(WOMAN) That's right. There is a plane that leaves for Barcelona this morning. The ticket counter for AeroEspaña is at the end of this hallway on your right.

(MAN) Do you have the time?

(WOMAN) Yes, it is nine o'clock. I will accompany you to the counter if you wish. I am also going to Barcelona this morning.

(MAN) Well yes, of course, it would be my pleasure. I am Ricardo Herrero.

(WOMAN) Delighted to meet you. I am Teresa Vara.

(MAN) Are you by chance the attorney for the Arturo Águila Company?

(WOMAN) Yes, I am. And you are the chief financial officer. We have met before, haven't we?

(MAN) Yes, I think we met at the annual meeting last year in London. What a coincidence!

(WOMAN) I suppose that you are going to the meeting in Barcelona with the president of the company?

(MAN) Of course, what a small world!

Translated Questions and Answers for Dialogue 2

5. What is AeroEspaña?

   (A) It is the airline.

   (B) It is the law firm.

   (C) It is the name of the airport.

   (D) It is the woman's name.

AeroEspaña is the name of the airline, answer choice (A). We know this because once inside the airport, the man asks the woman where the ticket counter is for the airline he is taking to Barcelona.

6. What work does the woman do?

   (A) She is a flight attendant.

   (B) She works at the ticket counter.

   (C) She is an attorney.

   (D) She is the head of administration.

Choice (C) is the correct answer. The woman is an attorney for the Arturo Águila Company.

7. Where is the woman going?

   (A) She is going to London.

   (B) She is going to Barcelona.

   (C) She is going to Burgos.

   (D) She is going to the ticket counter.

This should be an easy one for you. Barcelona is mentioned several times in the dialogue, so if you picked (B), you had your ears open! London is mentioned in the dialogue as well, but only in reference to the fact that the two had met there last year.

Translation for Dialogue 3 Found on Page 104

(NARRATOR) A telephone conversation

(WOMAN A) Hello?

(WOMAN B) Aunt Mari-Carmen? It's Ángela.

(WOMAN A) Angelina, how are you?

(WOMAN B) I'm well, and how are things with you? Are you very lonely?

(WOMAN A) You see, my dear, since your Uncle Manolo died I am lonelier, yes. But it is not that bad. And furthermore, your mother calls me every day to chat. How are your classes going at the university?

(WOMAN B) Pretty good. Now I'm on vacation until September. I am going to look for a summer job. But I would like to come and see you before starting to work. I wanted to take you out to the movies.

(WOMAN A) Great, I would love that! When are you coming?

(WOMAN B) How about next Sunday? Why don't we go to the cinema? I think they are showing the new Italian film in the Metropol Cinema, which is near your house.

(WOMAN A) What a good idea. What time should we meet?

(WOMAN B) Why don't we meet around 7:00 at your house? I'll pick you up, and we can go directly to the movie theater.

(WOMAN A) Very well, and after the movie, I will treat you to dinner at the Italian restaurant that is next door to the house.

(WOMAN B) Excellent. So let's plan to meet at 7:00 at your house on Sunday.

Translated Questions and Answers for Dialogue 3

8. Why is Mari-Carmen very lonely?

   (A) Because her husband died.

   (B) Because her mother died.

   (C) Because her uncle died.

   (D) Because her sister died.

The correct answer is (A), because her husband died. There is no mention of her mother, (B), nor of her sister, (D). Choice (C) may trick you since Mari-Carmen refers to Manolo as *tu tío Manolo*. But remember that Manolo is the husband of Mari-Carmen, and she is the one who is lonely.

9. What is Ángela going to do this summer?

   (A) Travel

   (B) Study

   (C) Work

   (D) Go to the movies

The correct answer is (C), she is going to work. There is no mention made of travel, so you can cancel choice (A). She studies at the university during the school year but not in the summer, which eliminates (B). She is talking about going to the movies with her aunt next Sunday, but not for the entire summer, which eliminates (D).

10. What are Ángela and Mari-Carmen going to do on Sunday?

   (A) They are going to the movies and then to dinner.

   (B) They are going home.

   (C) They are going to a party.

   (D) They are going to work.

The correct answer is (A), they are going to the movies and then to dinner. Ángela tells her aunt she wants to take her to see the new Italian film at the Metropol Cinema, and then Mari-Carmen is going to take Ángela to an Italian restaurant.

NARRATIVES

Translation for Narrative 1 Found on Page 105

(NARRATOR)   The Argentine, Alfonso García, wins the golf championship in Scotland.

(WOMAN)   The tumultuous and cold weather here in St. Andrew's, Scotland, yesterday was the catalyst for some extraordinarily high scores in the international golf championship, which was won by the young Argentine, Alfonso García. García, who is only twenty-two years old, is the first Argentine who has won this championship at St. Andrew's, the most historic and perhaps the most prestigious golf course in the world. The efforts of the golfers were complicated throughout the three-day tournament by an implacable wind and intermittent rain squalls.

"I have never experienced such a violent and tempestuous wind," the young Argentine said yesterday. And when he was asked how the weather affected his game, García replied, "At the beginning, I didn't know how to adapt well to the wind and calculate it into each shot. Later, the rain squalls bothered me quite a bit. The first day when I scored a 75, I was feeling very frustrated. But during the second day, when I realized that the other players were also struggling, it was much easier for me to concentrate. I began to think I might actually be able to win this tournament."

García, who comes from a family of athletes, is the first of his family to play golf at the professional level. His father was a tennis champion in the seventies and his younger sister, Patricia, is also a tennis player. Alfonso spends the majority of his time traveling on the PGA tour, but when he is not traveling, he lives with his parents in Buenos Aires. They say that he acquired his passion for golf from his maternal grandfather, who used to take him out on the golf course regularly.

Certainly, Alfonso García is a new star in the sport of golf.

Translated Questions and Answers for Narrative 1

11. What is the golf course like in St. Andrews, Scotland?

    (A) New and modern

    (B) Picturesque

    (C) Historic and prestigious

    (D) Innovative

The correct answer is (C). The golf course is said to be historic and prestigious. Something historic is certainly not new and modern, so that eliminates (A). The golf course may be picturesque, choice (B), but it is not described that way in the narrative. Choice (D), innovative, is never mentioned.

12. What was the weather like during the tournament?

    (A) The weather was nice.

    (B) The weather was hot.

    (C) It was snowing.

    (D) The weather was tempestuous.

The correct answer is (D). There are various references to the tempestuous weather, primarily the wind and the rain squalls.

13. How did Alfonso García react to the variable weather in Scotland?

    (A) He felt frustrated.

    (B) He felt very happy.

    (C) He felt nostalgic.

    (D) He felt sad.

The correct answer is (A); he felt very frustrated initially. Later, he realized that the other players were experiencing the same challenges, and he was able to regain his focus.

14. How did Alfonso García become interested in golf?

    (A) He played golf with his father.

    (B) He accompanied his grandfather to the golf course.

    (C) He played golf with his sister.

    (D) He played golf with his grandmother.

The correct answer is (B). It is stated in the narrative that he accompanied his maternal grandfather to the golf course frequently. Reference is made to his father and his sister, but not in reference to golf, so (A) and (C) are eliminated. His grandmother is never mentioned, which easily eliminates (D).

Translation for Narrative 2 Found on Page 105

(NARRATOR) The modern zoological park "My House"

(MAN) At its grand opening yesterday, March 12, the zoo "My House," which is located in the northern part of the state of Virginia, was named the most innovative zoo in the country. Arthur Richardson, the director of the park, declared that the park is devoted to the preservation of animals in natural, clean, and animal-friendly environments. The construction of the habitats took three years to complete and cost more than ten million dollars. The elephant habitat has received much attention because it includes more than two hectares of land and includes other animals that are part of the elephants' natural habitat such as the African cranes and giraffes. Richardson, who is a naturalist known for his work with "Freedom for Animals" and other naturalist organizations, has devoted himself entirely to this project from its inception to its completion. At the moment, he is working as director of the park while he tries to establish a series of educational courses offered to the public in zoological and preservation studies.

Translated Questions and Answers for Narrative 2

15. According to the narrative, to what cause is the park "My House" devoted?

    (A) Innovation of construction

    (B) Elephants and giraffes

    (C) Fund-raising

    (D) Preservation of animals

Choice (D) is the correct answer. The park is devoted to the preservation of animals. Choice (A) may seem logical because it is a new zoo and makes use of recent technological capabilities, but that is not the zoo's goal, which cancels (A). The narrative talks about the elephants and giraffes, but they are not the sole focus of the zoo, which eliminates (B). Fund-raising is never mentioned in the narrative, which cancels (C).

16. The elephant habitat received a lot of attention because:

    (A) it cost ten million dollars

    (B) it is very big and contains elements of their natural habitat

    (C) it is very clean

    (D) it offers educational courses

The correct answer is (B). The elephant habitat received a lot of attention because it is very big, more than two hectares of land. It alone did not cost ten million dollars; the entire zoo did, which eliminates (A). The cleanliness of the elephant habitat is never mentioned, so that cancels (C). Of course, the elephant habitat would not be offering educational courses, which cancels (D).

17. Arthur Richardson is:

    (A) director of the park and a naturalist

    (B) the local veterinarian

    (C) a publicist

    (D) governor of Virginia

Even if you missed this part of the narrative, common sense should guide you to the correct answer, choice (A).

FIVE-MINUTE NARRATIVES

Translation of Selection 1 Found on Page 107

Feminism in Spain is a strong force. For some it is a political battle. For others it is an economic struggle. Yet others search for a theoretical liberation, including a sexual liberation. One thing is certain: It is a movement that continues growing with increasing force. What interests us here is the situation in Spain today. We will examine how the peninsular movement sprang out of Spanish culture and what directions it is likely to take. It is very important that we look at this brand of feminism as a product of the Spanish culture. Of course, there is a universal movement going on outside of Spain. However, there are some specific characteristics of the movement in Spain that play a key role in its development there. Let's examine a few facets of Spanish culture and later turn our attention to the current state of feminism in Spain today.

One characteristic well-rooted in the Spanish culture, and perhaps the most opposed to feminism, is "machismo." Historically, in Spanish society, it is the man who makes decisions. It seems that the informal social laws are written by men to favor men. The concepts of honor and dignity are also very important. What comes out of all of this, then, is the idea of the strong and dignified man, who protects and assures the future of the woman. Similarly, the concept of "marianismo" establishes the desired qualities in the ideal Spanish woman. Also influenced by the ideas of honor and dignity, "marianismo" defines the domain of the woman in the home. Subordinated by the man, the woman personifies the qualities of obedience and self-sacrifice. Almost as if she were to exist through her association with the man, the woman is seen as fulfilled by her union in marriage to the man. After leaving the home of her father, the woman moves on to the home of her husband. Historically, in this culture there was no room for feminist independence.

The reverberations of these basic concepts from the Spanish culture provide the foundation for the feminist movement today. According to its own ideology, the feminist movement looks for an individual identity for the woman. Feminists want to reject the traditional concepts of "machismo" and "marianismo." The difficult part, however, is penetrating deeply into a culture that has a long history with these cultural values.

Now, let us turn our attention to the contemporary situation in Spain today. The reign of Franco marks a period of rigid censure. This oppressive regime reinforced the traditional values of the Spanish culture. It was almost as if it had resuscitated the concepts of "machismo" and "marianismo" in the society of the forties. Or perhaps they never died. In any case, there is most decidedly an important cultural foundation. What comes out of the Franco period are the reverberations of thought that have carried over from the Middle Ages. For that reason, the feminist movement was faced with a monumental obstacle. The feminists in Spain were looking for a way to express and communicate their protest. There are, among the feminist movement in Spain, those who want greater social or political freedom while others seek the complete elimination of traditional roles for women. There are militant groups and intellectual groups. Thus, the feminist movement in Spain is diverse and growing.

How can we evaluate such a movement? Surely, the extremes and excesses of a "machista" society should be eliminated. It is also essential that the independent identity of the woman be recognized. But with a radical approach, are we also prepared to lose all of the characteristics of femininity? It would seem that there are some traditional feminine roles worth maintaining, such as the nurturing mother figure, even in a society that is not gender biased. A search for complete equality, without limits or distinctions, it seems, would be a great loss. The role of women in the family, as mentioned above, is uniquely, distinctly, and positively feminine. Furthermore, the characteristics typically considered feminine, such as sensitivity, have a value for society in and of themselves. It is important, of course, that in this search for the true feminine identity, we don't lose femininity itself.

18. How do some interpret the feminist movement in Spain?

   (A) As a political battle

   (B) As an artistic issue

   (C) As a competition between equals

   (D) As a beauty pageant

The correct answer choice is (A), a political battle. There is no reference made to artistic issues, which eliminates (B). It is clearly not a competition between equals, which cancels choice (C). Choice (D) goes against all of the ideals described in the selection regarding a feminine identity.

19. Which characteristic of the Spanish culture can be considered as opposed to the ideals of the feminist movement?

   (A) *Marianismo*

   (B) Honor

   (C) Dignity

   (D) *Machismo*

The correct answer is (D). It should be pretty clear that honor and dignity would not go against feminist ideals, so choices (B) and (C) should be eliminated immediately. That leaves *marianismo* and *machismo*. If you understood what was said about *marianismo*, you know that *marianismo* defines the role of women in the home and idealizes the qualities of obedience and sacrifice. While these ideals do not seem to support the feminist movement, they are minor in comparison with the ideals that go along with *machismo*. In reality, both terms refer to cultural attitudes that clash with the modern feminist movement. However, the more obvious choice is *machismo*, which the selection, in fact, describes as "opposed to the feminist movement."

20. According to the selection, what is the ideological objective of the feminist movement?

   (A) The victory of the woman over the man

   (B) The acceptance of *marianismo* in all parts of the world

   (C) The individual identity for women

   (D) The appreciation of the traditional culture

The correct answer is (C), the individual identity for women. Choice (A) is extreme, and the selection did not advocate extremist measures. Choice (B) may be tempting because it uses the term *marianismo*, but *marianismo* is really a cultural view of women that grew out of the veneration of the Virgin Mary, and should not be confused with the feminist movement. Choice (D) is actually the opposite of what the selection is describing. The baggage of the traditional culture must be shed to find an individual identity for women.

21. According to the selection, what type of thinking surfaced during the Franco era?

   (A) Radical thinking

   (B) Traditional thinking

   (C) Progressive thinking

   (D) Feminist thinking

The correct answer is (B), traditional thinking. Franco was very traditional and very conservative. That cancels choices (A) and (C). Feminist thinking, (D), came about much later in Spain.

22. According to the selection, what should we keep from the traditional *machista* society?

(A) The role of the woman as mother

(B) *Marianismo*

(C) The role of the woman as subordinated to the man

(D) *Machismo*

The correct answer is (A), the role of the woman as mother. Both *marianismo* and *machismo* need to be overcome to move on to a greater state of gender equality, which cancels out both (B) and (D). Choice (C) is clearly one of the reasons to create a feminist movement and would most certainly not be desirable in a culture free of gender bias.

Translation of Selection 2 Found on Page 108

(NARRATOR)   Now you are going to hear an interview with Alejandro Martínez, victorious coach from the recent competition of the Special Olympic Games held in Vermont last April.

(MAN A)   Alejandro, first of all, how did you get involved with the world of the Special Olympic Games?

(MAN B)   Well, I have always been interested in sports. When I was in college, I played four sports during all four years, so sports have been a fundamental part of my life. The other fundamental part of my life, in chronological order, not order of importance, is my son, Carlos. Carlos was born eight years ago with a mild form of cerebral palsy. I noticed that with increased movement and physical activity, he felt better. For that reason, I have devoted myself to Special Olympics. We have met other children like Carlos and other families like ourselves. It has been a very positive experience.

(MAN A)   Do you work with the Special Olympics all year long?

(MAN B)   I wish I could devote myself to the Special Olympics 100 percent, but I also have a job. I am a high school mathematics teacher. So I work with the Special Olympics during the weekends and during the summer all week, which is the busiest time for us.

(MAN A)   It seems that you are drawn to professions that deal with children. Do you have any other children?

(MAN B)   Yes, I have a daughter who just turned four last month. It is true that I enjoy working with children. They are more innocent and honest than adults.

(MAN A)   What would you say is the most difficult part of your work with the Special Olympics?

(MAN B)   Well, we are faced with new obstacles every day. Perhaps the most difficult part for me is recognizing my own limitations. Frequently, I try to do much more than is reasonable in a day. And the worst thing is that the kids are the same way. Once they have become enthused by an idea or a training exercise, for example, they want to practice for hours. They are very dedicated.

(MAN A)   It seems that you too are very dedicated. How do you explain the phenomenal success of your teams?

(MAN B)   Well, I think there are two important factors. The first factor is that physical exercise has a very positive effect on the mind and body. It is incredibly therapeutic. It makes the kids feel better physically. And mentally, they are more alert. Of course, they also enjoy the benefits that we all gain when we participate in a physical sport. Our kids feel the pride and dignity that medicine or medical treatment cannot give them. The second factor that contributes to our success is the dedication of our kids. The kids are completely dedicated to their team. They understand instinctively the importance of the group and of working together. Each one of them is completely dedicated to the program. Without them, it would never work. Without our kids, the Special Olympics would not exist.

(MAN A)   What is Carlos's favorite sport?

(MAN B)   Without a doubt, his favorite sport is American football, perhaps because he knows that I played in college.

(MAN A)   What would you recommend to other families with children who at the moment do not participate in the Special Olympic games? Maybe they think these games are silly or too juvenile.

(MAN B)   I recommend that they call as soon as possible to find out about the upcoming events that are planned. One only has to go to one competition to see the advantages of this program. It's a great organization. The volunteers are very generous and dedicated. It's a very important experience for the children and for the families.

(MAN A)   Well, Alejandro Martínez, many thanks for being here with us.

Translated Questions and Answers to Selection 2

23. How did Alejandro Martínez become interested in the Special Olympic Games?
    (A) He had always participated in the Special Games.
    (B) His brother participated in the Special Games.
    (C) His son responded favorably to sports.
    (D) His wife is very involved in the Special Games.

The correct answer is (C), his son responded favorably to sports. There is no mention of his wife or brother, which eliminates both (B) and (D) easily. Choice (A) is really a restatement of the question and not an answer to the question.

24. When does Alejandro devote himself entirely to the Special Olympics?
    (A) On weekends
    (B) During school vacations
    (C) In the winter
    (D) In the summer

Because Alejandro is a high school teacher, he has his summers off and devotes himself to the Special Olympics. There is no mention made of the school vacations (B), except the summer vacation, which is best described by answer choice (D). It is stated in the narrative that Alejandro spends time working for the Special Olympic Games on weekends, choice (A). However, it's pretty clear that he is *entirely* devoted to the games during the summer.

25. According to the interview, why does he not work full time for the Special Olympics?
    (A) Because he doesn't earn enough money
    (B) Because he is a math teacher
    (C) Because he doesn't have time for everything
    (D) Because he couldn't take it

The correct answer is (B); he mentions that he would dedicate 100% of this time, but he also has a full time job as a Math teacher. There is no mention made of money, so that eliminates (A). At first glance, choice (C) would seem possible as children generally occupy a person's time, but this is not stated in the selection. (D) is an excuse that many people make, but Alejandro does not.

26. Why does Alejandro enjoy working with children?
    (A) Because they are young
    (B) Because they are honest
    (C) Because they are very interested
    (D) Because they are gifted

The correct answer is (B), as he mentions that he prefers working with children because they are more "honest and innocent." There are no specific mentions of age, interest level or talents, so the other answers are not correct in this situation.

27. According to the interview, why is physical exercise therapeutic?

   (A) Because they practice therapeutic exercises

   (B) Because the coaches have studied physical therapy

   (C) Because it's fun

   (D) Because it makes the kids feel better mentally and physically

The correct answer is (D), because it makes the kids feel better mentally and physically. Choices (B) and (C) may be true, but they are not mentioned in the interview. Choice (A) simply does not answer the question.

28. How is the collective spirit of the kids characterized?

   (A) They don't know how to collaborate in a group.

   (B) They understand instinctively how to collaborate.

   (C) They don't know how to function physically.

   (D) There is a lot of competition among the groups.

The correct answer is (B), they understand instinctively how to collaborate. Choice (A) is the exact opposite of the correct answer. Choices (C) and (D) are either completely false, or simply not mentioned in the interview.

29. According to the interview, which characteristic best describes the children who participate in the Special Olympic Games?

   (A) They are very thin.

   (B) They are very delicate.

   (C) They are very dedicated.

   (D) They are delegates.

The correct answer is (C), they are very dedicated. The other answer choices are designed to sound and look alike in an effort to confuse you. You, of course, will know your vocabulary and will not be fooled!

30. What does Alejandro recommend to the families who don't participate in the Special Olympic Games?

   (A) That they find out about the planned events

   (B) That they follow their hearts

   (C) That they organize their own games

   (D) That they don't participate

The correct answer is (A), that they find out about the planned events. None of the other answers were mentioned in the interview, although they may be true. Be sure to answer the questions according to the interview.

SECTION I: PART B

READING COMPREHENSION

Translation and the Questions and Answers for the First Reading Comprehension Passage Found on Page 109

We arrived at the Charles de Gaulle airport at six in the morning on Friday. We had spent a long time traveling, and we were exhausted. The combination of the uncomfortable seats, the recirculated air, and the generic food left us in an unreal, dream-like state. We felt dirty and smelly. After waiting two more hours (and what are two more hours after a ten-hour trip?) at the baggage claim, we finally found out that our bags had been lost. Well, in reality they were not lost. They only took a different route than we did and were about to arrive in Heathrow Airport in London. Okay, the baggage had to pass through London first but would soon be en route to us in Paris. It would be on the first plane that leaves for Charles de Gaulle. It didn't make any sense to become angry with the airline employees. They didn't understand the soporific state in which we found ourselves at the moment. Our crisis was of little importance to them. They had been able to have a hot shower this morning. They probably also had their usual morning coffee and their breakfast. Perhaps they arrived at work without encountering any jams or other traffic problems. But life for us this morning was not quite so easy. And how we love to travel! We decided to leave the airport and go look for the hotel. Later that day a bellhop would bring our baggage to the hotel. What service! We were frightened to think of the tip we would have to give him. In any case, we left the airport looking for a taxi. Everyone was looking at us strangely. They probably wanted to know where our baggage was. Finally we found the taxi stand. Our driver was older, but had a friendly face. "We are going to the Washington Hotel, please," my husband declared casually in his best French. The taxi driver looked at us in the mirror like a wolf when it sees a flock of sheep through the branches of a tree. He nodded his head and began our trip into Paris.

31. What is this selection about?

    (A) **The difficulties of some travelers**

    (B) The life of a pilot and his wife

    (C) The Charles de Gaulle airport in Paris

    (D) The best baggage for short trips

This is a general question asking about the general meaning of the passage. It would be difficult to answer this question without reading the passage. If you misunderstood bits of the passage, you may be fooled by answer choices (B), (C), or (D). Choice (B) is quite obviously a misunderstanding of the narrator and her traveling companion. Choices (C) and (D) are alluded to in the passage: The airport name and the word for "baggage" do appear but are not the focus of the passage.

32. What is the point of view of the selection?

    (A) From the point of view of the pilot

    (B) From the point of view of the flight attendant

    (C) **From the point of view of the wife**

    (D) From the point of view of the taxi driver

This is a popular type of question, so as you read the passages, be sure to pay attention to point of view. In this passage the key to the correct answer is located at the end of the passage: *declaró mi marido casualmente en su mejor francés*, "my husband declared casually in his best French." The correct answer is (C).

33. Why did they feel dirty and smelly?

   (A) They hadn't showered before getting on the plane

   (B) It was very hot

   (C) Because of the recirculating air in the cabin

   (D) Because they had been waiting for a long time

The best answer is (C). Although answer choices (A) and (B) could be true, neither is explicitly stated in the passage. Choice (D) may be true according to the passage, but it is not a likely answer to the question.

34. What happened with the baggage?

   (A) Some bags arrived broken.

   (B) They were not carrying bags.

   (C) It was lost.

   (D) There was no problem with the bags.

Choices (A) and (B) are not mentioned in the passage. Choice (D) can be immediately ruled out because there is clearly a problem with the bags. It is stated that the bags were on a different route to Paris, one that would pass through London first. Choice (C) is correct.

35. Why don't they get angry with the airline employees?

   (A) Because they are all friends

   (B) Because the employees are imbeciles

   (C) Because the employees are not there

   (D) Because the employees don't care about their problem

This answer is straightforward. The other answer choices may be true based on your own personal experience or someone else's experience, but are clearly not true according to the passage.

36. What does the "soporific state" refer to in line 16?

   (A) Not being able to breathe well

   (B) Feeling dirty

   (C) Tiredness

   (D) The state of crisis

This is a cognate, or word that looks and means the same in both languages. Unfortunately, it may be a vocabulary word that you don't know in English. "Soporific" refers to sleepiness or tiredness.

37. How does the narrator imagine the life of the airline employees?

   (A) Following their daily routine without problems

   (B) They have a lot of tension in their lives

   (C) They eat breakfast free in the airport

   (D) They're very interested in the lives of those who pass through the airport

Some of these answers, such as choices (B), (C), and (D) are simply thrown in there to confuse the unsophisticated test taker. You of, course, will not be fooled! Remember that the answer to these questions must come from the passage.

38. The following sentence can be added to the text. **"He'll surely try to take advantage of us."** Where would this sentence fit best?

   (A) Position A (line 12)

   (B) Position B (line 24)

   (C) Position C (line 30)

   (D) Position D (line 34)

This type of question is somewhat difficult because it requires you to have a strong grasp on vocabulary, but from some of the context clues, you might be able to deduce that the word *estafar* means *to swindle* or *trick*. This refers to the taxi driver, who has already been described with a negative metaphor. Lines 24 and 30 are mentioning positive comments about helpful or nice people, where the inserted sentence would make no sense. Thus, the correct answer is (D).

Translation and the Questions and Answers for the Second Reading Comprehension Passage Found on Page 110

My grandmother would have been around twelve years of age. She came with her mother. The two of them had abandoned forever their homeland and their family, or what was left of the family after the beginning of the war. They came to live in America. It was her first time in America and her first time in New York. My grandmother was very impressed by the hurried masses of people. All of them seemed to be following a secret clock that she didn't understand. But it wasn't a negative impression. She didn't feel offended by the gray suits that passed by her on the sidewalk of Park Avenue. She felt more like a curious little ant that had just discovered a complete lunch abandoned on the side of a peaceful stream. She had all of the time she needed to explore New York. In fact, she would spend her entire life exploring the nooks and crannies of this city famous throughout the world. Her mother was working as a seamstress in a large and famous department store. My grandmother spent mornings in the apartment, and in the afternoons she went to the park to care for the children of strangers. Her mother had met a rich lady who had two small children, and she always wanted my grandmother to go to her house to play with them, or to take them to the park or on some special excursion. It paid pretty well for what it was then, about fifty cents an hour. The best part was that she always took my grandmother to the museums, the theater, the shops, and the best restaurants. My grandmother only had to take care of the children and make sure they behaved properly. The rich lady bought her pretty dresses and new shoes, and always paid for the tickets to the museums, the theater, and the meals in the restaurants. My grandmother was like the eldest daughter in the family. And the children adored her. Both of them keep in contact with her today and treat her like a beloved aunt.

39. Why did the grandmother come to America?

    (A) She came over on vacation.

    (B) She fled the war in her native land.

    (C) Her brothers and sisters died.

    (D) She came to study.

This question is very clearly answered in the first part of the passage. Look for answers to first questions in the early part of the passage.

---

40. What was the grandmother's impression of New York?

    (A) She had a negative impression.

    (B) She was frightened by the large crowd of people in New York.

    (C) She felt like a small insect.

    (D) She saw many opportunities and new things that interested her.

This is a tricky question. Although the passage says she does feel like a little ant, the point of that comparison is the abandoned picnic (of the city of New York) she (the ant) is about to devour. So what it really means is best explained by choice (D). Both (A) and (B) would be misreadings of the passage.

---

41. How did the grandmother and her mother make money to live?

    (A) They lived on the street corners.

    (B) The grandmother cared for children, and her mother worked in a department store.

    (C) They lived on Park Avenue.

    (D) They lived in poverty.

The text says that the grandmother would spend her life exploring the corners and nooks and crannies of New York, but that doesn't mean she will be living on the street corners, so that eliminates choice (A). Choices (C) and (D) are simply not true. There are various references to the two jobs the women secured.

---

42. How did the grandmother spend her time in New York?

    (A) She spent the afternoons in the park with the children that she cared for.

    (B) She worked in a department store.

    (C) She studied in the high school.

    (D) She worked on Park Avenue.

Her mother worked in the department store, which cancels (B). There is no mention of school, which cancels (C). There is only a reference to Park Avenue early on in the passage when describing her first impression of the city. That leaves you with the right answer, (A).

43. What can we infer about the grandmother?

    (A) That she wasn't very cultured before meeting the rich woman

    (B) That during the day she helped her mom at her job

    (C) That she didn't attend school

    (D) That her salary was a great help to the family

The inference questions are sometimes tricky because you have to draw conclusions with only limited information. It's best to eliminate answers here. Choice (A) could be true, as she was taken to exciting and cultured places, but it doesn't mean she wasn't cultured. Choice (D) could be an inference, but there is no mention of the family's economic conditions in the passage. Choice (B) has no factual information to prove that she worked during the day, as the article says "she spent mornings in the apartment." This very sentence though, makes (C), the right answer, as she was home instead of being in school.

44. Why did the grandmother used to go to the theater, the stores, the museums, and the best restaurants?

    (A) Because the rich lady used to invite her to accompany the children

    (B) Because she was looking for work

    (C) Because she was very interested in everything

    (D) Because her mother wanted her to go

Other than the correct answer, (A), the only answer choice that appears in the passage above is (C), which is stated early on in the reading, so choices (B) and (D) can be easily eliminated. Choice (A) is clearly the best choice when you reexamine the text.

45. What relationship did the grandmother have later with the children of the rich lady?

    (A) They hated her.

    (B) They treated her poorly.

    (C) They ignored her.

    (D) They loved her very much.

The correct answer, choice (D), stands out because it is the one that is different from the others. When that happens, the one different answer is generally the correct answer.

Translation and the Questions and Answers for the Third Reading Comprehension Passage Found on Page 111

I wasn't able to fall asleep. I was so obsessed with the idea of the grand opening of the new restaurant next Saturday that millions of ideas were passing through my head. Had I invited all of the friends from the sports club? Had I invited all of the brothers and sisters and cousins of Eliza? I didn't want to offend anyone, much less my wife's family. I was listening to the slow rhythm of her calm breathing. She was so beautiful, and I loved to watch her sleep. She seemed so serene, like a white lily. In comparison, I felt as though I were on the verge of a heart attack. There were so many details, and I was certain that I was forgetting something important. I had called the critics from the local press. I had spoken with the chefs and waiters. I ordered all the food for the buffet. Shall I go over the menu once more in my head? We will start with squid, mussels, oysters, serrano ham, canapes, Swedish meatballs, and asparagus bathed in a cream sauce with caviar. Later, we will have a roast lamb and a poached salmon. We will also have salad and roast potatoes. For dessert, we will have various sorbets, an exquisite apple tart, and some chocolate truffles. The music, ah, the music. That's what I was forgetting! I forgot to call the band to confirm the time. I'll call them right now. What time is it? Oh, it's three in the morning. No problem. I can call them tomorrow.

46. Why can't the narrator sleep?

    (A) He's sick.

    (B) He's not sleepy.

    (C) He's nervous.

    (D) He's sad.

Once again it is important to understand the point of view to answer this question. The second and third sentences almost appear to be thoughts he is thinking out loud. Choices (A) and (D) are not mentioned. Answer choice (B) may be true, but (C) is most accurate.

47. Why does the narrator feel this way?

    (A) He's going to open a new restaurant.

    (B) He's going to speak in public.

    (C) He's going to play some music.

    (D) He's going to cook.

This information comes from the second sentence in the passage. Remember to look for answers to the earlier questions in the beginning of the reading. The correct answer is (A).

48. How does he describe his wife?

    (A) As a sleepy person

    (B) As an exemplary mother

    (C) Like a flower

    (D) Like a siren

He compares her with a *lirio blanco*, which means "white lily." He describes her calm breathing but doesn't describe her as a sleepy person. Choices (B) and (D) are never mentioned.

49. What is meant in lines 10-11 when the narrator says that he feels as if he were on the "verge of a heart attack"?

    (A) He is going to die.

    (B) He is depressed.

    (C) He is anxious.

    (D) He is sick.

He is exaggerating for effect. He is not really on the verge of a heart attack; he is only nervous and anxious. Answer choices (A) and (D) would be more literal readings of the passage. Choice (B) is not mentioned.

50. All of the following foods appear on the menu EXCEPT:

(A) squid

(B) mussels

(C) oysters

(D) shrimp

This is a detail question. You don't even have to know what the English equivalents of these foods are. A quick review of the items on the menu will reveal the correct answer, choice (A). Shrimp is not offered.

51. What meat will be served as the main course?

(A) Serrano ham

(B) Canapes

(C) Salmon

(D) Lamb

Remember that the first seven or so foods listed are all starters. The two main courses mentioned are lamb and salmon. Lamb is the only meat mentioned as a main course. The correct choice is (D).

52. What had the narrator forgotten?

(A) To set the alarm clock

(B) To call the band

(C) To set the table

(D) To call the press

Choice (B) is correct. At the end of the passage, when the narrator reflects upon the music to be played at the restaurant, he realizes that he's forgotten to call the band to confirm the time.

53. The following sentence can be added to the text. **"How could I forget about the apricots and the berries for the fruit salad?"** Where would this sentence fit best?

(A) Position A (line 16)

(B) Position B (line 19)

(C) Position C (line 21)

(D) Position D (line 22)

This is a vocabulary question testing your knowledge of fruit vocabulary. In Hispanic culture, fruit salad is often served as a dessert, making choice (C) the best place for the sentence, as the narrator is speaking about the desserts.

54. What is the narrator going to do tomorrow?

(A) Take a nap

(B) Eat a lot

(C) Call the band

(D) Call the critics

Choice (C) is correct. Recall that he wants to call them just when he thinks of it, but soon realizes that it's three in the morning so he decides to call the next day.

Translation and the Questions and Answers for the Fourth Reading Comprehension Passage Found on Page 112

When train number 65 stopped at the small station located between kilometers 171 and 172, almost all of the second- and third-class passengers remained asleep inside their cars because the penetrating cold of the dawn did not allow them to walk on the abandoned platform. The only first-class passenger to come on the train descended hurriedly, and turning himself to the crew, asked them if that place was the Villahorrenda station.

"We are in Villahorrenda," responded the conductor, whose voice became lost in the clucking of hens, which at that moment were underneath the caboose. "I believe they are there waiting for you with the horses."

"But it's cold as hell here!" said the passenger, wrapping himself in his blanket. "Is there any place in the station where I may rest and recover before I begin a trip by horse through this country of ice?" They had not finished speaking when the conductor, called by the pressing obligations of his job, left, leaving our anonymous gentleman as he was in the middle of his sentence. The passenger saw that another member of the crew was approaching with a lantern hanging from his left hand, which was moving to the rhythm of his walk.

"Is there a room or boarding-house in Villahorrenda station?" asked the passenger to the man with the lantern.

"There is nothing here," he said brusquely.

"It is best to leave here as quickly as possible," said the gentleman to himself. "The conductor told me that the horses were over there." The passenger left with his blanket in his hands.

55. What is this selection about?

   (A) The advantages of traveling by train.

   (B) The disadvantages of traveling by train.

   (C) Two friends traveling by train with animals.

   (D) The trip of a discontented man.

If you could not understand the passage, you could have used this question to help you understand the general topic. All four answer choices indicate traveling and (A), (B), and (C) explicitly mention that this traveling is done by train. If the passage were a list of advantages or disadvantages, as in (A) and (B), there would probably not be dialogue and literary description, so you can eliminate those two answer choices without reading much at all. The passage has nothing to do with two friends or traveling with animals, so you can eliminate (C), making (D) the correct answer.

56. What is the gentleman searching for in Villahorrenda?

   (A) A place to rest

   (B) His friends and their animals

   (C) Work and a home

   (D) The crew of the train

The conversations between the first-class passenger and the crew repeatedly show that the man is looking for a place to rest and relax, so (A) is the correct answer. There are no friends mentioned, so (B) is out. We have no idea as to what his long term plans are, so (C) is also entirely made up. Answer choice (D) does not make sense considering that the man was talking to the crew, which was still on the train.

57. According the conversations between the gentleman and the conductor, what adjective best characterizes the attitude of the conductor?

(A) Kind

(B) Disenchanted

(C) Busy

(D) Doubtful

The conductor seems hurried and overly busy as a result of his work on the train, so (C) is the correct answer to this question. He has nothing about which to be disenchanted or doubtful, so we can eliminate (B) and (D). His rudeness to the gentleman (leaving him mid-sentence) means that (A) is very weak in light of (C).

58. The narrator describes Villahorrenda as _____ place.

(A) an abandoned

(B) a dangerous

(C) a quiet

(D) The narrator does not describe Villahorrenda.

While you will not see many overtly "trick" questions on the AP exam, keep your eyes open for ETS's deceptive wording. The correct answer here is (D) because the narrator never describes Villahorrenda himself, but allows the characters to describe it through dialogue. The one common adjective used to describe the station is "cold," which, fortunately, is not an answer choice.

59. Whom is the gentleman addressing when he says, "It is best to leave here as quickly as possible"?

(A) The hens

(B) The conductor

(C) Himself

(D) The other member of the crew

The phrase "decir...para su capote" (27–28) is an idiomatic expression meaning "to say to oneself." The correct answer is (C).

60. Who are those waiting with the horses?

(A) The crew

(B) The women of Villahorrenda

(C) The men of Villahorrenda

(D) Unknown people

We are never told of any "women" or "men" of Villahorrenda, so (B) and (C) can be eliminated. Choice (A) seems ridiculous in light of the fact that it was the conductor who told him, so (D) is the only possible answer.

61. Why does he wrap himself in his blanket?

(A) Because it is cold.

(B) Because he needs to give the blanket to the train's crew.

(C) Because the hens are clucking beneath the train.

(D) Because he is afraid of demons.

This is a simple vocabulary and comprehension question, which relies on basic Spanish skills and common sense. Choice (B) is never mentioned in the passage, (C) makes no sense whatsoever, and (D) is an out-of-context and overly literal reading of the passenger's outburst. The correct answer is (A).

62. The following sentence can be added to the text. **"The idea of a two-day horseback ride through unfamiliar mountains with their windstorms, rainstorms, and snowstorms didn't appeal to him."** Where would this sentence fit best?

(A) Position A (line 6)

(B) Position B (line 17)

(C) Position C (line 21)

(D) Position D (line 31)

In this type of question, it is helpful to define the tone of the sentence to see where it would be complementary to other sentences in the passage. Then see where semantically it would make more sense; that is, find a sentence before or after the proposed position that will show flow and topic development. Lines 15-17 are showing the protagonist's desire to rest before a journey. As such, line 17, choice (B), would be the best answer for this question.

Translation and the Questions and Answers for the Fifth Reading Comprehension Passage Found on Page 113

Mamá, Ana, and the baby went to visit Grandpa, but poor Papá could not go because he had to stay at home to work.

"What shall I do without you?" he asked.

"I will write you letters, three letters," Ana answered. "I will tell you what we are doing here without you."

"Do you know how to write a letter?" asked Papá.

"Oh, yes, I can write one," said Ana. "I am seven now. You will see that I can write a letter."

Ana had a very good time. One day she said, "Grandma, may I take a pen? I want to write to Papá."

"Yes," said Grandma, "there are pens on the desk."

Ana ran to Grandpa's desk. "Oh, Grandma! Here is such a strange pen!"

"That is a quill pen," said her Grandma. "Grandpa made it for me. It is a goose quill; in old times everybody used to write with quill pens."

"I think it is very pretty," said Ana. "I don't think I can write with it."

She took another pen and went off. In a little while she went back to the desk. And there she saw that the baby had taken the quill pen and she had been writing to Papá with it. And what a letter she had written! Ana realized that she had spilled the ink over the desk.

"Oh, baby, baby! What did you do that for?"

Mamá sent baby's letter to Papá, and he said he was glad to get both letters.

ANA'S LETTER TO HER FATHER.

Aracataca, July 12, 1917.

Dear Papá:

We are having a very good time. Grandpa has a big bay horse. Sometimes he puts me on the horse's back. It is such fun! I play in the field a great deal. Grandpa lets me walk on the haycocks and I pick berries for Grandma. They give us cheese with our coffee. I wish you were here with us. Baby has written you a letter. She took Grandma's quill pen, and she spilled the ink. Can you read her letter? She says she wrote, "How are you, Papá? I love you a great deal."

Your little girl,

Ana

63. How can one understand what the baby's letter is about?

(A) according to the letter itself

(B) according to Ana's letter

(C) according to what the grandmother says to the father

(D) according to the narrator

Because the baby's "writing" consists of spilling ink all over the desk, her letter cannot be understood by itself (A), which is why Ana facetiously asks her father if he can read it and then offers a translation of what the baby was trying to say. She does this within her letter to her father, making (B) the correct answer. You could have eliminated (C) because the grandmother and the father do not have a conversation in this selection. The narrating voice does not offer any information about the contents of the letter, so (D) is also incorrect.

64. Who doubts that Ana can write the letter?

(A) her grandmother

(B) her father

(C) her grandfather

(D) the baby

This is a straightforward comprehension question. After Ana indicates that she will write letters, Ana's father introduces doubt by asking her if she knows how to write a letter in the first place, making (B) the correct answer.

65. According to the selection, why does Ana write, "Can you understand her letter?" in lines 39-40 to her father?

(A) Because she knows he has poor vision.

(B) Because she knows the letter has arrived.

(C) Because she knows he cannot read the baby's letter.

(D) Because she knows that in old times everyone used to write with quill pens.

Ana asked her father if he could read the baby's letter, knowing that he could not because it was illegible. Answer choice (C) is correct. Answer choice (D) merely rehashes some of the text and choices (A) and (B) are entirely unrelated.

66. The following sentence can be added to the text. **"Fascinated by the novelty, she handled it for a moment, and then she returned it to its proper place."** Where would this sentence fit best?

(A) Position A (line 14)

(B) Position B (line 19)

(C) Position C (line 29)

(D) Position D (line 38)

This passage becomes confusing because the word "pluma" here is used to refer to both a feather pen and a regular pen. The reader may have difficulty is distinguishing between the two. As the feather pen is source of fascination to the young girl, she would naturally pick it up and examine it. In line 14, she hasn't discovered the feather pen yet. Line 19, would be the best fit, as she remarks how beautiful it is and that doesn't think she can write with the feather pen. Immediately afterwards, she takes a regular pen and leaves, implying she had put the feather pen back. Thus, (B) is the best answer.

67. Who is the "her" ("it") with whom the baby writes the letter (line 24)?

    (A) the grandmother

    (B) the pen

    (C) Ana

    (D) the mother

Since the mother is not mentioned in this scene, you can eliminate choice (D) right away. If you look closely at the line, the only possible answer is (B), as the "ella" ("it" in English) refers to "la pluma," which is a feminine noun and not a person. You know that no one wrote the letter with the baby because she was unsupervised.

---

68. Why does Ana look for a pen?

    (A) Because she wants to write a letter.

    (B) Because she wants to write a book.

    (C) Because she wants to spill the ink.

    (D) Because she needs her father.

This is an easy question, but notice how far into the question set you had to work to get here. Because the questions do not move in a clear order of difficulty, be sure not to trap yourself by spending too much time on a difficult question. Doing this would rob you of the easy points you could earn with questions like this. The entire plot of this passage is Ana writing a letter to her father: (A) is the correct answer.

---

69. Who sends the letter to Papá?

    (A) the grandmother

    (B) Ana

    (C) the baby

    (D) the mother

This question may seem strange, but it is actually the mother who *sends* the letter, not the baby (C), the grandmother (A), or Ana (B), who is the one who *writes* the letter. Therefore answer choice (D) is the correct answer.

SECTION II: PART A

Translation for the Essay Topic Given in the Practice Test Found on Page 115

Write an email to a friend indicating that you will be moving to his/her town. You should include in your letter:

- An appropriate greeting

- The reason why you are moving

- How you feel about the changes you will face

- Your hopes concerning having to change homes and schools

- Your desire to see each other soon

- An appropriate closing

Sample Student Response

Mi querida amiga Olga:

Espero que te encuentres bien. Tengo que decirte algo muy importante. Recientemente mi padre obtuvo un trabajo nuevo. Recibirá un aumento de salario, pero es necesario que nos mudemos a una ciudad nueva. ¡Y las buenas noticias son que nos mudaremos a tu ciudad! ¡Es posible que seamos vecinos!

Pero por otra parte, tengo que cambiar de escuela. Espero poder conocer a nuevos amigos. Preferiría quedarme aquí con mis amigos, pero por lo menos sé que tú puedes ayudarme con el proceso. Me encantan mis maestros aquí, pero espero que los nuevos maestros sean igual de agradables. Si fuéramos vecinos, no haría mis tareas para nada y jugaríamos al béisbol todos los días.

No puedo esperar verte muy pronto y ver a tus padres también. No he visto a tu familia en muchos años. Será buenísimo verte todos los días. ¡Espero que estés lista para mí!

Muchos abrazos,

Josh Messinger

Translation of Sample Student Response

My dear friend Olga:

I hope this finds you well. I have to tell you something very important. Recently my father obtained a new job. He will receive a salary increase, but it is necessary for us to move to a new city. And the good news is that we will be moving to your town! It's possible we may even be neighbors!

But on the other hand, I have to change schools. I hope to be able to make new friends. I would prefer to remain here with my friends, but at least I know that you can help me with the process. I love my teachers here, but hope that the new teachers are equally pleasant. If we were neighbors, I wouldn't do my homework at all and we would play baseball every day.

I can't wait to see you and your family soon. I haven't seen your family for many years. It will be great to see you every day. I hope you are ready for me!

Many hugs,

Josh Messinger

Evaluation

This response fulfilled the requirements of the letter and provided pertinent details. It also made an attempt to show varied verb tenses: future, conditional, past and present subjunctive; and several good expressions (igual de agradable; espero que te encuentres bien) as well as good transitions between sentences. Where the essay falls short is in its structure, style, and tone. Many of the sentences are translations from English (Espero que estés lista para mí: I hope you are ready for me, or No puedo esperar verte pronto: I can't wait to see you soon) which give an awkward tone and are simply not expressed that way in Spanish. Be sure to know the idiomatic expressions for these (Espero que puedas recibirme and Me muero de ganas de verte or Estoy loco por verte). In addition, the sentences are short and choppy, which call attention to their English dominance. These letters are a snapshot of your style and knowledge, and this student did a great job of incorporating all the complex structures he could. However, a little more maturity and flow in the content would have worked wonders for the score. The letter would probably get a 3 from the graders. However, in order to score more points, it is necessary to make the letter sound more "native" sounding. A nice example of a similar letter would be:

Querida Olga:

Espero que al recibir estas líneas te encuentres bien de salud, al igual que tu familia. ¿Adivina qué? ¡Pronto seremos vecinos! Mi padre consiguió una tremenda oferta de trabajo, y tenemos que trasladarnos a tu ciudad. ¡Me muero de ganas de verte! Hace tanto tiempo que no nos vemos.

Obviamente esto representa una buena oportunidad, pero al mismo tiempo me preocupan los cambios que me esperan. El dejar lo conocido de mi casa y escuela me es difícil, pero hay que experimentar nuevas cosas en la vida, ¿no? Espero que puedas ayudarme a familiarizarme con el nuevo ambiente para que pueda sentirme a gusto lo más pronto posible. Sé que puedo contar contigo.

Bueno, te avisaré cuando llegue a tu ciudad. Gracias de antemano por tu apoyo.

Muchos abrazos de tu amigo.

Josh Messinger

Translation for the Essay Topic Given in the Practice Test Found on Page 116

How does global warming affect our lives?

Sample Student Essay

El calentamiento global trae consigo graves riesgos al bienestar del planeta. El ritmo al cual han crecido tanto la población mundial como la expansión industrial han puesto en peligro las defensas naturales del planeta. Como resultado, en la Tierra hay una mayor tendencia a ocurrir acontecimientos perjudiciales como desastres naturales, escasez de comida, brotes de enfermedades, y una disminución de recursos vitales para sobrevivir. Por consiguiente, nuestras vidas han cambiado también.

Yo diría que los cambios más drásticos se han presenciado en nuestra vida diaria. Los precios de gasolina, comida, y transportación han aumentado muchísimo recientemente. Por ello, nuestra vida económica cotidiana es más difícil. Muchas personas han sufrido ya que sus sueldos no rinden comoantes y les es difícil que su presupuesto les alcance para todo lo necesario. Y como recientemente ha surgido conciencia para preservar el planeta, estamos viendo programas de reciclar, ahorrar energía, compartir viajes, explotar recursos locales, descubrir fuentes de energía, y hasta salvar a los animales que están en peligro de extinción, particularmente en las zonas antárticas. La calidad de nuestras vidas ha bajado también por el calentamiento global. Por ejemplo, en muchos países subdesarrollados, las cifras de muertes causadas por el calentamiento global han crecido. Las enfermedades como la malaria tendrán más víctimas como nunca ya que el calentamiento global permite que los insectos proliferen y sobrevivan con más facilidad. El derretimiento del hielo de Antártica traerá más inundaciones y consigo más casos de cólera y otras enfermedades. Yo mismo he observado el crecimiento de alergias y problemas cardiorrespiratorios entre la gente de mi familia. Y tal como predijeron los expertos, estos problemas están manifestándose ahora. Si hubiéramos hecho caso a las advertencias de los expertos hace años, tal vez no nos habríamos encontrado en esta situación tan desconsolada.

Finalmente, el calentamiento global ha cambiado nuestra forma de pensar. Se han despertado nuevas maneras de planificar el futuro. Los expertos están educando al público para que varíe su forma de pensar y su percepción en el mundo. El individuo se ha dado cuenta de que sí se puede hacer una diferencia al preservar el planeta y consumir más prudentemente. La gente está tratando de hacer lo posible para preservar el medio ambiente. Cada día se ve más programas para ayudar a preservar los recursos naturales, minerales y humanos del planeta. Solo esperamos que no sea demasiado tarde.

En resumen, se reconoce que el planeta en si es la base de nuestra existencia y supervivencia. El calentamiento global, fenómeno creado por el hombre, ha llegado a tal punto que por fin el mundo ha reconocido su importancia, y como resultado, ha tratado de modificar su forma de pensar y actuar. Sin embargo, el daño es extenso, y requiere que también los gobiernos apoyen toda opción necesaria para salvar al mundo. Solo el tiempo dirá si este esfuerzo es suficiente.

Translation of the Student Essay

Global warming brings with it severe risks to the well being of the planet. The rhythm at which both the world population as well as the industrial expansion has grown have endangered the natural defenses of the planet. As a result, on Earth there is an increased tendency of detrimental events such as natural disasters, food shortages, sickness outbreaks and a decrease of the vital resources necessary for survival. As a result, our lives have changed as well.

I would say that the most drastic changes have been evident in our daily lives. The prices of gas, food and transportation have gone up tremendously recently. For that reason, our daily economic life is even more difficult. Many people have suffered since their salaries don't go as far as before and it is difficult for their budget to pay for all of their needs. And given that recently there has been an increase in consciousness towards preserving the planet, we are seeing programs for recycling, saving energy, ride sharing, using local resources, discovering alternative energy sources, and even saving animals that are in danger of becoming extinct, particularly in the Antarctic zones. Our quality of life has also gone down as a result of global warming. For example, in many underdeveloped countries, the number of deaths caused by global warming has grown. Sicknesses like malaria will have more victims than ever because global warming allows insects to thrive and to survive more easily. The melting of Antarctic ice will bring more floods and with that more cases of cholera and other sicknesses. I myself have observed an increase in allergies and cardio-respiratory problems among my own family members. And just as the experts predicted, these problems are becoming evident now. If we had paid attention to the expert's warnings years ago, perhaps we wouldn't have found ourselves in this sad situation.

Finally, global warming has changed our way of thinking. New ways of planning the future have been formed. Experts are educating the public to change its way of thinking and its perception of the world. The individual has realized that one can indeed make a difference by preserving the planet and consuming more wisely. People are taking the necessary steps to save the environment. Each day we see more programs to help preserve the planet's natural, mineral, and human resources. We only hope that it is not too late.

In summary, it is known that the planet itself is the key to our existence and survival. Global warming, a phenomenon created by man, has come to point where the world has finally recognized its importance, and as a result, has modified its way of thinking and acting. However, the damage is extensive and requires that governments also support all the necessary options in order to save the planet. Only time will tell if this effort is enough.

Explanation

This essay expresses ideas clearly and in an organized manner. It has a good flow and transitions, and it displays excellent grammatical control and breadth of vocabulary. At the end of the introduction, there should be some reference to the topics of the following paragraphs to ease transitions. Another improvement would be to tie the articles in a little bit more, as it referenced them in mostly general terms. Some specifics from the articles could have strengthened the essay. The writer didn't specifically identify the sources mentioned. Perhaps a few lines where he could have said "According to Source #1…" However, given the strong style, grammar, and organization, this essay would have still scored extremely well.

This essay has some very good grammatical points that you should try to use in your essay: Use of good transitions: *Por ello, en resumen, Finalmente, Tal como*. Advanced vocabulary: *ya que, consigo, se reconoce que*. Good use of subjunctive: *Esperamos que, Requiere que, para que*. Good use of verbs: *surgir, rendir, predecir, manifestarse, proliferar, sobrevivir, modificar*. Advanced/Native structures: *tanto…como; les es difícil*.

A good way to make a winning essay is to find vocabulary and expressions that you can use or modify to fit most essays. Choose a few expressions in each of the above categories from essays and readings and try to start inserting them in your essays each time you write in class. For example, "Por ello" is a more sophisticated way to say "por eso," and this is exactly the type of thing the readers are looking for in the essays. Keep a checklist and always try to incorporate some of them into your essay. It will definitely make a good impression with the readers. In addition, try to use a variety of tenses: The above essay used present tense, present progressive, present subjunctive, future, preterit, and conditional. Readers especially like to see the advanced tenses and past subjunctive as well. Don't be afraid to go over the minimum word requirement either; generally you do better by writing more as opposed to less.

Sample Script of Student Response with Translation, Page 121

Narrador: Has solicitado una posición de aprendiz en una empresa multinacional latinoamericana. Imagina que recibes una llamada telefónica del director del Departamento de Recursos Humanos para hablar sobre la posición que has solicitado.

You have applied for an internship in a Latin American multinational company. Imagine that you receive a phone message from the director of Human Resources to speak about the position that you have applied for.

Ahora tienes un minuto para leer el esquema de la conversación.

Now you have one minute to read the conversation outline.

Ahora imagina que recibas una llamada del señor Rivero para realizar una entrevista.

Now imagine that you receive a phone call from Mr. Rivero to speak about the position.

MA: Buenos días, le habla el señor Luis Rivero director de Recursos Humanos de la Empresa Mundiales. Me gustaría hacerle algunas preguntas por teléfono sobre su solicitud. Primero, cuénteme por favor. ¿qué le motivó a solicitar una posición de aprendiz en nuestra compañía?

Good morning, this is Mr. Luis Rivero from the Human Resources Department of the Mundiales Company. I would like to ask you a few questions by phone about your application. First, please tell me, what prompted you to apply for a position in our company?

Tú: Pues, como su compañía cuenta entre los líderes de su industria, me pareció buena idea solicitar una posición con ustedes para poder aprender más sobre la industria.

Well, since your company is among the leaders of its industry, it seemed like a good idea to me to apply for a position to learn more about the industry.

MA: Muy bien. ¿Qué destrezas y habilidades podrá aportar a nuestro lugar de trabajo?

What skills and abilities could you contribute to our workplace?

Tú: Hablo tres idiomas: el español, el inglés y el francés. Además, domino varios programas de computadora y soy muy bueno resolviendo problemas.

I speak three languages: Spanish, English, and French. In addition, I am proficient in many computer programs and I am very good at resolving problems.

MA: ¿Qué dirían sus patrones o jefes anteriores sobre personalidad y calidad de trabajo?

What might your previous employers say about your personality and quality of your work?

Tú: Dirían que soy puntual, leal, y que trabajo bien en grupos. En cuanto a mi calidad de trabajo, dirían que soy trabajador, organizado, y diligente.

They would say I am punctual, loyal and that I work well in group situations. In terms of my work quality, they would say I am hard working, organized, and diligent.

MA: Quisiera saber, ¿cuándo está disponible para trabajar y cuándo podrá empezar?

I would like to know when you are available to work and when you could start.

Tú: Como las clases terminan a finales de junio, puedo trabajar los meses de julio y agosto. Puedo comenzar el 5 de julio.

As school finishes the end of June, I can work in July and August. I can start July 5th.

MA: Me gustaría que pasara por nuestra oficina para que conociera a algunos de mis compañeros de trabajo. ¿Podrá pasar por la oficina mañana a las 10 de la mañana?

I would like for you to pass by our office in order to meet some of my work colleagues. Could you stop by tomorrow at 10?

Tú: Desafortunadamente, asisto a la escuela hasta las tres de la tarde. Sería posible que le visitara a las 4?

Unfortunately, I have school until 3 pm. Would it be possible for me to visit at 4pm?

MA: No hay ningún inconveniente. Nos vemos entonces en esa fecha y hora.

No problem. We'll see you then at that date and time.

Tú: Espero con ganas poderle conocer mañana. Que pase buen día. Adiós.

I look forward to seeing you tomorrow, have a nice day. Goodbye.

Explanation

The answers were clear, appropriate, and had some complex structures like conditional and past subjunctive (*sería posible que le visitara*), and subjunctive (*que pase buen día*). The rest of the responses advanced the conversation and more than fulfilled the requirements. It would receive at least a 4 due to the quality of its grammar and topic development.

Translation and Script for the Two-Source Composition on Pages 123 and 124

Printed Text/Source 1

The following document was created by the Board of Supervisors for Educational District #242, Los Angeles on the possibility of offering parents the option of reducing the school week from five days to four.

June 15, 2008

Re. Changing the routine: Reducing the school week from 5 days to 4

Dear Parents:

I understand how recent inflation and the rising cost of living have affected you and your families. This is a difficult time for all. Already affected by the rising costs of fuel for buses, for heating and cooling buildings, feeding students and of almost all materials, school districts across the country are considering the idea of reducing the school week from five days to four. It's an option we should seriously consider.

More than 150 schools across the country have already adopted this option and seem to be happy with the results. A district in Topeka, Kansas has adopted a Tuesday to Friday schedule and has saved $248,000 of its $8.7 million budget. This money was used for refunds to district residents. They also reported improved student attendance and better results on standardized tests.

There are other benefits. A three-day weekend would provide more family time, something lacking in today's society. In addition, students could spend more time on school assignments without the pressure of a 5-day school week.

The costs associated with the maintenance of our buildings and the transportation of our students are staggering. As we are faced with future uncertainty in fuel costs, we have to act now. Obviously, reducing costs is the answer, and cutting 1.5 hours from each school day, thus eliminating a full day represents economic savings without the necessity of sacrificing jobs, academic instruction or student programs. Without these savings, students living less than 2 miles from their schools will lose the free transportation provided by the district, and various jobs and programs will be affected.

I invite you to attend a public forum at Fleetwood July 23, 2008 at 7PM. There we can discuss this issue further.

Sincerely,

Luis Maldonado

Superintendant, District 242

Audio/Source 2

Meeting of parents, School Management Board, July 23, 2008, Fleetwood School

The following residents of Los Angeles expressed their opinions on the proposal to change the school week from five to four days.

Myrta Morales:	"No estoy segura que no exista un límite sobre lo que un estudiante pueda aprender durante un día escolar. Y me preocupo especialmente por los niños del primer grado y del jardín infantil, con la posibilidad de que tengan que sentarse 90 minutos más. Se trata de calidad, no cantidad".

I'm not sure that there isn't a limit to what students can learn in a school day. And, I'm especially worried for children in the first grade and kindergarten possibly having to sit for an additional 90 minutes. It's about quality, not quantity.

Rene López:	"Esto no ahorraría dinero, es más, los costos subirían. Para los que creen que se trata de ahorros de combustible, se equivocan. Muchos edificios grandes tienen que mantener un nivel especifico de temperatura por varios motivos, pero desde el punto de vista económico es más eficiente mantener un edificio a 65 grados por 3 días en vez de apagar la calefacción y tratar de calentar el edificio los lunes por la mañana. Además, no ahorraríamos dinero en sueldos, ya que los profesores estarían trabajando la misma cantidad de horas. Además, la ayuda fiscal estatal depende de horas de contacto diarias, que tiene que llegar a 180 días de asistencia. Si bajamos el numero de asistencia, corremos el riesgo de perder la ayuda fiscal estatal, y pagaríamos más impuestos".

This would not save money. What's more, costs would rise. For those who think this is about saving fuel, they are mistaken. Many large buildings have to maintain a specific level of temperature for various reasons: From the economic perspective, it's more efficient keep a building at 65 degrees for 3 days instead of turning off the heat and trying to heat up the building on Monday morning. In addition, we wouldn't save any money on salaries, as the teachers are still working the same number of hours. What's more, state financial aid is linked to the length of the school day, which has to equal 180 days of attendance. If we lower the attendance figures, we run the risk of losing state financial aid—and we would pay more taxes.

Roberto Méndez	"Nuestros hijos necesitan más tiempo en la escuela en vez de menos tiempo. La educación es la base de nuestra sociedad. Tal vez esto se podría hacer con los estudiantes del colegio pero no se podría en la escuela primaria. Algunos niños tendrán problemas en acostumbrase a la escuela después de un fin de semana, ¡tres días libres serían un desastre! Como país necesitamos buscar fuentes alternativas para reducir el costo de energía. Reducir el tiempo que los niños pasan en la escuela, nos detendrá como nación. Necesitamos educarlos y abrirles la mente…. ¡son nuestro futuro!"

Our children need more time in school, rather than less. Education is the basis of our society. Perhaps this would work with high school students but not with grade school students. Some children will have problems getting used to school after the weekend. Three days off would be a disaster! As a country we need to find alternative ways to reduce energy costs. Reducing the time children spend in school will hold us back as a nation. We need to educate them and open their minds...they're our future!

Irene Ramos "Ya tenemos estudiantes que pasan más de una hora en el bus para llegar a la escuela. Agregar más horas a eso es simplemente demasiado para ellos".

We already have students who spend more than an hour on the bus to get to school. Adding more hours to this is simply too much for them.

Sample Student Answer with Translation

Con los precios altos de energía, nos vemos comprometidos a encontrar nuevas maneras de ahorrar dinero y recursos. Ya no se puede dar por sentado todo lo que tenemos hoy, ya que puede que mañana no lo haya. Para tratar de ahorrar dinero, y controlar los gastos ascendientes, algunos distritos están considerando la opción de sólo operar 4 días por semana y extender cada día unos 90 minutos.

El superintendente explica que esto ahorraría dinero, mejoraría asistencia, y mejoraría rendimiento estudiantil en términos académicos. Sin embargo, la comunidad, demuestra que les importa más el éxito de sus niños que el ahorrar dinero. Además, señalan que es posible que no ahorren dinero. Cerrar las escuelas sin calefacción ni aire acondicionado podrá resultar más caro que simplemente mantenerlas a una temperatura estable. También, cuestionan la utilidad de extender el horario escolar. Sin embargo, un estudiante explica que el tiempo libre le permitiria dedicarle más tiempo a sus estudios, de acuerdo a lo que explica el Superintendente Maldonado.

Según la Fuente 2, los padres insisten en que sus hijos pasen más tiempo en la escuela, no menos. Y la ayuda financiera del estado exige 180 días, no menos. La conservación durante el día escolar podrá ser una manera de ahorrar energía: no hace falta tener luces todo el tiempo, y tal vez otras tecnologías pudieran ayudar a ahorrar energía. En realidad no hay una solución al problema; hay que considerar las dos caras de la moneda. Tal vez si todos los miembros de la comunidad se sentaran a conversar, y así considerar las opiniones de muchos, podrían llegar a un acuerdo y ver como resolver el problema.

With the high prices of energy we are obliged to find new ways of saving money and resources. We can no longer take for granted what we have today, because it may not be here tomorrow. In order to try to save money and control rising costs, some districts are considering the option of operating only 4 days a week and extend each school day 90 minutes.

The superintendent explains that this would save money, improve attendance, and improve student academic performance. However, the community demonstrates that they are more interested in the success of their children than saving money. In addition, they show that it is possible that money would not be saved. Closing the schools without heat or air conditioning could be more expensive than simply maintaining them at a stable temperature. And they question the usefulness of extending the school schedule. However, one student explains that the free time would allow him to dedicate more time to his studies, in accordance with what Superintendent Maldonado explained.

According to Source 2, parents want their children to spend more, not less, time in school. And the financial aid of the state demands 180 days, nothing less. Conservation during the school year could be a way to save money; it's not necessary to have lights on all the time and perhaps other technologies could help save energy. In reality, there isn't a solution to the problem; we have to consider both sides of the coin. Maybe if all of the members of the community sat down to speak and thus consider the many opinion, then they could come to an agreement and solve the issue.

Explanation

This response was adequate in addressing the three areas of topic development, task completion, and language usage. It was somewhat short and did summarize, although there is evidence of comparing and contrasting. It is well organized as well, and given that the student had only 2 minutes to say all of this, he would probably be receiving a 4 on this task.

PART ◆ III

AP SPANISH LITERATURE: HOW TO CRACK THE SYSTEM

OVERVIEW

The AP Spanish Literature Exam consists of two sections:

Section I is the multiple-choice section, which tests *reading comprehension* and *literary analysis*.

Section II is the free-response section, which tests *interpretation analysis* and *writing skills*.

The College Board provides a breakdown of the types of questions on the exam. Below is a summary of the various components of the test.

Multiple-Choice Section I	Description	Number of Questions	Percent of Grade	Time
Reading Comprehension and Literary Analysis	Multiple-Choice	Approx. 65 questions	40%	80 mins.

Free-Response Section II	Description	Number of Questions	Percent of Grade	Time
Poetry Analysis	Free-Response	1	20%	30 mins.
Thematic Analysis	Free-Response	1	20%	40 mins.
Text Analysis	Free-Response	1	20%	40 mins.

As you can see, the three essays are heavily weighted and contribute to more than half of your final grade on the test. The evaluation of your essay content will account for 70 percent of your score, while your language usage will account for the other 30 percent. No need to worry; we will discuss each of the essay questions in greater detail in the coming chapters. Also, note the weight of the reading comprehension exercises in Section I. We will examine in detail some techniques to help you tackle these reading comprehension passages.

THE READING LIST

The AP Spanish Literature Exam contains questions about specific works from the reading list below. Therefore, you should try to read—in their non-abridged, original-language versions—all the titles included in the list. In the case of Gabriel García Márquez, you can select any three stories from the list of six.

MEDIEVAL AND GOLDEN AGE LITERATURE

- Anónimo, "Romance de la pérdida de Alhama" ("Ay de mi Alhama")
- Anónimo, "Romance del Conde Arnaldos" (Versión de 26 versos)
- Anónimo, Lazarillo de Tormes: tratados 1, 2, 3 y 7
- Cervantes Saavedra, Miguel de, *El ingenioso hidalgo, don Quijote de la Mancha*: Primera parte: capítulos I, II, III, IV, V y VIII
- Cruz, Sor Juana Inés de la, "En perseguirme, Mundo, ¿qué interesas?", "Hombres necios que acusáis"

- Góngora y Argote, Luis de, Soneto CLXVI ("Mientras por competir con tu cabello")
- Juan Manuel, Infante de Castilla, *Conde lucanor:* Ejemplo XXXV ("Lo que sucedió a un mozo que casó con una mujer muy fuerte y muy brava")
- Núñez Cabeza de Vaca, Álvar, *Naufragios:* Capítulos XII ("Cómo los indios nos trajeron de comer"), XX ("De cómo nos huimos"), XXI ("De cómo curamos aquí unos dolientes") y XXII ("Cómo otro día nos trajeron otros enfermos")
- Quevedo y Villegas, Francisco de, *Heráclito cristiano:* Salmo XVII ("Miré los muros de la patria mía")
- Téllez, Gabriel (Tirso de Molina), *El burlador de Sevilla y convidado de piedra*
- Vega, Garcilaso de la, Soneto XXIII ("En tanto que de rosa y de azucena")

NINETEENTH-CENTURY LITERATURE

- Alas, Leopoldo (Clarín), "Adiós, Cordera"
- Bécquer, Gustavo Adolfo, Rima IV ("No digáis que agotado su tesoro"), XI ("Yo soy ardiente, yo soy morena") y LIII ("Volverán las oscuras golondrinas")
- Darío, Rubén (Félix Rubén García Sarmiento), *Cantos de vida y esperanza:* Otros poemas, VI ("Canción de otoño en primavera") y XLI ("Lo fatal"); *Cantos de vida y esperanza,* VIII ("A Roosevelt")
- Espronceda, José de, "Canción del pirata"
- Heredia, José María, "En una tempestad"
- Larra, Mariano José de, "Vuelva Ud. mañana"
- Martí, José, "Dos patrias" ("Dos patrias tengo yo: Cuba y la noche"); *Versos sencillos,* I ("Yo soy un hombre sincero")
- Palma, Ricardo, "El alacrán de Fray Gómez"
- Pardo Bazán, Emilia, "Las medias rojas"

TWENTIETH-CENTURY LITERATURE

- Allende, Isabel, "Dos palabras"
- Borges, Jorge Luis, "El sur", "La muerte y la brújula"
- Burgos, Julia de, "A Julia de Burgos"
- Castellanos, Rosario, "Autorretrato"
- Cortázar, Julio, "Continuidad de los parques", "La noche boca arriba"
- Fuentes, Carlos, "Chac Mool"

- García Lorca, Federico, "La casa de Bernarda Alba", dos romances del "Romancero Gitano"
- García Márquez, Gabriel, tres cuentos de la lista siguiente:

  "El ahogado más hermoso del mundo"

  "Un día de éstos"

  "La prodigiosa tarde de Baltazar"

  "Un señor muy viejo con unas alas enormes"

  "La siesta del martes"

  "La viuda de Montiel"
- Guillén, Nicolás, "Balada de los dos abuelos", "Sensemayá"
- Machado, Antonio, "He andado muchos caminos", "La primavera besaba", "Caminante, son tus huellas"
- Martín Gaite, Carmen, "Las ataduras"
- Neruda, Pablo (Ricardo Neftalí Reyes Basoalto), "Oda a la alcachofa"; *Residencia en la Tierra 2*, "Walking around"; *Veinte poemas de amor y una canción desesperada*, Poema 15 ("Me gustas cuando callas porque estás como ausente")
- Quiroga, Horacio, "El hijo"
- Rulfo, Juan, "No oyes ladrar los perros"
- Storni, Alfonsina, "Peso ancestral", "Tú me quieres blanca"
- Ulibarrí, Sabine R., "Mi caballo mago"
- Unamuno y Jugo, Miguel de, *San Manuel Bueno, mártir*
- Vodanovic, Sergio, *El delantal blanco*

8

THE MULTIPLE-CHOICE SECTION

READING COMPREHENSION AND LITERARY ANALYSIS

Section I, the multiple-choice section of the Literature exam, evaluates how well you can analyze and interpret literature. The majority of the passages in this section will be prose fiction, but you may also see literary criticism, poetry, or essays in this part of the exam. You will see references to literary terminology in the questions in this section.

How to Read the Literary Selections

Let's look at some pointers on how to approach the questions in the multiple-choice section.

You should spend about 30 seconds, never more than a minute, skimming a passage. Look at the beginning of the passage and take in the first sentence for the main idea or the gist of the passage. Then, do a quick read-through of the rest of the passage, paying closer attention toward the end. This probably isn't the way you learned to read in school all these years, but skimming the passage in this manner can be more helpful than you think. True, you won't comprehend many details in 30 seconds, but your brain will register things like the level of vocabulary and lengths of paragraphs, which will make it easier to spot details later.

Next, you should reread the passage at a much more comfortable pace. It may not be as gripping as the latest John Grisham thriller, but you get the idea. And remember not to worry about a few unfamiliar words. You will be looking for the overall picture and will probably be able to get the meaning from the context of the passage.

Poetry Selections

Poetry selections require a bit of special attention. You will probably have one poem among the reading comprehension passages. Read poems at least twice before looking at the questions. The first read of the poem will help you get all the vocabulary into your head. Read from top to bottom. Don't stop at individual verses to try to understand them. On the first read of a poem, you want to get a basic sense of what is going on—that's all. The second read of the poem should be phrase by phrase. Again, focus on getting the main idea. Don't worry about symbols or metaphors or any poetic devices. Read for literal meanings and stay simple. Let the questions do their work directing you to the meaningful parts of the poem.

After the second read, you should move on to the questions, even if part of the poem is giving you trouble. Don't obsess or panic over the verses you don't understand. Keep in mind that the other students in the room are probably having difficulty with the same poem. Also keep in mind that the questions will direct you to the important parts of the poem, and oftentimes they will hint at the general idea. As you go through the questions, be prepared to return to the poem several times. You're not expected to memorize it, so refer back to it and reread as often as necessary.

Read the Poetry as if It Were Prose

The most efficient way to read poetry is to ignore the poetic elements. Ignore the rhythm, the musicality of the language, and the form.

- Ignore the versification or line breaks.

- Read in sentences, not in verses or lines.

- Emphasize punctuation.

- Ignore any rhyme.

- Be prepared for ideas that develop over several verses or lines.

This will make it much easier to grasp the meaning of the poem and probably make you feel more comfortable with it. Now let's practice a drill.

SAMPLE LITERARY ANALYSIS

The directions will look like this.

> **Directions:** Read the following selections carefully for comprehension. Each selection is followed by a number of questions or incomplete statements. Choose the answer or completion that is BEST according to the selection and fill in the corresponding oval on the answer sheet.

XXIV

Caminante, son tus huellas

el camino, y nada más;

caminante, no hay camino,

se hace camino al andar.

Al andar se hace camino,

y al volver la vista atrás

se ve la senda que nunca

se ha de volver a pisar.

Caminante, no hay camino,

Sino estelas en la mar.

1. Con respeto al tono, este poema se puede describir como:
   - (A) un poema de amor
   - (B) una meditación filosófica
   - (C) una descripción de las ideas estéticas del autor
   - (D) una lección moral

2. Según el poema, ¿qué hace el caminante?
   - (A) Camina en la mar
   - (B) Canta canciones
   - (C) Calla secretos
   - (D) Crea caminos

3. ¿Qué efecto crea la repetición de la palabra "caminante"?
   - (A) Es monótono para el lector.
   - (B) Hace que el lector se identifique con el caminante.
   - (C) Crea un tono alegre.
   - (D) Introduce un elemento de la naturaleza.

4. ¿Cuál imagen del poema se puede comparar con las "huellas" del primer verso?

   (A) Mirar atrás

   (B) Andar

   (C) Nada

   (D) Estelas

5. En el poema, el camino representa:

   (A) la vida

   (B) el pasaje

   (C) el individuo

   (D) la muerte

6. El artificio poético ilustrado por "Caminante, son tus huellas" se llama:

   (A) analogía

   (B) aliteración

   (C) apóstrofe

   (D) anécdota

Translation

XXIV

Traveler, your own tracks

are the trail, and nothing more;

traveler, there is no trail,

The trail is made by walking on it.

And by walking on it we make the trail,

and as we look behind,

we see the trail that will

never again be traveled.

Traveler, there is no trail,

but only wakes in the sea.

Here's How to Crack It

Keep in mind that there will be a variety of questions on the literary analysis passages. With respect to the poetry questions, they will usually (but not always) start out with a general question. You should do the questions in the order that is best for you. If you felt pretty comfortable with the main idea of the poem, do the questions in the order presented. If you felt pretty lost, start with the more specific questions to improve your overall understanding of the poem and its main idea. Let's look at Question 1.

1. With respect to the tone, this poem can be described as:

   (A) a love poem

   (B) a philosophical meditation

   (C) a description of the aesthetic ideas of the author

   (D) a moral lesson

The correct answer is (B). General questions ask about the whole passage, not some detail of the passage. It compares life with the travels of the traveler and the trail he creates in life. That sounds like a philosophical meditation to us. Choice (A) is easily eliminated because there is no reference to love or a loved one in the poem. Choices (C) and (D) may be tempting, but if you examine the poem closely, you'll see that there is no real moral lesson identified, nor is any reference made to art or aesthetic ideals.

2. According to the poem, what does the traveler do?

   (A) Walk in the sea

   (B) Sing songs

   (C) Keep secrets

   (D) Create tracks

The correct choice is (D). The traveler creates tracks by living his life and undertaking his travels. Choices (B) and (C) are both sort of silly and do not appear anywhere in the poem. Choice (A) may tempt you because of the last line of the poem, particularly if you don't know the meaning of *estelas*. Nevertheless, you can determine that *estelas* is a noun because of the way it is used in the last verse. If it were a verb, answer choice (A) would be more plausible, but it is not, so it can be canceled.

3. What effect is created by the repetition of the word *caminante*?

   (A) It is monotonous for the reader.

   (B) It enables the reader to identify with the traveler.

   (C) It creates a happy tone.

   (D) It introduces an element from nature.

The correct choice is (B). Choice (A) is highly unlikely because the poet is not trying to bore the reader. If the tone of the poem were boring, or the subject boredom, that would be a different matter. However, the tone of the poem is not really a happy one either. It is more solemn and serious, or at best, philosophical. Choice (C) can be eliminated. Choice (D) is simply not true, especially if you know the meaning of *caminante*. If you don't know the meaning of *caminante*, it may be a bit more challenging. Let's say that you had never even seen the word before. There's no need to panic. Look for root words with which you are probably familiar. In *caminante* you have *camino* (which also appears in the poem) and *caminar* (which appears in the poem in its synonym form, *andar*), both related to *caminante* and both are more commonly used words. *Caminante* is one who practices the activity of *caminar* or walking, or traveling in this translation.

4. Which image from the poem can best be compared with the "tracks" of the first verse?

   (A) Looking behind

   (B) The trail

   (C) Nothing

   (D) The ship's wake

The tracks are best compared with the ship's wake, which are the tracks left in the water. If you are a bit unclear of the vocabulary, you can still use POE to cancel answer choices. *Huellas* is clearly a noun. Of the answer choices, (D) is the only corresponding noun. Choice (A) is a prepositional phrase, and choice (B) is a verb, so both can be canceled. (C) is an odd choice, but don't be fooled simply because the word *nada* appears in the second verse of the poem. It has no poetic or conceptual link to *huellas* in this poem.

5. In the poem the trail represents:

   (A) life

   (B) a trip

   (C) the individual

   (D) death

If you understood the poem well, this question is easy. The poet compares life with a trail that we create as we go about our daily task of living. If you didn't really understand the poem, once again use POE. Choice (D) can be canceled because there are no images that refer to death, nor is it mentioned at all in the poem. Choice (B) is incorrect because it is synonymous with "camino" so it wouldn't be accurate poetically. Choice (C) would correspond best to *caminante* because it refers to the person traveling.

6. The poetic device illustrated by "Traveler, your own tracks" is called:

   (A) analogy

   (B) alliteration

   (C) apostrophe

   (D) anecdote

These questions will be easy for you because you will study the list of literary terms at the back of this book before test day. Nevertheless, the poetic device illustrated above is called apostrophe, choice (C), which is when the poetic voice addresses someone or something directly. The other answer choices are designed to see if you really know your terminology, which you will by test day! Here are the other definitions, very briefly: Analogy is a correspondence or comparison; alliteration is the repetition of the initial letter or sound of closely connected words; and anecdote is a short narrative.

THE SEVEN-MINUTE STRATEGY

When you reach the last passage on the test, check your time. If you have seven minutes or fewer, you need to change your strategy. You don't have time to proceed in the normal fashion. It's time for drastic measures. There is no need to panic; just be sure to adjust your strategy accordingly. There is still plenty of time to harvest points. You need to be familiar with the seven-minute strategy just in case. Consider it your backup plan.

Here it is.

- Don't reread the passage. It may seem like a good idea. But if you don't have time for it, don't do it.

- Proceed directly to the questions.

- Answer the questions in the following order:
  1. Answer any literary-term identification or grammar questions. Use POE as necessary to gather those points.
  2. Go to any question that asks for the meaning of a single word or phrase. These questions include a line reference that makes it easy for you to go back to the text and answer the specific question.
  3. Go to any other question with a line reference, read the reference, and answer the question.
  4. Go to any question on tone or attitude. You'll probably have a good idea about the author's tone after answering the questions above.
  5. Do whatever is left over. Keep working until time is called.

CHRONOLOGICAL ORDER AND THE LEVEL OF DIFFICULTY

Keep in mind that the writers of the exam try to vary the literary passages, including some easier passages and some challenging passages. They also try to vary narrative passages by using creative passages and by varying the point of view. You may see poems in this section, just as we saw in the previous example. If you find yourself faced with what seems to be an impossible literary passage with very difficult questions, you may find comfort in the fact that most other students will feel the same way you do. You can also put POE to work for you and conquer that challenging passage.

SUMMARY FOR THE LITERARY ANALYSIS PASSAGES

- Study the list of literary terms at the back of this book.

- Skim through the text once, taking in the words and the endpoint.

- Read through the poetry as if it were prose; look for the main idea.

- Look for general answers to general questions.

- Use POE aggressively.

9

The Free-Response Section

WHAT DO THE AP ESSAY GRADERS LOOK FOR?

All the AP Literature essays are graded using two rubrics, one for quality of content and the other for overall language usage. The content rubric follows a 0 to 9 scale for the poetry analysis and the thematic analysis essays and a 0 to 5 scale for the text analysis. The Language Usage rubric, which is used to grade ALL essays, goes from 0 to 5. Here is a brief explanation of the language usage rubric:

FIVE: EXTREMELY GOOD COMMAND

This essay is virtually error free, with accurate and varied vocabulary and nearly perfect control of the writing components (organization, accentuation, punctuation, and spelling).

Four: Strong Command

This essay contains some errors, uses appropriate vocabulary, and has good overall control of the writing components.

Three: Average Command

This essay contains frequent errors, but the essay is understandable. Vocabulary usage is not varied and there may be numerous errors in the writing components.

Two: Weak Command

This essay contains serious grammatical errors which interfere with comprehension. The vocabulary is basic and repeated. There are very many errors in the writing components.

One: Virtually No Command

There are constant errors in grammar which make the essay very difficult to understand. The vocabulary and writing components are insufficient.

Zero

The response is too brief to be considered a meaningful essay, or the response is written in English or some language other than Spanish.

About a week before the actual grading session, the AP chief readers go through about 100 essays to get a feel for how students did. They comb through the essays looking for the "perfect nine" essay, the "perfect seven" essay, the "perfect three," and so on. These representative essays are the sample essays that are used in the training sessions for all of the AP essay readers. The graders study the samples, compare them with other student essays, and discuss the grades that they would assign. The readers then begin grading essays in small reading groups or tables, while the table leaders check graded essays at random for consistency. Each reader grades one type of essay. ETS puts a great deal of effort into creating fair grading practices and a consistent grading standard, but keep in mind that everyone is human and the nature of holistic scoring is very subjective. The readers also work from a scoring guide for each question, which we will examine later in our detailed discussions of the three essay questions.

Answer the Question You Are Given

Make sure that you answer the question you are given for each of the three essays. Remember that none of the specific works is listed on the AP reading list, only the authors to be studied. You may have different examples, even opposing viewpoints on certain questions from other students who have read different works. That's no problem. The important thing is that you formulate a strong thesis based on the specific question given, structure the essay in an easily identifiable manner, follow a clear and condensed outline format (which we discuss in detail later with each essay question), and illustrate with concrete examples from the readings. You can assume that the readers of your essays have read the works in question but have not sat in on any class discussions about the works. You must cite concrete examples and explain how they illustrate your ideas. You shouldn't waste your time trying to fake your way through the essay portions of the exam. The readers know the authors and the works in question, and they also know what constitutes a good essay. As we mentioned earlier, they go through a considerable amount of effort in the beginning of each reading to ascertain that they are all on the same page regarding grading. They discuss the scoring guide, evaluate sample essays in a group format, and reach consensus on the scoring guide before beginning to grade any of the essays. Thus, it is important to prepare thoroughly for the essay portion of the exam. Read the texts with care, practice writing sample thesis statements with outlines, and illustrate your ideas with easily identifiable examples from the readings. Remember to explain *how* your examples illustrate your ideas. We will look at a few basic guidelines to improve any essay in a moment.

You should also keep in mind the fact that the readers of the AP exams will have very little time to read your three essays. In fact, your three essays will be scored by three different readers. They spend only a few minutes per essay. At that rate, the AP readers are not looking for anything especially profound. What they will look for is a concrete opening paragraph that addresses the question being asked. (We examine some techniques for writing concrete opening paragraphs later when we discuss each essay question in detail.) They will mark down essays burdened by plot summary—you should avoid plot summary at all costs. Remember that the readers of your essays know the works that you've studied as well as or better than you do. Thus, it seems obvious that the best way to score well on the AP Spanish Literature Exam is to master the material. It also helps to be a good writer. Let's look at some tips to make any essay stronger.

WEAVING

In Question 3, if you are writing a two-author comparison, you will want to discuss examples from each author. Rather than discussing all of your examples from one author and then moving on to the other author, you should try to "weave" from one author to the next. That is, talk about how the theme of solitude is present in the works of both García Lorca and García Márquez by choosing three different characteristics of solitude in each author. Discuss each characteristic individually, and compare and contrast how each characteristic is present, similarly or distinctly, in each author. In each paragraph, therefore, you will be discussing each author and citing different examples from each to illustrate your ideas. We will talk more about "weaving" when we examine the essay questions in detail.

SOUND DAUNTING?

It really shouldn't sound too daunting. The AP readers know that you have only thirty minutes each to prepare the poetry question and the one-author question, and only forty minutes to complete Question 3, which can be one of three choices (two-author comparison, the excerpt from an AP author, or a critical excerpt about one of the AP authors). They also realize that you really don't have enough time to cover each question in tremendous detail. Therefore, it is not important that you include every example that may illustrate your ideas, but rather choose three strong examples that you can explain thoroughly. Certainly three strong examples combined with a well-stated thesis that addresses the topic given along with the question presents a very strong essay.

WRITING TIPS

As you are writing, you may want to keep a few of our writing guidelines in mind.

Neatness

Do everything you can to make your essay legible. Your writing doesn't have to be pretty, but it does have to be readable. Print if at all possible. Graders look at an enormous number of exams for an extended period of time and trying to decipher your handwriting only adds to their grumpy moods. Neatly written essays, in contrast, make their job a great deal easier. If you need to cross out or insert a paragraph, do it neatly and be certain to indicate all changes clearly.

First Impressions Last

Your reader's first impressions are crucial. Think about first impressions. You wouldn't want to show up for a job interview with messy hair and wrinkled or torn clothing, would you? The overall look of your essay gives the first impression. Make your paragraphs obvious by indenting clearly. Neat presentation, clear handwriting, and obvious paragraphs will make a great first impression. The reader will already be thinking, "This looks like a high-scoring essay" when he or she hasn't even read a word yet.

Take extra care to write two really good first sentences. You want your reader to see that you can write. If you are unsure of the usage of a particular word, don't use it. If you are not sure whether you should use the subjunctive or any other verb form, rewrite the sentence in a way that makes you feel confident. Don't make any mistakes in the first two sentences. After that, you can relax into the rest of your essay. The glow of a good beginning carries over the entire essay.

Do the essays in the order you choose. Start with the one you like the best. It will loosen you up a bit. Be sure to take your watch and be mindful of the time. You'll have thirty minutes for Question 1 and forty minutes for Questions 2 and 3.

Keep Your Essay Simple...

Your language-skills level will dictate the level of sophistication in your writing, but simple is generally clearest and best. It is also easiest to read.

...But Add a Little Pizzazz

Don't let the test environment or the tension get the best of you. Take risks. Show your enjoyment of the works you studied by demonstrating your love of language. If you write like someone who enjoys writing, the readers will be impressed.

We don't want you to think that you have to write long, complex sentences. In fact, that would be bad advice. Just choose your words carefully. Be as descriptive as you can. Avoid generic verbs and nouns, and use their more descriptive counterparts.

A few sophisticated words will demonstrate a strong, literary vocabulary. NEVER use a word if you are uncertain of its meaning or proper usage. Rather than always saying the work of Lorca, Borges, or Matute, you may want to refer to the works of the authors in the following ways: *la obra lorquiana, la obra borgesiana, la obra matuteana, la obra marquesiana, la obra unamuniana*, although again it is best not to overdo it.

DEFINE YOUR TERMS

The thematic or essay questions may refer to "nostalgia" in a particular poem or the theme of social criticism in a particular author's work. Define exactly how you see the social criticism, or what the nostalgia means to you, or the poetic voice. It will help to keep you focused on the specific question and will remind the graders that you are addressing the question.

- **Use transition words to show where you are going**. When continuing an idea, use words such as *además de* (besides, furthermore), *adicionalmente* (additionally), *del mismo modo* (in the same way), *por eso*, *por lo tanto* (therefore, for that reason), *así (que)* (thus), *debido a* (because of). When changing the flow of thought, use words such as *al contrario* (on the contrary), *aunque* (although, even though), and *en cambio*, *por otra parte* (on the other hand). Transition words make your essay easier to understand by clarifying your intentions. They also demonstrate to the graders that you can express yourself in clear, fluid Spanish.

- **Use structural indicators to organize your paragraphs**. Another way to clarify the direction you are taking with your essay is to use structural indicators such as *primero*, (first), *segundo* (second), and *tercero* (third). You could also use transitional words such as *sin embargo* (however), *en cambio*, *por otra parte* (on the other hand), *en contraste con* (in contrast to) to introduce contrasts if you are writing a comparison essay between two authors.

- **Vary your verbs**. Useful verbs that may come in handy include *ilustrar* (to illustrate), *sugerir* (to suggest), *revelar* (to reveal), *indicar* (to indicate), *mostrar* (to show), and *representar* (to represent).

- **Stick to your condensed outline**. Unless you get a truly brilliant idea while you are writing, you should not deviate from your earlier outline. If you do, you may risk submitting a garbled mess instead of a coherent essay.

- **Express one main idea per paragraph**. Keep it simple. Each paragraph should make one point and be illustrated by concrete textual examples.

- **Use concrete textual examples**. Explain how they illustrate your ideas. Remember textual details such as the characters' names, roles, symbolic significance if they have one, and so on. Confusing the characters' names suggests a hurried essay, a poor reader, or both.

- **Fill up the essay form**. An overly short essay will hurt you more than an overly long essay.

- **Make certain that your first and last paragraphs address the question directly**. A good way to begin your last paragraph is by restating the thematic question given along with the essay question. If you have developed a strong thesis, this last paragraph should serve as a good conclusion.

SUMMARY

- Answer the question you have been asked.

- When discussing two different authors, weave your textual examples rather than listing them. Explain the differences in the treatment of the theme of solitude, for example, in the works of García Lorca versus those of García Márquez.

- Be neat and indent clearly.

- Write simple, clear, but descriptive sentences. Don't be afraid to have fun.

- Write two good sentences at the beginning.

- Keep in mind that practice makes perfect. One of the best ways to prepare for the Literature exam is to make numerous outlines of various hypothetical questions. Practicing creating condensed outlines and citing concrete examples from the works you have read is an excellent way to get in shape for exam day. You may even get lucky and guess one of the questions that appears on your exam!

PART ◆ IV

THE AP SPANISH
LITERATURE REVIEW

10

THE POETRY
ESSAY QUESTION

THE BASICS

For the poetry question, you will need to analyze a poem that you may not have studied before. You are expected to employ the terminology used in the study of poetry and also be able to relate structure to meaning. It is very important that you explain why the poet uses a specific poetic device, and not simply identify it.

THE SCORING GUIDELINES FOR THE POETRY QUESTION

NINE: DEMONSTRATES CLEAR SUPERIORITY

This is a very well-written essay that addresses the theme and how it is presented in the poem. It also includes a clear discussion of literary devices or poetic techniques and language and how they convey meaning in the poem. The essay demonstrates insightful reading and clear analytical writing. The essay leaves no doubt in the reader's mind that the student has an excellent understanding of the text. In addition, there are clear textual references.

SEVEN TO EIGHT: DEMONSTRATES CLEAR COMPETENCE

This is a good essay that explores the theme and includes appropriate examples from the text. There is mostly textual analysis versus paraphrasing of the verses of the poem. The reader may have to do some interpretation because the essay is not always full and explicit. May contain some errors, but they do not interfere with the ideas the student is trying to express. An essay that gives a good discussion of theme but gives only superficial and vague references to the language would earn a score of 7.

FIVE TO SIX: POSSIBLE COMPETENCE

This essay demonstrates a basic understanding of the poem and the question but is very poorly focused. The analysis is burdened by paraphrasing. There may be erroneous statements that interfere with the overall content of the essay. The thematic discussion may be satisfactory, but there is little or no effective discussion of the poetic technique and language. The thematic discussion may be weak, but the discussion of poetic devices and language is strong.

THREE TO FOUR: POSSIBLE LACK OF COMPETENCE

This is a poorly organized and vague essay with little or no focus. The student demonstrates a limited understanding of the question and the poem. Irrelevant or erroneous comments predominate. May also contain gross errors.

ONE TO TWO: CLEAR LACK OF COMPETENCE

This essay clearly demonstrates incompetence. The student misunderstands the question or answers a question different from the one given. This essay is difficult to understand.

ZERO: CANNOT BE EVALUATED

The response is too brief to be considered a meaningful essay, or the response is written in English or some language other than Spanish.

So you see, to get a high score on the poetry question, you need to find the meaning in the poem and relate it to the language and poetic techniques. Notice that the higher score categories all refer to meaning, language, and technique. These are the three areas that you need to focus on in your poetry essay.

Let's examine the following essay-writing techniques and see how they apply to the poetry question. Use the condensed outline as a general guideline to zero in on *meaning*. The detailed outline, which follows, will help you apply a more concrete *structure* to your poetry essay.

THE CONDENSED OUTLINE

I. What is the literal meaning of the concept or theme?
   A. Can you explain the theme and how that theme or concept is treated in the poem?
   B. What feelings does the theme or concept evoke? What feelings do the images suggest? What feelings does the poem evoke in you, the reader?

II. How does the poet treat that concept or topic in this particular poem?
   A. What are the important examples (images) in the work, and how do they relate to the concept or theme?
   B. What specific examples produce the strongest feelings?
   C. What elements are in opposition?

JUST SAY NO TO PARAPHRASING

You must avoid simply paraphrasing the poem. Heavy paraphrasing immediately puts your essay into the five-maybe-six-if-you're-lucky range. Discuss the emotions suggested by the images in the poem and how they relate to the concept or theme, and you will be discussing meaning right away.

So you know what you have to do. Be clear and concrete. Look for meaning in the poem. Read it as if it were prose. Remember to use the condensed outline for meaning and the more detailed outline on the next page to flesh out your poetry analysis. It is very important that you address each part of the outline in your poetry essay. It is equally important that you direct your response to the specific question that you are given for the poem. For example, the readers of a question will be looking for essays that deal specifically with the passage of time in the poetry question. Thus, in your opening statement, it is crucial that you address the notion of the passage of time in the poem. You will lose points if you do not address the question you are given, even if your essay is a great analysis of the poem. Before examining the sample essay, let's examine a theme. The notion of the passage of time is the theme to be analyzed. Depending on how the poet treats the passage of time, you will want to identify how you perceive his or her portrayal of the passage of time.

Here are a few possible interpretations.

A. The poet laments the quick passage of time (emotion).

B. The poetic voice finds that time seems to stand still for nature (the mountains, the sea, the birds in the sky, and so on) in contrast to human kind's mortality (opposition).

C. The poetic voice feels subject to the mechanical and relentless tick-tock of the clock in the train stations, in the office, at appointments, and so on (emotion).

There may be another portrayal of the passage of time not described above. The important thing is that you study the wording of the question and then the presentation of the specific idea in the poem to formulate your thesis. A strong opening paragraph is very impressive to the AP readers, especially after reading numerous essays of garbled Spanish with no apparent goal or focus.

THE DETAILED OUTLINE

Memorize and follow this outline to give structure to your poetry essay. Remember to study the wording of the question in order to formulate a strong opening paragraph.

HOW TO WRITE A TEXTUAL COMMENTARY ON A POEM

I. The Subject of the Poem
   A. Formulate an opening paragraph based on the question that comes with the poem. Briefly identify the subject of the poem. Why was the poem written? Is it a description? A love poem? A social criticism? A poem about esthetic ideals or beauty? Does it express the vision or philosophy of life of the poet? Is it about a personal relationship?

II. The Form of the Poem
   A. Comment on the organization of the poem. Does it rhyme? Is it organized into specific stanzas? Can you identify the type of verse or poem? (Is it a sonnet?)
   B. How can you describe the language used? Are the words easy or difficult to understand? Are they familiar or formal? Do many words have double meanings? (You'll want to mention one or two examples here, but discuss all examples in greater detail when discussing the poem stanza by stanza.) In what verb tenses are the verbs used? Why?
   C. How can you describe the tone of the poem? Are there changes in voice? Is it a dialogue or a monologue? Why? Who is speaking? The poet? A character? Is the tone familiar or formal? Ironic? Satiric? Critical? Didactic? Serious? Solemn? Tragic? Comic? Why? What does the tone contribute to the overall significance of the poem?
   D. Identify the poetic devices and figurative language in the poem. Are there allusions to myths, other stories, other histories? Synesthesia? Apostrophe? Metaphor? Simile? Personification? Anaphora? Hyperbole? Antithesis? Paradox? What do all of these contribute to the significance of the poem?

III. The Conclusion
   A. Conclude with a rapid synthesis of your impression of the text. Remember to restate your thesis at the beginning of your conclusion. What is your personal reaction to the poem? Can you relate the poem to anything in your daily life? Does it relate to any of the other works you have studied?

Feeling ambitious? How about memorizing this detailed outline *en español*?

Cómo Comentar a un Texto Poético

I. El tema del poema
   A. Escribe un párrafo inicial basado en la pregunta que viene con el poema. Identifica brevemente el tema del poema en 2 ó 3 oraciones. ¿Por qué se escribió el poema? ¿Es una descripción? ¿Es un poema de amor? ¿De crítica social? ¿Sobre la belleza o las ideas estéticas? ¿Sobre el arte en general? ¿Sobre el arte poético? ¿Expresa la visión del poeta? ¿Se trata de una relación personal?

II. La forma del poema
   A. La organización del poema:
      ¿Tiene rima? ¿Tiene organización estrófica? ¿Puedes identificar el tipo de verso? ¿Cómo contribuye la forma al sentido del poema?
   B. ¿Cómo se puede identificar el lenguaje?
      ¿Son fáciles o difíciles las palabras? ¿Son familiares o formales? ¿Cúales palabras tienen doble sentido? ¿Cómo contribuyen al sentido del poema (ejemplos concretos)? ¿En qué tiempos se emplean los verbos?
   C. ¿Cómo se puede describir el tono?
      ¿Hay cambios de voz? ¿Qué significan? ¿Es un diálogo? ¿Un monólogo? ¿Quién habla? (¿La voz poética? ¿Un personaje?) ¿Es un tono formal o familiar? ¿Irónico? ¿Satírico? ¿Crítico? ¿Didáctico? ¿Serio? ¿Solemne? ¿Trágico? ¿Cómico? ¿Cómo contribuye el tono al sentido del poema?
   D. Identifica los procedimientos estilísticos/recursos poéticos:
      ¿Hay alusiones a otros mitos? ¿Otras historias? ¿Otras obras? ¿Hay ejemplos de personificación? ¿Anáfora? ¿Apóstrofe? ¿Metáfora? ¿Símil? ¿Sinestesia? ¿Hipérbole? ¿Antítesis? ¿Paradoja? ¿Cómo contribuyen al significado del poema?

III. La conclusión
   A. Concluye con una síntesis rápida de tu impresión de la relación entre la pregunta concreta y el poema. Da tu opinión personal si quieres. ¿Cómo se relaciona con otras obras de éste u otros autores? ¿Cúal es tu reacción personal? ¿Cómo se aplica a tu propia vida?

SAMPLE POETRY ESSAY QUESTION

The directions for the sample essay question look like this.

Directions: Write a well-organized essay in SPANISH on the topic below.

Discute la noción del pasar del tiempo en el siguiente poema, dirigiendo tu respuesta al uso de recursos poéticos, imagenes y lenguaje que emplea el poeta para comunicar sus ideas.

XXIV

Caminante, son tus huellas

el camino, y nada más;

caminante, no hay camino,

se hace camino al andar.

Al andar se hace camino,

y al volver la vista atrás

se ve la senda que nunca

se ha de volver a pisar.

Caminante, no hay camino,

Sino estelas en la mar.

SAMPLE STUDENT ESSAY

En el poema XXIV, vemos que el pasar del tiempo es algo que no podemos controlar. En este poema el "caminante" es una metáfora para el ser humano y su "camino", una metáfora para la vida. El poeta nos dice que nosotros creamos nuestra vida y el tiempo pasa. No podemos volver al pasado. El pasar del tiempo es irrevocable.

El poeta nos está dando su visión hacia la vida. Es un poema breve, de una sola estrofa de diez versos. No tiene rima. Tiene una forma simple para comunicar sus ideas claramente y simplemente. La forma simple refleja su punto de vista hacia el tiempo; el pasar del tiempo es un concepto simple. Por mucho que queramos, no podremos cambiar, modificar ni parar el tiempo.

El lenguaje es relativamente simple, pero tiene varios niveles de interpretación. Es informal. Hay tres verbos en la forma infinitiva. También usa la forma impersonal con 'se'. El uso de estos verbos crea un elemento impersonal, mejor dicho, un elemento universal. Parece que el poeta habla con el lector, pero el poema se aplica a todos los seres humanos. Hay también muchas palabras con doble sentido. Por ejemplo, el caminante, representa al ser humano, o incluso al lector. El camino es su vida en la tierra. Repite mucho las palabras "Caminante" y "camino" para impresionar más al lector su papel, su responsabilidad en el "camino" de la vida. La vida es lo que nosotros hacemos de ella. Las huellas son las marcas que dejamos atrás en la tierra. También son las marcas o las formas que damos a nuestra vida. El camino, según el poema, consiste en las huellas que dejamos nosotros en la tierra. Creamos el camino a medida que vamos "caminando" por la tierra (la vida). La forma negativa también se ve en el poema en el segundo verso, "nada más" y en el séptimo verso, "nunca se ha...". El uso de la forma negativa crea una sensación de finalidad en el poema. Como el pasar del tiempo es irrevocable, también el uso de "nunca se ha de volver a pisar" es algo que no podremos cambiar.

El tono del poema es serio y filosófico. Sobre todo, al final del poema cuando el poeta nos advierte, "no hay camino sino estelas en la mar," vemos que incluso el camino que creamos en la tierra también se borra. Desaparece como las estelas en la mar. Es una imagen un poco deprimente. Nos hace sentir pequeños e insignificantes frente al esquema mayor de la vida.

Hay varios recursos poéticos. Hemos visto que el poeta está comparando el Caminante con el ser humano y el camino con su vida. El andar o el caminar es el ejercicio de vivir la vida. Las huellas que dejamos en la tierra representan las obras importantes en nuestra vida, pero también se borrarán con el pasar del tiempo. El poeta usa apóstrofe para dirigir su poema directamente al 'Caminante', el lector. Al emplear el apóstrofe el poeta llega más profundamente al corazón del lector. Sus ideas aplican a cada ser humano. Me gusta el poema. Es un poema universal. Todos tenemos que enfrentarnos con el pasar del tiempo. Es un concepto filosófico pero práctico porque todos hacemos nuestros propios caminos "que nunca se ha de volver a pisar."

Translation

Discuss the notion of the passage of time in the following poem, addressing the use of literary devices, poetic images, and language that the poet employs to convey his/her ideas.

XXIV

Traveler, your own tracks

are the trail, and nothing more;

Traveler, there is no trail,

The trail is made by walking on it.

And by walking on it we make the trail,

and as we look behind,

we see the trail that will

never again be traveled.

Traveler, there is no trail,

but only wakes in the sea.

In the poem XXIV, we see that the passage of time is something that we cannot control. In this poem the "traveler" is a metaphor for the human being and his "trail" a metaphor for his life. The poet tells us that we create our lives and time passes. We cannot return to the past. The passage of time is irrevocable.

The poet is giving us his vision of life. It is a brief poem, of only one stanza with ten lines. There is no rhyme. It has a simple form to communicate his ideas clearly and simply. The simple form reflects his point of view toward time; the passage of time is a simple concept. No matter how much we would like to, we cannot change, modify, nor stop time.

The language is relatively simple, but it has various levels of interpretation. It is informal. There are three verbs in the infinitive form. The poet also uses the passive voice with *se*. The usage of these verbs creates an impersonal or universal element. It seems that the poet is talking with the reader, but the poem really applies to all human beings. There are also many words with double meanings. For example, the traveler represents the human being, or even the reader. The trail is his life on earth. The poet repeats the words "traveler" and "trail" to impress upon the reader that we each have a role or responsibility in the "trail" of life. Life is what we make of it. The "tracks" are the marks that we leave behind as we go walking through life. They are also the marks or the form that we give to our own lives.

The negative form is also used in the poem in the second verses, "nothing more" and in the seventh verse, "never again." The usage of the negative form creates a sensation of finality in the poem. Because the passage of time is irrevocable, so too is the usage of the negative form something that we cannot change.

The tone of the poem is serious and philosophical. Above all, at the end of the poem when the poet warns us, "there are no trails, only wakes in the sea," we see that even the trails we create on earth, that are our lives on earth, will be eventually erased. They disappear like the wake of ships in the sea. It is a depressing image. It makes us feel small and insignificant in comparison with the greater scheme of life on earth.

There are many poetic devices. We have seen that the poet is comparing the traveler with the human being, and the traveling is the action of daily living. The tracks that we leave on earth represent important points in our lives, but they too will be erased by the passage of time. The poet uses apostrophe to address the poem directly to the traveler, or the reader. By using apostrophe, the poet is able to penetrate the heart of the reader. His ideas apply to every human being. I like the poem. It is a universal poem. We all have to face the passage of time. It is a philosophical concept but also a practical one because we all create our own pathways through life that we will "never travel again."

Explanation

This is a clear and concrete essay. It is not perfect, but it does follow the scoring guideline requirements for clear discussion of the theme (the passage of time) and imagery in the poem. Notice how this student starts her essay by discussing the theme. Rather than simply stating that time is the theme of the poem, she states that the poem presents it as something that "we cannot control." She roughly followed the outline we gave you on writing a poetry essay, which gave her essay good organization. Remember that strong organization of your essay will make it easier for the grader to give you a higher score.

This essay clearly demonstrates insight and analytical ability. Concrete examples from the text are discussed (the image of the traveler, his tracks, the trail as metaphors, and so on). The use of language is also discussed but particularly as it *relates to the theme in question*. The use of the negative verb forms "creates a sense of finality," the passage of time is also final. The sentences are rather simple, but concrete.

Like this student, you will be armed with some really strong tools to help you pull the meaning out of the poem and get it down on paper with a clear understanding and thorough explanation.

SPANISH GLOSSARY OF POETIC DEVICES

Aliteración—Es la repetición del sonido inicial.

Antítesis—Es un contraste, la juxtaposición de una palabra u otra con la palabra de contraria significación.

Asonancia—Es la rima de los últimos sonidos entre palabras cuyos vocales son iguales.

Climax/Gradación—Es una serie que desciende o asciende.

Consonancia—Es la rima de los últimos sonidos entre palabras cuyos vocales y consonantes son iguales.

Encabalgamiento—Es cuando la unidad rítmica del verso empieza en un verso y continúa en el siguiente verso.

Epíteto—Es una palabra o frase que no es necesaria para describir algo—"la fría nieve".

Estrofa—Es un grupo de versos sujetos a un orden metódico.

Fábula—Es un poema alegórico que incluye una enseñanza moral.

Hipérbole—Es la exageración de las cualidades de un ser, normalmente con intención satírica.

Imagen—Es la representación de una cosa determinada con detalles definitivos.

Metáfora—Es la trasposición del significado en virtud de una comparación tácita.

Métrica—Es la ciencia y el arte que trata de los versos.

Metonimia—Es el tropo que identifica algo por su origen.

Onomatopeya—Es la imitación del sonido de una cosa.

Paradoja—Es una figura que se expresa a través de una contradicción.

Personificación—Es atribuir cualidades humanas a un objeto o animal.

Rima—Es la semejanza o igualdad entre los sonidos finales del verso a contar desde la última vocal acentuada.

Romance—Es una serie indeterminada de versos octosilábicos con rima asonante en pares en la que los impares quedan sin rima.

Símbolo—Es una cosa concreta que sugiere una cosa abstracta.

Símil—Es una figura que consiste en comparar un cosa con otra para dar una idea viva.

Sinestesia—Es una descripción sensorial en términos de otro sentido.

Soneto—Es una obra poética de catorce versos, generalmente con un cambio de tono al final.

11

ANALYSIS OF A THEME IN ONE TEXT

THE BASICS

The thematic analysis question comes in one of two varieties. The question can be either an analysis of a theme in one text taken from the reading list, or a request to compare a certain theme in two texts on the reading list. You will choose the text from a list of works provided; generally two or more are listed. In this chapter, we will address the one text question.

With our approach to writing AP essays, you will be able to focus your analytical skills quickly and efficiently. Our approach is not necessarily similar to the methods of writing you have learned in the past. AP time limits really don't allow for that. That's why many students with strong writing skills earn lower scores on the AP essays. They may be good writers, but they need a different set of tools for the AP essays.

SCORING GUIDELINES

NINE: SHOWS SUPERIORITY

These are well-developed essays that fully discuss the theme or question topic. They demonstrate insightful reading and analytical writing. They use concrete textual examples and thoroughly explain how the examples illustrate their ideas. They don't have to be perfect; they may contain a few minor errors, but do not contain erroneous or unnecessary information. They may show some originality too. These essays leave no doubts in the reader's mind that the student has a superior understanding of the concept discussed in the given author's work.

SEVEN TO EIGHT: SHOWS COMPETENCE

The content of these essays is similar to that of higher-scoring essays, but it is less precise and less thoroughly supported. These essays are well developed and may show careful reading and sensitive interpretation. There is more analysis and less description. There may be a bit of plot summary but only to illustrate the theme of the question. Although these essays may contain some inaccurate information, the errors do not affect the final quality of the essay. The reader must do some interpretation because the response is not always sufficiently explicit.

FIVE TO SIX: SUGGESTS COMPETENCE

These essays are superficial. The student basically understands the question, but the essay is not well-focused. There is more plot summary than analytical writing. May include factual errors or errors of interpretation.

THREE TO FOUR: POSSIBLE COMPETENCE

These essays are poorly organized. They reflect a poor understanding of the question and do not fully address the question. The discussion is unclear or simply misses the point. May consist almost entirely of plot summary. Comments are overly generalized and include major errors. These essays may demonstrate little understanding of the texts.

ONE TO TWO: NOT COMPETENT

These essays contain even more pronounced errors than those found in the previous category. They may demonstrate a misunderstanding of the question, or they may answer a question that is different from the specific question asked. Typically, these essays are incoherent and too short. The writing demonstrates no control of written Spanish, either grammatically or organizationally.

ZERO: CANNOT BE EVALUATED

This is a response that completely fails to address the question. There is no response, or the response is written in English or any language other than Spanish.

ANALYSIS OF THE SCORING GUIDE

There are two major points we want you to remember from the scoring guidelines. First, the high-scoring essays are clear. You don't have to aspire to perfection, just clarity of thought and expression. The essays in the eight-to-nine category are, above all, legible, lucid, and comprehensible.

Second, there is a vast difference in what kind of essay only aspires to the five-score category. Notice how the tone of the scoring guide changes. Suddenly, it no longer talks about the fine points of answering the question; it speaks of the dull, commonplace plot-summary essay that every reader dreads to grade. Surprisingly, there are lots of five essays written by good students—even A-students. Some of those students probably thought they wrote a pretty good essay. But in reality, they just wrote a generic essay.

If you understand what you read and can write in grammatically correct Spanish, a five is your absolute low-end score. You will almost certainly do better than a five with our help. Read on.

THE CONDENSED OUTLINE REVISITED

As we saw in Chapter 10, the condensed outline is a set of questions designed to help you focus on the material you need to incorporate into your essay. For the AP Spanish Literature Exam, you must keep in mind that you will need to supply the literary works. The questions generally supply a concept or recurrent theme from a variety of the author's works. You may also see a question about the feminine characters, or general character development in the work of one of the authors. You decide which books you studied will make the best examples to support what you'd like to say about the given question.

THE CONDENSED OUTLINE

I. What is the literal meaning of the concept or theme?
   A. Can you explain the theme and how that theme or concept is treated in the works that you studied?
   B. What feelings does the theme or concept evoke? What feelings do the characters demonstrate? What feelings does it evoke in you, the reader?

II. How does the author treat that concept or topic in the works that you studied?
   A. What are the important examples (images) in the work, and how do they relate to the concept or theme?
   B. What specific examples produce the strongest feelings?
   C. What elements are in opposition?

JUST SAY NO TO PLOT SUMMARY

We've said it before, but it's so important, we'll say it again: Avoid writing a plot summary at all costs. Excessive plot summary immediately puts your essay into the five-maybe-six-if-you're-lucky range. Discuss the characters' emotions and your emotions and how they relate to the concept or theme. Do this and you're well on your way to discussing meaning right away.

THE CLASSIC AP ONE-TEXT THEME ANALYSIS QUESTION

El tema de la ironía está presente en numerosas obras de la literatura latinoamericana. Escoge UNA de las obras siguientes. Escribe un ensayo que analice este tema en la obra. Incluye ejemplos del texto para apoyar tus ideas.

La muerte y la brújula, Jorge Luis Borges
El delantal blanco, Sergio Vodanovic

The theme of irony is present in numerous works of Latin American literature. Choose ONE of the following works. Write an essay that analyzes this theme in the work. Use examples from the text to support your ideas.

This seems like a simple enough question, until you try to answer it. Most students begin like this:

En las obras de Jorge Luis Borges, la ironía es un tema frecuente. En La Muerte y la Brújula, vemos varios ejemplos de la ironía. La muerte del protagonista y las semejanzas entre los dos rivales son dos manifestaciones de la ironía en el cuento.

In the works of Jorge Luis Borges, irony is a frequent theme. In "Death and the Compass," we see various examples of irony. The death of the protagonist and the similarities between the two foes are two manifestations of irony in the story.

This student is not really telling the reader anything that is not already included in the reading. The AP readers know what happens in the books; there is no need to summarize the plot. If you look at the condensed outline, you may first ask yourself these questions: How is irony portrayed in the works of Borges? Is it a result of past actions of the characters? How do characters react to the ironic situations? Is this irony within another context, or compounded by other factors? How does Borges describe irony in this text? What are the most striking images or results of irony in the work? What elements, if any, are in opposition?

If you had thought of those questions first, you might have answered the question this way:

En "La Muerte y la Brújula", un detective trata de resolver unos crímenes que están relacionados unos con los otros. Piensa que estos crímenes siguen un patrón triangular cuando en realidad siguen un patrón rectangular. Irónicamente, todos los hechos y claves del misterio fueron creados por Scharlach, que pretende destruir a su enemigo, Lonröt. Al final, Scharlach dirige a Lonröt al cuarto lugar del misterio donde lo mata, terminando un juego de ironía, lógica circular e ilusiones. Lonröt va al cuarto lugar para supuestamente arrestar al criminal, pero entra en un ambiente de simetría y repeticiones maniacas, y hasta ve su imagen en un cuarto de espejos. Todas son claves que predicen su papel como la víctima del cuarto crimen, pero no logra desenredarse de la telaraña del rival.

Muchas veces Lonröt y Scharlach, cuyos nombres significan rojo en alemán, funcionan como una sola entidad a pesar de su conflicto. Sus mentes utilizan la misma lógica, pero Scharlach actúa como Dios, porque desde el principio ha puesto a Lonröt en un laberinto sin salida ni escape. Al tratar de escapar de este laberinto y resolver el crimen, Lonröt irónicamente crea su propio laberinto, y en vez de ser el perseguidor, se convierte ahora en la presa de Scharlach. También, sus papeles de detective y criminal se intercambian. Lonröt no sabe que la realidad que percibe es otra, creada por otra persona. Es como si Scharlach estuviera en la mente de Lonröt y controlara lo que éste percibe. La muerte de Lonröt al final justifica todo lo que hizo Scharlach porque el falleci-miento de Lonröt es la venganza por el encarcelamiento de su hermano hace tres años. Al estar en el laberinto sin salida, Lonröt es como el hombre mortal sin control sobre su destino, mientras que Scharlach, un criminal y asesino, irónicamente personifica a Dios, ya que controla el destino, el pensamiento y, finalmente, el momento de morir de otros. Este conflicto entre dos personas tan parecidas pero a la vez semejantes hace resaltar la ironía del cuento.

Translation

In "La Muerte y la Brújula," a detective tries to resolve several crimes that are related to each other. He believes that these crimes follow a triangular pattern, when in reality they follow a rectangular pattern. Ironically, all the facts and clues of the mystery were created by Scharlach, who plans to destroy his enemy, Lonröt. At the end, Scharlach directs Lonröt to the fourth scene of the mystery, where he kills him, ending a game of irony, circular logic, and illusions. Lonröt goes to the fourth scene in order to supposedly arrest the criminal, but he enters a world of symmetry and manic repetition, and even sees his own image in a room of mirrors. All of these are clues that predict his role as the victim of the fourth crime, but he doesn't manage to disentangle himself from the web of his rival.

Many times Lonröt and Scharlach, whose names mean red in German, function as one being in spite of their conflict. Their minds use the same logic, but Scharlach functions as God, because since the beginning he has put Lonröt in a labyrinth without exit or escape. When he tries to escape from the maze and solve the crime, Lonröt ironically creates his own labyrinth, and instead of being the chaser, he now becomes the prey of Scharlach. In addition, their roles as detective and criminal are exchanged. Lonröt does not realize that the reality he sees is indeed another, created by another person. It is as if Scharlach were in Lonröt's mind and controlled by what he perceives. The death of Lonröt at the end justifies everything that Scharlach did because his death is revenge for the jailing of his brother three years ago. By being in a maze without exit, Lonröt is like the mortal man without control of his destiny, while Scharlach, a criminal and killer, ironically personifies God, given he controls the destiny, thinking, and ultimately, the moment of death of others. This conflict between two people so different yet alike highlights the irony of this story.

Is this the most brilliant piece of analytical writing the student has ever written? No, but notice how he has taken the question and applied it to the condensed outline to develop the idea that readers are looking for in the essay. The student began by describing the theme in greater detail, not simply saying that it was present in the works of that author. Then he showed how the characters relate to that theme. The student is on his way to a really good score on this essay. Now, because you do not have any textual quotes before you on this question, you must discuss images that you can recall from the works you have read. But that shouldn't be a problem. You want concrete textual examples anyway, so be certain that you explain how your examples of irony define the existence of the characters.

OPPOSITION

The last part of the condensed outline is opposition. Opposition is a sharp contrast between two elements. It may be as obvious as black and white or as subtle as a naive character and a sophisticated character. Opposition often occurs between an author's style and subject. It is very easy to miss if you aren't looking for it. Take the time to look for it. You don't have to resolve the contrast; simply identify it. Explain the opposition and how it adds further meaning to the text you are discussing. Opposition will bring you to the heart of the story. AP readers will be very impressed if you can identify any key elements that are in contrast. Find them and then relate them to the thematic question you were given.

SAMPLE QUESTION

Directions: Write a well-organized essay IN SPANISH on the topic that appears below.

Instrucciones: El poder es un tema importante en las obras de muchos autores latinoamericanos. Muchas veces parece que ciertos personajes tienen todo el poder y otros no lo tienen. Discute el tema del poder en **una** de las obras siguientes haciendo referencia concreta a la obra.

Un día de éstos, Gabriel García Márquez
El sur, Jorge Luis Borges

Power is an important theme in the works of many Latin American authors. Many times, it seems that certain characters have power while others do not. Discuss the theme of power in **one** of the following works, making concrete reference to the works that you have studied.

Un día de éstos, Gabriel García Márquez
El sur, Jorge Luis Borges

SAMPLE STUDENT ESSAY

En sus cuentos cortos Gabriel García Márquez le pone gran énfasis al tema del poder. Se enfoca particularmente en el problema del abuso del poder, que casi siempre es un poder político, y cómo este abuso afecta tanto a los que sacan ventaja del abuso como a los perjudicados. Los cuentos "Un día de estos" y "La prodigiosa tarde de Baltazar" nos presentan los dos tipos básico de reacciones que tiene la gente frente al abuso del poder. Estas reacciones son la reacción activa y la pasiva. En ambos casos, los afectados hacen un esfuerzo para ganar el poder para ellos mismos, pero casi nunca lo logran por más de un tiempo bien corto.

En "Un día de estos", un dentista llamado Don Aurelio Escobar, un dentista "sin título y buen madrugador" se enfrenta a el abuso del poder que demuestra el alcalde. De los dos personajes principales de los cuentos mencionados arriba, Escobar es quizás el que mejor entiende su situación de abusado. Él siempre trae "una mirada que raras veces corresponde a la situación, como la mirada de los sordos". El dentista tiene aquella mirada porque él sabe que en un mundo lleno de corrupción es muy peligroso saber demasiado. Por dentro, el dentista está lleno de odio y resentimiento por el sistema y el alcalde que lo representa. Cuando el alcalde viene a pedir que le saque una muela, lo hace amenazando al dentista, y le dice al hijo de este que le diga a su padre: "Si no le sacas la muela, te pega un tiro". El dentista tiene su propio revolver y está más que preparado para enfrentar los tiros del alcalde. Si muriera, sería un mártir más, un símbolo de las víctimas del abuso del poder. Pero cuando el alcalde entra al consultorio del dentista, con "muchas noches de desesperación en sus ojos marchitos", al dentista le viene una idea mucho mejor. Allí estaba su oportunidad de tomar un poco del poder que el alcalde abusa. El dentista ha sufrido mucho tiempo bajo la tiranía del alcalde, y siente mucho remordimiento, no por el mismo pero por las otras víctimas y las personas que han muerto. Escobar le saca la muela al alcalde sin anestesia. Márquez nos pinta el dolor del alcalde describiendo sus lágrimas, el "sudor frío" y el "crujido de huesos". En este momento, el alcalde es quien está débil y sin poder. El poder pasa al dentista y se da a entender que él se está aprovechando de la vulnerabilidad. Márquez pregunta si el abuso del poder es apropiado en algunos casos, como en el caso de la venganza del dentista. Él le dice al alcalde inmediatamente antes de sacarle la muela: "Con esto nos está pagando veinte muertos, teniente". El poder del dentista dura poco. Finalmente, el poder regresa al alcalde, pero la experiencia es una que él no olvidará muy pronto.

En sus cuentos, los personajes que Márquez nos presenta en sí son víctimas. El más fuerte de todos es el dentista, pero aunque termina en una desgracia obvia y concreta, él tiene que vivir con su conocimiento de la maldad. Márquez nos muestra todas las consecuencias de la corrupción y el abuso del poder, diciéndonos que escapar del círculo vicioso es casi imposible porque cuando el poder sale de las manos de un abusador, es muy probable que caiga en manos de alguien que sienta la tentación de hacer lo mismo.

Translation

In his short stories, Gabriel García Márquez puts a lot of emphasis on the theme of power. In particular he focuses on the abuse of power that is almost always political power and how that abuse affects those who benefit from the abuse and those who are injured by it. The stories "Un día de estos," and "La prodigiosa tarde de Baltazar" present us with two basic types of reactions that people have when faced with the abuse of power. These reactions are the active reaction and the passive reaction. In each of these instances, those affected by the abuse make an effort to gain power themselves, but they almost never attain it for more than a fleeting moment.

In "Un día de estos" a dentist called Don Aurelio Escobar, a dentist "without a title, and an honest early riser" is faced with the mayor's abuse of power. Of the two characters from the stories mentioned above, Escobar is perhaps the one who best understands his situation of abuse. He always wears "an expression that rarely corresponds with the situation, like the expression of the deaf." The dentist has that expression because he knows that in a world filled with corruption, it is very dangerous to know too much. On the inside the dentist feels hatred and resentment for the system and for the mayor who represents the system. When the mayor comes to ask that he removes a molar, he does it with threats. He tells the dentist's son to tell his father that "if he doesn't remove (my) tooth I'm going to shoot him." The dentist has his own revolver and is more than prepared to face the shots of the mayor. If he died, he would be one more martyr, a symbol of the victims of abusive power. But when the mayor enters his office with many nights of desperation in his withered eyes, the dentist thinks of another, much better idea. There was his opportunity to grab a little bit of the power that the mayor abused. The dentist has suffered for a long time under the tyranny of the mayor, and he feels much regret, not for himself, but for the other victims and the people that have died. Escobar removed the mayor's tooth without anesthesia. Márquez paints the pain of the mayor for us with the descriptions of his tears, the "cold sweat" and the "cracking of bones." In this instance, the mayor is the weak one without power. The power passes to the dentist in this moment. There is an implication that the dentist is taking advantage of the vulnerability. Márquez (asks) the question if it is appropriate to abuse power in some instances, such as the vengeance of the dentist. He tells the mayor immediately before removing the molar, "With this you pay us for twenty deaths, Lieutenant." The power of the dentist is short-lived. Eventually, the power returns to the mayor, but the experience is one that the mayor will not soon forget.

In his stories, the characters who Márquez presents to us are themselves victims. The strongest of them all is the dentist. But although he ends up in obvious and concrete disgrace, he has to live with his knowledge of the malice. Márquez shows us all of the consequences of corruption and the abuse of power, telling us that escaping the vicious circle is almost impossible because when the power leaves the hands of one abuser, it is very likely that it will fall into the hands of someone who feels the temptation to do the same.

Explanation

This is a perfect example of an essay that, although written by a strong student, doesn't score well on the exam. He writes this essay as if he were writing a longer, more complex assignment like a research paper. In the AP essays you don't have time for that sort of development. This essay is burdened by plot summary. And it doesn't make use of our condensed outline technique that makes it so much easier to write essays the readers look forward to grading. Let's examine his opening paragraph and see how it could be improved.

En sus cuentos cortos Gabriel García Márquez le pone énfasis al tema del poder. En particular enfoca el problema del abuso del poder, que casi siempre es un poder político, y cómo este abuso afecta tanto a los que sacan ventaja del abuso como a los perjudicales. Los cuentos "Un día de éstos" nos presentan a los dos tipos básicos de reacciones que tienen la gente frente al abuso del poder. Estas reacciones son la reacción activa, y la pasiva. En todas las instancias, los afectados hacen un esfuerzo para cobrar el poder para ellos mismos, pero casi nunca lo logran por más de un tiempo bien corto.

If we consider the literal meaning of the notion of power in García Márquez, we must discuss the meaning of power in his work. Our student above identifies the abuse of power in his second sentence, but he doesn't formulate a strong enough opening sentence. His first sentence is virtually a wasted restatement of the question. The power that we see in García Márquez is the ability to influence or control others. In many instances, power is used for personal gain. In *"Un día de estos"* the abusive power of the mayor is clearly for his own financial gain, particularly when asked whether he would like the bill sent to his home or to the municipal offices, he replies with *"es la misma vaina"* (it's all the same). We, the readers, can be confident that the government pays for all of his personal expenses. This is one type of abuse. The twenty deaths that the dentist holds him accountable for are yet another type of abuse. Your opening paragraph should define power and abuse of power, if that is how you see power in the works of García Márquez.

Let's compare the previous opening paragraph with the following one for virtually the same essay:

El poder en las obras de García Márquez es la capacidad de controlar o abusar de otros, con la fuerza militar, la fuerza política o la riqueza económica. En muchas de sus obras, los perjudicados sufren tanto, que en un momento dado cuando ellos mismos toman el poder por un tiempo corto, lo abusan de la misma manera que sus opresores. Sus personajes son humildes, honestos y inocentes hasta el momento en que toman el poder. Sienten tan profunda noción de venganza que no pueden evitar la tentación de abusar del poder también.

Con el dentista de "Un día de éstos", García Márquez nos pinta a un individuo oprimido por una autoridad abusiva. El siente frustración y humillación frente la figura del opresor.

Translation

Power in the works of García Márquez is the capacity to control or abuse others with military force, political force, or economic wealth. In many of his works, the oppressed suffer so much that in a given moment when they seize power for a short time, they abuse it in the same fashion used by their oppressors. His characters are humble, honest, and innocent until the moment in which they seize power. They feel such a deep notion of revenge that they cannot avoid the temptation to abuse power also.

With the dentist from *"Un día de éstos,"* García Márquez paints for us an individual oppressed by an abusive authority. He feels frustration and humiliation in front of his oppressor.

While this may not be the most profound or deep analytical writing you have read in Spanish, it at least gives the AP reader what he or she wants: a clear, well-focused discussion of the theme of power in García Márquez. Notice how the first paragraph discusses, and indeed defines, the literal meaning of power in the author's work. It also talks about the characters right away, how they react to and feel about the theme. This is how you get to the concrete details of the concept in question. And that is what the AP readers want. So be sure to take advantage of the condensed outline technique and all that it offers. It will help you earn high scores on the AP essay questions.

SUMMARY

- Remember the importance of clarity of thought and expression. Above all, the readers are impressed by clarity in your essay.

- Define your terms, even terms used in the wording of the question to demonstrate your understanding of them.

- AVOID plot summary at all costs.

- Follow our condensed outline format to get to the heart of the essay fast.

12

THEMATIC ANALYSIS OF TWO TEXTS AND THE EXCERPT ESSAY QUESTIONS

Other possible topics for the thematic and text analysis questions include the following:

- the two-author comparison involving one theme
- an excerpt from one of the AP authors
- an excerpt from a critical commentary on one of the AP authors

THE BASICS OF THE TWO-TEXT THEMATIC ANALYSIS

The two-author question is asking you to compare and contrast the treatment of a theme in one author's work with that of another author. The treatment may be similar in both authors' works or it may be different. You decide. There isn't really a right or wrong way of interpreting this question. Generally the test writers choose a theme or concept that appears in the works of the two authors. All you have to do is compare and contrast the topic.

Let's review again the condensed outline we worked with in Chapters 10 and 11.

CONDENSED OUTLINE

I. What is the literal meaning of the theme or concept?
   A. Can you explain the theme and how that theme or concept is treated in the work?
   B. What feelings does the theme or concept evoke? What feelings do the characters demonstrate? What feelings does it evoke in you, the reader?
   C. What feelings does the theme or concept evoke in you, the reader?

II. How does the author treat that theme or concept?
   A. What are the important images that relate to the theme?
   B. Which are the strongest examples of the theme?
   C. What elements are in opposition?

OPPOSITION

We spoke briefly about the concept of opposition in an earlier chapter. Let's take a closer look at how opposition applies to Two-Text Thematic Analysis. Opposition refers to any pair of elements that contrast sharply. It may be obvious, like black and white or hot and cold. It may be more subtle, such as in a story that begins with creativity and richness and ends with poverty and despair. It is easy to miss if you are not looking for it. Opposition can often be found between an author's style and his subject. You may also see opposition in the works of two authors, which is why it is so important to think about it here. It is a pairing of images or concepts whereby each becomes more striking and powerful when considered together. When you see two elements opposed to each other, you should identify them and interpret them. There is no one right answer. That is the beauty of literature. You do, however, have to find concrete textual examples in the readings to support your ideas. For example, you may feel that women characters in Unamuno have traditional, feminine, nurturing roles. In Lorca, you may think that women are the masculine, aggressive character types. This is a contrast or opposition. Your entire essay could be built around opposition in this section, depending on the question you get and your interpretation of the books you read.

WEAVING

The two-author comparison essay is written for weaving. Weaving, as we saw briefly in an earlier chapter, is a technique in which you choose a theme and discuss different aspects of the theme using examples from each author. This way you would be comparing aspects of a character from one author with aspects of a character from another author throughout your essay. It's also a great way to avoid deadly plot summary. **Remember: You want to avoid plot summary at all costs.**

SCORING GUIDELINES FOR THE TWO-AUTHOR QUESTION

NINE: SHOWS SUPERIORITY

This is a well-developed and focused essay that compares the theme or characters from the works of one author with those of another author. The essay demonstrates the ability to read insightfully and write analytically. It also may show some originality of thought. This essay uses at least one fully developed example from each author's work. There is no irrelevant or erroneous information. This essay leaves no doubt in the reader's mind that the student possesses a high level of understanding of the works of both authors.

SEVEN TO EIGHT: SHOWS COMPETENCE

This is also a well-developed essay that shows some creativity and insight. This essay has at least one strong example from each author's work. There may be some plot summary, but it serves to illustrate the theme. This essay may include some errors, but the errors do not affect the overall quality. The reader must make some interpretation because the response is not always fully explained. A strong treatment of both authors without any comparison would earn a score of seven.

FIVE TO SIX: SUGGESTS COMPETENCE

This essay suggests that the student may have understood the question, but the essay is not well focused. It is not very analytical. Plot summary may predominate. It may include errors of interpretation or plot. A satisfactory treatment of one example may earn a five.

THREE TO FOUR: POSSIBLE COMPETENCE

This is a poorly organized essay. There is little focus and understanding of the question. It may include exclusively plot summary. Comments may be irrelevant and erroneous. The student appears unable to thoroughly discuss the theme. There are limited or no connections to the topic.

ONE TO TWO: NOT COMPETENT

This essay suggests that the student misunderstood the question or that the student answered a question different from the question asked. Reader has no doubt that the student did not read or understand the texts.

ZERO: CANNOT BE EVALUATED

The essay is meaningless, or it's written in English or any language other than Spanish.

SAMPLE TWO-TEXT THEMATIC ANALYSIS

The two-text thematic analysis question looks like this.

Directions: Write a well-organized essay on the topic that appears below.

Instrucciones: En algunas de las obras que has leído, la muerte es un tema recurrente. Escoge DOS de las siguientes obras y escribe un ensayo que compare el trato de este tema en las dos obras. Tu ensayo debe contener ejemplos de los textos para apoyar tus ideas.

San Martín Bueno, mártir, Miguel de Unamuno
El sur, Jorge Luis Borges
No oyes ladrar los perros, Juan Rulfo
La casa de Bernada Alba, Federico García Lorca

Directions: In some of the works that you have read, death is a recurrent theme. Choose TWO of the following works and write an essay that compares the treatment of this theme in the two works. Your essay should contain examples for the texts to support your ideas.

San Martín Bueno, mártir, Miguel de Unamuno
El sur, Jorge Luis Borges
No oyes ladrar los perros, Juan Rulfo
La casa de Bernada Alba, Federico García Lorca

First, you should apply the condensed outline to each author's works. Look for similarities between the treatment of the theme in each author, but also look for opposition. Generally, the question writers come up with a question that includes some opposition and will be looking for it in your essays.

Your condensed outline may look like this.

1. The idea of death in Unamuno is an escape from the uncertainty of life.
   A. San Manuel Bueno wants to escape his doubts (*San Manuel Bueno, mártir*).

2. The idea of death in García Lorca is an escape from oppression.
   A. Adela wants to escape the oppressive environment created by her mother, dictated by society. (*La casa de Bernarda Alba*).

So you could choose an example of a character from each author's work and discuss how that character illustrates the treatment of the theme. Then alternate characters, works, or authors, discussing for example death as an escape from the uncertainty of life in contrast to death viewed as an escape from oppression. The weaving technique makes it easier for the reader to distinguish between the treatment of the same theme in the works of two different authors.

Sample Student Essay

La muerte es capaz de representar muchas cosas en la literatura, incluso un escape de la vida difícil. En las obras de Miguel de Unamuno, específicamente "San Manuel Bueno, mártir" y de Federico García Lorca, "La casa de Bernarda Alba" por ejemplo, la muerte se presenta como un huida de la incertidumbre y opresíon en la vida. En las obras de Unamuno, los personajes escapan, por medio de la muerte, la tortura de meditar sobre sus propias existencias. En Lorca, los personajes, típicamente mujeres, mueren a causa de y como escape de la sociedad opresiva. En los dos casos, la muerte alivia los problemas de la vida.

San Manuel, de "San Manuel Bueno, mártir," es torturado por las dudas en su fe. Como sacerdote, debe creer en todas las doctrinas de la iglesia, pero la narradora nota que el se calla durante la oración sobre la vida eterna después de la muerte. No cree en ningún paraíso después de la vida sino en el opuesto, algo terrible (como dice él.) Se supone que, para él, la muerte es el fin de la existencia. Manuel, entonces, se preocupa de la muerte (como no tiene la idea consolante de la vida eterna.) También se preocupa por su propia incapacidad de creer como debe creer un padre de la iglesia.

Adela, personaje de "La casa de Bernarda Alba", por Federico Gárcia Lorca, es torturada también. Es castigada como mujer en la sociedad española. Tiene que guardar luto por su padre, y no casarse, aunque está enamorada. Su madre, oficio de una sociedad opresiva, dice que solo su hermana mayor se puede casar porque está casi demasiado mayor. Este castigo lleva Adela a la frustración. Ella se mata cuando piensa que su amor ha muerto. Se ve como perdida en la sociedad, y el suicidio sirve como buen escape. La muerte de San Manuel también es bienvenida por el. Está tranquilo porque ahora puede descansar la mente y olvidarse de las dudas.

Entonces la muerte en las obras de Lorca y Unamuno sirve como un escape de las dificultades de la vida. A veces la muerte es aceptada por el individuo, y a veces no. Las dificultades pueden tener origen adentro de la mente, como las dudas de San Manuel, o fuera como la opresión de la sociedad. A pesar de todas estas diferencias, la muerte siempre se presenta como escape de la vida dura, especificamente en "San Manuel Bueno, mártir" por Unamuno"y "La casa de Bernarda Alba" por Lorca.

Translation

Death is capable of representing many different things in literature, including an escape from a difficult life. In the works of Miguel de Unamuno, specifically, *San Manuel Bueno, mártir* and "La casa de Bernarda Alba" by Federico García Lorca, for example, death is presented as a way to flee from the uncertainty and oppression of life. In the works of Unamuno, the characters escape, through death, the torture of meditating about their own existences. In Lorca the characters, typically women, die because of and as an escape from an oppressive society. In both cases, death alleviates the problems of life.

San Manuel, from *San Manuel Bueno, mártir*, is tortured by doubts in his faith. As a priest, he should believe all the doctrines of the church, but the narrator notices that he falls silent during the prayer about eternal life after death. He doesn't believe in any kind of paradise in the afterlife but rather something quite the opposite, something terrible (as he says). It seems that for him, death is the end of existence. Manuel, then, worries about death (because he doesn't have the consoling idea of eternal life). He also worries about his inability to believe as he should believe, being a priest of the church.

Adela, from "*La casa de Bernarda Alba*" by Lorca, is tortured too. She is punished as a woman in Spanish society. She has to be in mourning for her father, and she cannot marry even though she is in love. Her mother, (embodiment) of an oppressive society, says that only her elder sister may marry because she is almost too old. This punishment leads Adela to frustration. She kills herself when she thinks her lover has died. She sees herself as lost in society, and her suicide acts as a good means of escape. The death of San Manuel is also well received by him. He is calm because now he can rest his mind and forget about his doubts.

So it seems clear that death in the works of Lorca and Unamuno serves as an escape from the difficulties in life. At times death is accepted by the individual, and at other times it is not accepted. The difficulties can originate from within, like the doubts of San Manuel, or from the outside, like the oppression of society. In spite of all of these differences, death is always presented as an escape from a difficult life. Specifically in "San Manual Bueno, mártir" by Unamuno and "La casa de Bernarda Alba" by Lorca.

Explanation

Notice how this student, even in the first two sentences, gets right to the topic at hand: death is "an escape from a difficult life," and "from the uncertainty and oppression of life." She also does a good job weaving her discussion of the characters from each author's work. Although this essay is not perfect, it's pretty close. Minor errors, such as the persistent *personage* versus *personaje*, are minor irritations but don't really detract from the overall strength of the essay.

There is virtually no plot summary; although when it is present, it serves to support views expressed. Overall, this essay would probably receive a score of 4 because it is a very well-developed essay on the concept of death in the works of both authors. In other words, it demonstrates considerable insight and analytical ability while presenting a thorough discussion of death in Lorca and Unamuno.

THE BASICS OF THE AP AUTHOR-EXCERPT QUESTIONS (TEXT ANALYSIS)

The AP excerpt questions, also known as text analysis questions, are the final essay the student must complete on the exam. This essay may be one of two types, only one of which will appear on the test. One type is known as the author excerpt question where a student writes short answers to several open ended questions that refer to a passage from a work that comes from the required reading list. The second type is known as the Critical Excerpt question where a student must do an analysis of a critical commentary made by someone else about a work that appears on the required reading list.

SAMPLE AP AUTHOR-EXCERPT QUESTION

"La verdad, Lázaro es acaso algo terrible, algo intolerable, algo mortal; la gente sencilla no podría vivir con ella. Yo estoy para hacerles felices, para hacerles que se sueñen inmortales y no para matarles. Lo que aquí hace falta es que vivan sanamente, que vivan en unanimidad de sentido, y con la verdad, con mi verdad, no vivirían. Que vivan. Y esto hace la Iglesia, hacerles vivir. ¿Religión verdadera? Todas las religiones son verdaderas en cuanto hacen vivir espiritualmente a los pueblos que las profesan, en cuanto les consuelan de haber tenido que nacer para morir, y para cada pueblo la religión más verdadera es la suya, la que le ha hecho. ¿Y la mía? La mía es consolarme en consolarme a los demás, aunque el consuelo que les doy no sea el mío."

—"San Manuel Bueno, Mártir"

Miguel de Unamuno

1. ¿Cuál es el concepto de la religión para Unamuno?

2. ¿Cómo afecta la religión la búsqueda de verdad en la vida y la vida en la verdad?

SCORING GUIDELINES FOR THE SAMPLE AP AUTHOR-EXCERPT QUESTION

Unlike the other essays, both text analysis questions are graded on a 5-point scale:

FIVE: SHOWS SUPERIORITY

The responses are completely accurate and supported by textual reference. The writing is organized and virtually free of errors.

FOUR: SHOWS COMPETENCE

The response is convincing and supported by textual reference. However there may be errors in the analysis.

THREE: POSSIBLE COMPETENCE

The response shows a basic understanding of the question, and there is an attempt at an accurate response. However, there are errors and ambiguity in the response.

TWO: POSSIBLY NOT COMPETENT

This response does not answer the question completely. Summary outweighs analysis, and serious errors detract from the response, which may be irrelevant or inaccurate.

ONE: NOT COMPETENT

This response fails to address the question and is a mere summary with no analysis.

ZERO

This response cannot be evaluated.

CONDENSED OUTLINE

I. What is the literal meaning of religion in this excerpt? (Looking for truth in life and life in truth)
    A. Can you explain the idea of religion in the works you studied? (In *San Manuel Bueno, Martir*, religion is very important to Don Manuel.)
    B. What feelings does religion evoke in the characters in the work that you read? What feeling does it evoke in you, the reader? (Religion for Don Manuel produces anguish and angst because of his doubts. For Lazarus, it is a sideshow.)

II. How does Unamuno treat religion in relation to life and truth?
    A. What are the important examples (images), and how do they relate to the concept of religion? (Don Manuel)
    B. What specific examples produce the strongest feelings? (Don Manuel's inner turmoil and feeling of helplessness)
    C. What elements are in opposition? (faith versus doubt)
        Opposition is very important in the works of Unamuno. His work is filled with opposition.

There is tremendous contrast; perhaps you would call it irony or even heresy that Don Manuel in *San Manuel Bueno, Mártir* is a parish priest and yet does not believe in life after death. If you can identify elements such as these that relate to the excerpt you are given on the exam, your essay reader will be filled with awe. You will also be well on your way to a high-scoring essay.

SAMPLE STUDENT ESSAY

La religión para Miguel de Unamuno es una búsqueda de la verdad en la vida caracterizada por una oposición entre la fe y la duda. En muchas de sus obras, vemos la misma búsqueda, el mismo deseo ardiente de saber la verdad. Sus personajes cuestionan sus propias existencias como seres humanos y como seres ficticios. Sufren mucho al darse cuenta que son meros entes ficticios o entes humanos en un universo caótico e impersonal. Don Manuel de "San Manuel Bueno, mártir" es un fictio que personifica la oposición entre la fe y la duda que caracteriza el concepto de la religión para Unamuno.

Don Manuel, el párroco querido de Valverde de Lucerna esconde su secreto del pueblo. Según Don Manuel, su "terrible secreto" atormentaría al pueblo, a la persona corriente. No podrían vivir felices dudando de la vida eterna. Don Manuel se dedica, entonces, a la felicidad de las gentes en el pueblo. Les ayuda a "bien morir", significando que les ayuda a aceptar tranquilamente la muerte en la tierra sabiendo que se van a reunir con su Padre espiritual en la vida eterna. El único problema, por supuesto, es la oposición, o el contraste fuerte entre las acciones de Don Manuel y sus verdaderas creencias. Es la personificación del concepto de la religión de Unamuno porque enseña la fe en la vida eterna, pero no cree en ella. Parece que ha buscado la verdad en la vida y la vida en la verdad y ha concluido que no existe la vida eterna. De todas formas, Don Manuel se dedica completamente a su pueblo y a su felicidad. Hace todo lo que puede para mantener su fe fuerte.

La religión para Unamuno, en términos amplios, es un esfuerzo voluntarioso de entender nuestra propia existencia. Para Don Manuel, atormentado por sus dudas, el significado de su existencia era ayudar a los demás. Terminamos entendiendo que el valor de la "religión" es la búsqueda misma, no necesariamente la respuesta encontrada.

Translation of the Sample Question

"The truth, Lázaro, is perhaps something terrible, something intolerable, something deadly; the common people would not be able to live with it. I am here to make them happy, to make them believe themselves to be immortal, not to kill them. What is lacking here is that they live healthily, that they live in unanimity of meaning, and with the truth, with my truth, they wouldn't be able to live. Let them live. And this is what the Church does; it gives them life. True religion? All religions are true in that they make the people to whom they profess live spiritually, such that the give them comfort of having had to have been born in order to die, and for each people the most true religion is theirs, that which they have made. And mine? Mine is to take comfort in giving comfort to others, although the comfort I give them isn't necessarily mine."

Translation of the Sample Student Essay

Religion for Miguel de Unamuno is a search for truth in life characterized by the opposition, or sharp contrast, between faith and doubt. In many of his works, we see the same search, the same ardent desire to know the truth. His characters question their own existences as human beings and as fictional beings. They suffer greatly when they realize that they are merely fictional beings or human beings in a chaotic and impersonal universe. Don Manuel of *San Manuel Bueno, mártir* and Augusto Pérez of *Niebla* are two fictitious beings who personify the opposition between faith and doubt that characterizes the concept of religion for Unamuno.

Don Manuel, the beloved parish priest of Valverde of Lucerna, hides his secret from the people. According to Don Manuel, his "terrible secret" would torment the simple, ordinary people of the village. They wouldn't be able to live happily, doubting the truth of life after death. Don Manuel, then, dedicates himself to their happiness. He helps them to accept death peacefully; he comforts them with the knowledge that they will be meeting up with their heavenly father in the afterlife. The only problem, of course, is the opposition between the actions of Don Manuel and his actual beliefs. In this way he personifies Unamuno's concept of religion because he teaches about faith in eternal life, but yet in his heart of hearts he doesn't really believe in it. It seems he has searched for truth in life and life in truth and has come to the grim conclusion that there is no eternal life. Nonetheless, he is devoted to his followers and does his best to keep their faith strong.

In broad terms, religion for Unamuno is the willful effort to understand our own existence. For Don Manuel, tormented by his doubts, the meaning of his existence was helping others. We come to understand that the value of "religion" is the search itself and not necessarily the answer that was found.

Explanation

This is a very good essay. Notice how well she defines the terminology throughout the essay. She starts by stating the definition of religion given in the excerpt. Although it may seem redundant, it's not. You are explaining your understanding of the excerpt, so go ahead and spell it out in one or two carefully presented sentences. She then applies the topic (religion, in this case) to the author's work and specifically, to two concrete examples, all in the opening paragraph. Note also how often and accurately she refers to opposition in the author's work. This question is frequently written with opposition in mind, so be sure to look carefully for it. Although there is some plot summary, it serves to illustrate the ideas. And because the overall structure of the essay is so good, the minor amount of plot summary would probably go unnoticed. This is a high-scoring essay.

THE BASICS OF THE CRITICAL EXCERPT QUESTION

The critical excerpt question asks you to use your knowledge of the readings and the commentary from the excerpt. You must address your opening paragraph to the comment made in the critical excerpt. You need to apply the condensed outline technique to the excerpt and the works you studied of that author.

SAMPLE CRITICAL-EXCERPT QUESTION

Lee la cita siguiente que refiere a la obra *La casa de Bernarda Alba* de Federico Garcia Lorca para apoyar la afirmación de Raimundo Hernández.

En su acercamiento a la literatura del siglo veinte, Raimundo Hernández afirma que "la fuerza dominante en la obra de Lorca es la opresión. La opresión penetra toda faceta de sus dramas e incluso exige que el público comparta la frustración de los protagonistas. Es esa misma frustración, esa indignación frente al atropello del espíritu humano que nos hace identificar con los protagonistas de Lorca".

Analiza cómo las ideas planteadas de esta cita se reflejan en la obra *La casa de Bernarda Alba* de Federico García Lorca. Usa ejemplos para apoyar tus ideas.

Condensed Outline: Critical Excerpt—Oppression in Lorca

I. What is meant by oppression in the critical excerpt? (*atropello del espíritu humano* or trampling of the human spirit, lack of personal/individual freedom)
    A. What is the literal face-value meaning of the excerpt? (Oppression is present in every part of the Lorcan drama. Such trampling of the human spirit enables us to identify and sympathize with the characters.)
    B. What feelings does the oppression evoke in the characters and in you as a reader? (Outrage, indignance)

II. How does the author treat the theme of oppression?
    A. What are the important oppressive images in the works that you studied? (*Adela versus Pepe el Romano, el caballo garañón libre versus las potras encerradas, y el calor aplastante de* La casa de Bernarda Alba)
    B. Which are the strongest examples? (*Adela*)
    C. Which elements are in opposition? (Oppression of society in the form of Bernarda is in opposition to the desires/wishes of the protagonist.)

Sample Student Essay

Segun Raimundo Hernández, la opresión penetrante en los dramas de Lorca es el "atropello del espíritu humano". Vemos a personajes que no pueden seguir sus deseos, sus inclinaciones naturales, porque se enfrentan con una sociedad dominante que no permite la expresion individual. Al ver sus deseos completamente desbaratados, los personajes se sienten frustrados y desesperados. Sus acciones violentos resultan de una situación opresiva into-lerable. A pesar de su violencia, podemos compadecer con los protagonistas porque identificamos con sus básicos deseos humanos.

En "La casa de Bernarda Alba" la opresión está presente en el mismo calor sofocante del verano. Las hijas se quejan del calor aún de noche cuando se debería refrescar más. Muchas salen a buscar agua, para refrescarse, pero nunca pueden apagar la sed ardiente que tienen, símbolo de sus deseos sexuales frustrados. Bernarda, la personificación de la opresión y la voz de la sociedad dominada por los hombres, habla una tarde con una vecina mientras el caballo garañón, que está en el corral afuera, está dando patadas contra la pared de la casa. Bernarda da orden a los mozos a encerrar a las potras y dejar al caballo garañón libre. Es decir, encerrad a las potras, aunque hay varias, pero deben dejar libre al solitario caballo garañón. La comparación con las hijas de Bernarda y con Pepe el Roman no podría ser más clara. Pepe el Romano es el único macho en el drama, y ni siquiera aparece en escena, pero es una presencia palpable. Es el hombre el que manda y controla todo. Pepe elige a Angustias, la hija mayor y la más fea no porque esté enamorado de ella, sino porque es la que tiene una herencia grande. Pepe sigue visitando a Adela por la noche y amándola en secreto porque ella es el objeto de sus deseos. El tiene todo lo que quiere mientras que las hijas de Bernarda están condenadas a ocho años de luto por la muerte de un padre adultero.

Vemos a Adela, la hija menor y la más guapa de la familia de Bernarda Alba, quien es también la más rebelde y la única que se enfrenta con su madre opresiva. Al oír que su amante está muerto, Adela se suicida porque no puede resignarse a la vida oprimida sin su único escape, su única libertad en la vida. A pesar de que el suicidio no se considera normalmente admirable, en este caso, sentimos empatía por Adela porque así se escapa de la tiranía y opresión de su madre. El individuo se enfrenta con la sociedad opresiva y a costa de su vida, salió vencedora.

Hemos visto, entonces, que en los dramas de Lorca hay opresión penetrante que "atropella" el espíritu humano. Los deseos de los protagonistas no se pueden realizar cuando no están de acuerdo con las normas de la sociedad. De acuerdo con Raimundo Hernández, vemos que la opresión intolerante en los dramas de Lorca nos hace simpatizar con los protagonistas, aún cuando se vuelven violentos en busca de un escape de la opresión.

Translation of the Sample Question

Read the following quote that refers to the work *La casa de Bernarda Alba* by Federico Garcia Lorca.

In his *Approximation to the Literature of the Twentieth Century*, Raimundo Hernández affirms that "the dominant force in the work of Lorca is oppression. Oppression penetrates every facet of his dramas and even requires that the public share the frustration of the protagonists. It is that very frustration, the outrage at the trampling of the human spirit, that enables the public to identify fully with Lorca's characters."

Analyze how the ideas presented in this quote are reflected in the work *La casa de Bernarda Alba* by Federico Garcia Lorca. Use examples to support your ideas.

Translation of the Sample Student Essay

According to Raimundo Hernández, the penetrating oppression in the dramas of Lorca is the "trampling of the human spirit." We see characters who cannot realize their wishes or their natural inclinations because they are faced with a dominant society that does not permit individual expression. Upon seeing their wishes completely thwarted, the characters feel frustrated and desperate. Their violent actions result from an oppressive and unbearable situation. In spite of their violence, we can sympathize with the protagonists because we identify with their basic human desires.

In *La casa de Bernarda Alba* the oppression is present in the very suffocating heat of the summer. The daughters complain of the heat even at night, when it should be alleviated. In various instances, different daughters rise to get a drink of water, but none is able to quench the burning thirst they all feel, which symbolizes their frustrated sexual desires. Bernarda, the personification of oppression and the voice of the male-dominated society, talks one afternoon with a friend while the stud horse, out of the corral, begins kicking the side of the house. Bernarda orders the stable hand to lock up the fillies and leave the stud horse free, even though there are various fillies and only one solitary stud horse. The comparison with the daughters and Pepe el Romano could not be more explicit. Pepe el Romano is the only developed male figure in the play, and though he never even appears on stage, he is still a palpable force. The man is the one who rules in society and has control of everything. Pepe chooses to marry Angustias, the eldest and the ugliest, not because he loves her but because she has the greatest inheritance. Pepe continues to visit Adela at night, loving her in secret because she is truly the object of his desire. He has everything he could possibly want while Bernarda's daughters are left with eight years of mourning for a dead adulterous father.

We see Adela, who is the youngest and also the most rebellious daughter of Bernarda, who is the only one who stands up to her mother. Upon hearing that her lover is dead, Adela kills herself because she cannot be resigned to the oppressive life reserved for her without her only escape, her only freedom in her sad life. In spite of the fact that suicide is not normally an admirable act, we empathize with Adela because she escaped the tyranny and oppression of her mother. The individual went face to face with the oppressive society and at the price of her own life was victorious.

We have seen, then, that in the dramas of Lorca there is a pervasive oppression that tramples upon the human spirit. The wishes or desires of the protagonists cannot be realized when they do not follow the norms of society. We agree with Raimundo Hernández when he asserts that the intolerable oppression in the dramas of Lorca make us sympathize with the protagonists, even when they become violent in an attempt to escape oppression.

Explanation

This essay does a good job of relating the excerpt to *La casa de Bernarda Alba*. Notice how his opening paragraph addresses the excerpt, defines what the excerpt means to him: The "trampling of the human spirit" is ever present in the dramas of Lorca, and the frustration felt by both the characters and the public is shared because we all share the same basic human desires. Plot summary is kept to a minimum and used only to illustrate the ideas being expressed.

SUMMARY

- Define your terms, particularly if you have an excerpt question; define what the excerpt means to you. Also identify any specific terms used in the excerpt that may require clarification to make your point clearly.

- Follow the condensed outline to zero-in on your topic quickly and succinctly.

- Write a strong opening paragraph relating the excerpt or thematic topic to your essay.

PART **V**

THE PRINCETON REVIEW
AP SPANISH LITERATURE
PRACTICE TEST

13

LITERATURE
PRACTICE TEST

AP® Spanish Exam

SECTION I: Multiple-Choice Questions

DO NOT OPEN THIS BOOKLET UNTIL YOU ARE TOLD TO DO SO.

At a Glance

Total Time
1 hour
Number of Questions
65
Percent of Total Grade
40%
Writing Instrument
Pencil required

Instructions

Section I of this examination contains 65 multiple-choice questions. Fill in only the ovals for numbers 1 through 65 on your answer sheet.

Indicate all of your answers to the multiple-choice questions on the answer sheet. No credit will be given for anything written in this exam booklet, but you may use the booklet for notes or scratch work. After you have decided which of the suggested answers is best, completely fill in the corresponding oval on the answer sheet. Give only one answer to each question. If you change an answer, be sure that the previous mark is erased completely. Here is a sample question and answer.

Sample Question   Sample Answer

Chicago is a   Ⓐ ● Ⓒ Ⓓ Ⓔ
(A) state
(B) city
(C) country
(D) continent
(E) village

Use your time effectively, working as quickly as you can without losing accuracy. Do not spend too much time on any one question. Go on to other questions and come back to the ones you have not answered if you have time. It is not expected that everyone will know the answers to all the multiple-choice questions.

About Guessing

Many candidates wonder whether or not to guess the answers to questions about which they are not certain. Multiple choice scores are based on the number of questions answered correctly. Points are not deducted for incorrect answers, and no points are awarded for unanswered questions. Because points are not deducted for incorrect answer, you are encouraged to answer all multiple-choice questions. On any questions you do not know the answer to, you should eliminate as many choices as you can, and then select the best answer among the remaining choices.

This page intentionally left blank.

SPANISH LITERATURE

SECTION I

Time—80 minutes

Directions: Read the following selections for comprehension. Each selection is followed by a number of questions or incomplete statements. Choose the BEST answer according to the reading selection, and darken the corresponding oval on your answer sheet.

Instrucciones: Lee cada una de las siguientes selecciones. Después de cada selección verás varias preguntas u oraciones incompletas. Escoge la MEJOR respuesta según la selección y rellena el óvalo correspondiente en la hoja de respuestas.

Explosión

¡Si la vida es amor, ¡bendita sea!
¡Quiero más vida para amar! Hoy siento
Que no valen mil años de la idea
Lo que un minuto azul de sentimiento.

Línea

5 Mi corazón moría triste y lento…
Hoy abre en luz como una flor febea;
¡La vida brota como un mar violento
Donde la mano del amor golpea!

Hoy partió hacia la noche, triste, fría,
10 Rotas las alas mi melancolía;
Como una vieja mancha de dolor
En la sombra lejana se deslíe…
¡Mi vida toda canta, besa, ríe!
¡Mi vida toda es una boca en flor!

1. ¿Por qué se escribió el poema?
   (A) Para contemplar una idea abstracta
   (B) Para describir un problema concreto
   (C) Para celebrar un sentimiento fuerte
   (D) Para articular una creencia absurda

2. ¿Cómo se puede describir el tono del poema?
   (A) Caprichoso
   (B) Extático
   (C) Arrepentido
   (D) Perturbado

3. Según el poema, ¿qué valor tienen las ideas?
   (A) Mucho más que el amor
   (B) Mucho menos que una flor
   (C) No se puede medir
   (D) Mucho menos que el sentimiento

4. En los versos 7–8, "La vida brota como un mar violento/Donde la mano del amor golpea"

   Se llama:
   (A) aliteración
   (B) hipérbole
   (C) metonimia
   (D) símil

5. El título del poema se refiere a:
   (A) la muerte
   (B) una bomba
   (C) un infarto
   (D) la pasión

GO ON TO THE NEXT PAGE.

Mi abuela fue también la que me llevó a conocer el
mar. Una de sus hijas había logrado encontrar un marido
trabajador y éste trabajaba en Gibara, el puerto de mar
Línea más cercano a donde nosotros vivíamos. Por primera
5 vez tomé un ómnibus; creo que para mi abuela, con sus
setenta años, era también la primera vez que tomaba uno.
Nos fuimos a Gibara. Mi abuela y el resto de mi familia
desconocían el mar, a pesar de que no vivían a más de
treinta o cuarenta kilómetros de él. Recuerdo a mi tía
10 Coralina llegar llorando un día a la casa de mi abuela y
decir: «¿Ustedes saben lo que es que ya tengo cuarenta
años y nunca he visto el mar? Ahorita me voy a morir de
vieja y nunca lo voy a ver». Desde entonces, yo no hacía
más que pensar en el mar.

15 «El mar se traga a un hombre todos los días», decía mi
abuela. Y yo sentí entonces una necesidad irresistible de
llegar al mar.

¡Qué decir de cuando por primera vez me vi junto al
mar! Sería imposible describir ese instante; hay sólo una
20 palabra: el mar.

6. ¿Por qué lloró la tía Coralina?
   (A) Estaba muy enferma e iba a morir pronto.
   (B) Acababa de ir al mar, que le había dado miedo.
   (C) Pensaba que nunca iría al mar.
   (D) La abuela rehusó llevarla a conocer el mar.

7. ¿Cómo es la abuela del narrador?
   (A) Alegre
   (B) Vieja
   (C) Melancólica
   (D) Astuta

8. ¿Por qué quiere el narrador ir al mar?
   (A) Para visitar a sus tíos
   (B) Porque se había muerto el marido de su tía
   (C) Para tomar un autobús
   (D) Porque siente una atracción irresistible

9. ¿Qué describe esta selección?
   (A) La familia del narrador
   (B) Un viaje de autobús
   (C) El primer viaje al mar del narrador
   (D) La boda de la tía del narrador

10. ¿Cómo se puede describir el tono del pasaje?
    (A) Nostálgico
    (B) Triste
    (C) Sarcástico
    (D) Aburrido

GO ON TO THE NEXT PAGE.

Había una vez un hombre que vivía en Buenos
Aires, y estaba muy contento porque era hombre sano
y trabajador. Pero un día se enfermó, y los médicos le
Línea dijeron que solamente yéndose al campo podría curarse.
5 Él no quería ir, porque tenía hermanos chicos a quienes
les daba de comer; y se enfermaba cada día más. Hasta
que un amigo suyo, que era director del zoológico, le dijo
un día:
—Usted es amigo mío, y es un hombre bueno y
10 trabajador. Por eso quiero que se vaya a vivir al monte,
a hacer mucho ejercicio al aire libre para curarse. Y
como usted tengo mucha puntería con la escopeta, cace
animales del monte para traerme los cueros, y yo le daré
plata adelantada para que sus hermanitos puedan comer
15 bien.
El hombre enfermo aceptó, y se fue a vivir al monte,
lejos, más lejos que Misiones todavía. Hacía allá mucho
calor, y eso le hacía bien.
Vivía solo en el bosque, y él mismo cocinaba. Comía
20 pájaros y animales del monte, que cazaba con la escopeta,
y después comía frutas. Dormía bajo los árboles, y
cuando hacía mal tiempo construía en cinco minutos
una ramada con hojas de palmera, y allí pasaba sentado
y fumando, muy contento en medio del bosque que
25 bramaba con el viento y la lluvia.

11. La acción descrita en la segunda parte del pasaje
    tiene lugar en:

    (A) el zoológico

    (B) un bosque en el monte

    (C) la casa de los hermanitos del hombre

    (D) Misiones

12. Al principio, el hombre rehúsa ir al campo porque:

    (A) tiene que cuidar a sus hermanos

    (B) todavía se siente sano

    (C) a él no le gusta el aire libre

    (D) necesita curarse antes de ir

13. ¿Cómo reacciona el hombre al mal tiempo?

    (A) Le da miedo.

    (B) Caza varios animales.

    (C) Come frutas.

    (D) Se relaja.

14. ¿Qué hace el hombre para el director del zoológico?

    (A) Captura animales exóticos.

    (B) Le da plata para que sus hermanos coman bien.

    (C) Le construye una ramada.

    (D) Le da cueros de los animales del monte.

15. Al fin del pasaje el hombre está:

    (A) más enfermo

    (B) más sano

    (C) más pobre

    (D) más contento

GO ON TO THE NEXT PAGE.

La poesía y el verso

La poesía es la más alta expresión del arte literario. Se caracteriza, como ya se ha dicho, por tener un fin esencialmente estético; pero esto no quiere decir que *Línea* la obra poética haya de ser totalmente ajena a otros
5   propósitos: el autor puede glorificar a un héroe, exponer o defender una idea, servir a una empresa, enamorar a una mujer, etc., valiéndose de las obras mismas. Lo importante es que, al concebirlas y elaborarlas, el fin estético se sobreponga a los móviles ideológicos o vitales.

10   La forma habitual de la poesía es el verso; pero no son términos que se correspondan forzosamente. Hay poesía, finísima a veces, en prosa, y versos ramplones que no merecen el nombre de poesía. Esta distinción se hizo más honda al surgir hacia 1925 la tésis de la poesía
15   pura. Según esta doctrina, la verdadera poesía no consiste en ideas, imágenes, ritmos, palabras ni sonidos: es algo misterioso que de cuando en cuando se deja prender en lo que el poeta dice; entonces las palabras se contagian del encanto poético, se electrizan y cobran inusitado
20   poder. Descubrimos la huella de la poesía y sentimos la eficacia de su virtud, pero no podemos definirla porque es extrarracional e inefable. Mucho antes de que la idea de la poesía pura apareciera en Francia, suscitando una memorable polémica, nuestro Bécquer la había
25   formulado con toda claridad; en la rima V la poesía misma dice:

Yo, en fin, soy ese espíritu,

Desconocida esencia,

Perfume misterioso

De que es vaso el poeta.

16. Según la selección, ¿qué propósito general tiene la poesía?
   (A) Tiene un propósito didáctico.
   (B) Tiene un propósito estético.
   (C) Tiene un propósito de crítica social.
   (D) Tiene un propósito religioso.

17. ¿Qué es la forma habitual de la poesía?
   (A) Prosa
   (B) Drama
   (C) Versos
   (D) Líneas

18. ¿Qué es la poesía pura, según la selección?
   (A) Un secreto poético
   (B) Todo lo que el poeta dice
   (C) Algo inefable, indefinible
   (D) Una doctrina francesa modernista sobre la poesía

19. ¿Qué sugieren los versos citados arriba?
   (A) Que la poesía es como un licor misterioso
   (B) Que la poesía es desconocida por la mayoría de las personas
   (C) Que la poesía es una ciencia
   (D) Que la poesía es racional y lógica

GO ON TO THE NEXT PAGE.

El siglo XIX es una época que engendra una producción y desarrollo importante de la novela. Empieza con los antecedentes históricos y costumbristas vistos en la obra de Alarcón y Fernán Caballero. Luego sigue desarrollándose con el tradicionalismo y el regionalismo de Valera y Pereda. Al final del siglo, Pardo Bazán inicia un movimiento hacia el naturalismo, el cual desarrolla unos aspectos realistas con más libertad y menos inhibiciones. También parte de este esquema realista, y quizás más universal, es la obra de Benito Pérez Galdós. Casi como enlace de los dos extremos, la fecunda producción de Galdós va más allá de una mera época literaria. En concreto, nos gustaría examinar su novela *Miau*, como obra de esta época, pero más importante como novela universal.

Para empezar consideremos la obra en su época. Como parte de la preocupación de la realidad española en aquel entonces, Galdós plantea por medio de Villaamil, el tema del individuo en la sociedad. De este tema principal sale una variedad de temas; el establecimiento de la burocracia, el dinero, la religión, unos aspectos fantásticos, etcétera. Vemos la lucha de Villaamil con la burocracia, y al final, su abandono de la sociedad dominada por ella. Es una lucha simbólica también, simbólica de la lucha de España por encontrarse. Vemos que los ideales de su sociedad no coinciden con los de Villaamil. También notable es su incapacidad de solucionar los problemas sin utilizar los mecanismos de la sociedad burocrática. Es decir, que Villaamil es víctima de la sociedad, pero también de sus propios valores, los cuales caben dentro de la sociedad enemiga. Su falta de control en la vida del gobierno se complementa por su falta de control en la vida familiar. Es su esposa Doña Pura quien siempre le manda. O sea, que falta en grado severo su libertad en la vida profesional y también personal. Se entiende entonces su suicidio al final de la obra, donde por vez primera actúa por su propia cuenta utilizando hasta el punto máximo su preciosa libertad.

También interesante es el papel de Luisito. Casi paralelo a Villaamil, Luisito también busca su papel dentro de esta sociedad. Su punto de vista infantil le da más sensibilidad todavía a la lucha violenta de su abuelo por colocarse otra vez en el gobierno. Más acentuada, quizás, es la inocencia de Luisito vista en contraste con la mediocridad y corrupción de la sociedad burocrática. Los aspectos fantásticos planteados a través de sus sueños con Dios nos muestran otra inocencia o pureza que refleja su experiencia juvenil en la sociedad mucho más "adulta" y llena de corrupción.

Más importante nos parece es una lectura más abstracta, más universal. ¿No es la situación de Villaamil análoga a nuestra experiencia humana? ¿No tenemos cada uno de nosotros que "colocarnos" en la realidad humana? En términos abstractos podemos ver la lucha de Villaamil como la lucha del destino del hombre. También importante aquí es el libre albedrío del ser humano. ¡Qué tragedia que Villaamil no lo haya sabido utilizar hasta el momento de suicidarse! Hasta cierto punto, entonces, Galdós profundiza y trata la realidad del ser humano, con la cual no se limita con el personaje de Villaamil. Así que por medio de la forma novelística, Galdós nos da una obra que supercede clasificación literaria. Aunque parte de la obra realista del XIX, *Miau* va mucho más allá. A través de ello Galdós nos habla de cuestiones profundas de nuestra existencia. Son obras de este tipo, las que nos hacen pensar en nuestros propios seres, y que hacen valioso el estudio de la literatura.

20. ¿Cómo se caracteriza la narrativa de Galdós?

(A) Es una narrativa naturalista.

(B) Es una narrativa realista.

(C) Es una narrativa costumbrista.

(D) Es una narrativa surrealista.

21. ¿Cuál es el tema general de *Miau*?

(A) El papel del individuo en la sociedad

(B) El hombre en busca de su identidad

(C) La guerra

(D) El amor

22. Según la selección, todas estas ideas son subtemas de la novela MENOS:

(A) la religión

(B) el dinero

(C) el gobierno

(D) el amor

GO ON TO THE NEXT PAGE.

23. ¿Cómo se caracteriza la vida del protagonista Villaamil?

   (A) Le falta libertad en la vida profesional y la vida personal

   (B) Es religioso y piadoso

   (C) Es un criminal

   (D) Le falta amor

24. ¿Cuándo ejerce Villaamil su libertad por primera vez?

   (A) Cuando se mata

   (B) Cuando deja su trabajo

   (C) Cuando abandona a su familia

   (D) Cuando mata a su jefe

25. ¿Qué papel tiene Luisito?

   (A) Su inocencia es un contraste con la sociedad corrupta.

   (B) Le hace la vida difícil a su abuelo.

   (C) Simboliza el futuro del país.

   (D) Representa la decadencia de la juventud.

26. En términos universales, ¿cómo interpretamos la lucha de Villaamil?

   (A) Es indicativa de sus problemas personales.

   (B) Es una indicación de la decadencia en España.

   (C) Es análoga a la lucha del ser humano con su destino.

   (D) Es símbolo de su inocencia y simpleza.

GO ON TO THE NEXT PAGE.

Poesía lírica y su evolución

Poesía lírica es la que expresa los sentimientos, imaginaciones y pensamientos del autor; es la manifestación de su mundo interno y, por tanto, el
Línea género poético más subjetivo y personal. Hay lirismo
5 recluido en sí, casi totalmente aislado respeto al acaecer exterior; pero más frecuentemente el poeta se inspira en la emoción que han provocado en su alma objetos o hechos externos; éstos, pues, caben en las obras líricas, bien que no como elemento escencial, sino como estímulo
10 de reacciones espirituales. Así, en la oda 'Y dejas, Pastor santo' Fray Luis de León trata de la Ascensión del Señor, que envuelto en una nube va ocultándose a las miradas de los hombres; pero el fondo del poema es el sentimiento de desamparo que acomete a Fray Luis al
15 pensar en el término de la presencia sensible de Jesús en la tierra.

El carácter subjetivo de la poesía lírica no equivale siempre al individualismo exclusivista: el poeta, como miembro integrante de una comunidad humana —
20 religiosa, nacional o de cualquier otro tipo— puede interpretar sentimientos colectivos.

En relación a los demás géneros de poesía, la lírica se distingue por su brevedad, notable incluso en las composiciones más amplias; por la mayor flexibilidad
25 de su disposición, que sigue de cerca los arranques imaginativos o emocionales sin ajustarse a un plan riguroso; y por su gran riqueza de variedades, mucho mayor que la ofrecida por la épica o el teatro.

27. Según la selección, ¿por qué es la poesía lírica el género poético más subjetivo y personal?

    (A) Porque sólo expresa un punto de vista

    (B) Porque es limitado por las leyes del género

    (C) Porque expresa el mundo interior del poeta

    (D) Porque es la manifestación de las reglas líricas

28. ¿En qué se inspira el poeta lírico generalmente?

    (A) En las reglas líricas

    (B) En la emoción provocada en su alma por eventos exteriores

    (C) En la belleza del mundo natural

    (D) En la historia poética

29. En la oda de Fray Luis de León, ¿qué emoción siente el poeta al pensar en el término de la presencia de Jesús en la tierra?

    (A) Abandono

    (B) Tristeza

    (C) Alegría

    (D) Melancolía

30. La poesía lírica se diferencia de los otros géneros poéticos porque tiene

    (A) una forma rígida y rigurosa

    (B) una forma flexible

    (C) una forma tradicional

    (D) una forma épica

31. En términos generales, la poesía lírica se distingue por su

    (A) emoción

    (B) imágenes sensuales

    (C) ritmo musical

    (D) brevedad

GO ON TO THE NEXT PAGE.

La obra dramática está concebida y dispuesta con miras a la representación teatral. Son excepcionales los casos en que no ocurre así; en su mayor parte se trata entonces de
Línea poemas o novelas dialogados, como el *Fausto* de Goethe,
5 la *Celestina*, o la *Dorotea*, de Lope de Vega, que no la llamo comedia ni tragicomedia sino "acción en prosa", indicando su carácter irrepresentable. La finalidad escénica de las obras teatrales les impone determinadas condiciones. La unidad del asunto, deseable en toda
10 creación literaria, es precisa aquí para evitar que la atención de los espectadores, dispersa en hechos inconexos, se debilite o desaparezca. La acción necesita *dinamismo:* la inmovilidad que insiste en una misma nota es propia de la lírica, pues acentúa la expresión intensa
15 de un estado de alma; pero al teatro se va a presenciar un conjunto de hechos palpitantes de vida, cuya sucesión y fluctuaciones mantengan el interés. También se requiere *verosimilitud*, verdad artística profunda en el desarrollo de la acción y los personajes: cada momento, cada rasgo
20 debe tener motivación armónica en lo que antecede. Pero esta verosimilitud no implica forzosamente realismo, pues la obra dramática no es reproducción de la realidad, sino interpretación suya, por lo cual ofrece siempre convencionalismos. El autor puede contar con la
25 fantasía de los espectadores, dispuestos a colaborar con él situándose en el plano conveniente, ideal o real, y a admitir los supuestos necesarios.

32. Según la selección, ¿para qué está creada la obra dramática?

(A) Para ser leída por todos

(B) Para ser examinada por escolares del teatro universal

(C) Para ser presentada

(D) Para formar parte de una celebración religiosa

33. ¿Por qué es importante la unidad del asunto en la obra dramática?

(A) Porque es una de las leyes del género dramático

(B) Porque es una ley de Aristóteles

(C) Porque está relacionada con la limitación escénica

(D) Porque hay que respetar la atención del público

34. ¿En qué manera se requiere dinamismo en la obra dramática?

(A) La acción tiene que ser dinámica.

(B) Los actores tienen que ser dinámicos.

(C) Las reglas del género tienen que ser dinámicas.

(D) La expresión intensa de un estado de alma tiene que ser dinámica.

35. ¿Qué es la verosimilitud?

(A) Realidad

(B) Creatividad

(C) Calidad artística

(D) Acción dinámica

36. ¿En qué sentido es necesario que la obra dramática sea verosímil?

(A) Las acciones tienen que ser una reproducción de la realidad.

(B) Las acciones tienen que tener valor artístico.

(C) Las acciones tienen que tener relación realista y armónica.

(D) Las acciones tienen que ser dinámicas.

GO ON TO THE NEXT PAGE.

El doble

Ya no sé si soy yo o es aquel hombre
que está ahí, frente a mí, o en cualquier parte;
aquél que se disfraza con un nombre
que no es el mío, aunque mi ser comparte.

Línea
5   Aquel ser temeroso y reverente
que mi amistad tímidamente implora,
que unas veces me mira indiferente
y otras sonríe, o se desespera y llora.

El ser que me acompaña y me persigue
10 fatalmente en la ruta, donde sigue
la duda ahondando el porvenir incierto…

No sé quién soy ni sé quién esto escribe,
si soy yo o es el otro, que concibe
y labora por mí, porque yo he muerto.

37. ¿Por qué se escribió el poema?

    (A) Para ilustrar una lección moral

    (B) Para pintar un cuadro

    (C) Para lamentar el pasar del tiempo

    (D) Para expresar la dualidad de la identidad

38. Según el poema, ¿qué hace la voz poética?

    (A) Medita sobre su identidad

    (B) Explica sus ideas estéticas sobre la poesía

    (C) Expresa su amor por sí mismo

    (D) Expresa su visión de la vida

39. ¿Qué contribuye la forma al significado del poema?

    (A) Es una forma alegre para un tópico triste.

    (B) Es una forma clásica dirigida a la identidad, un tópico clásico.

    (C) Es una forma moderna dirigida a la contemplación moderna del "yo".

    (D) Es una forma musical que alivia el tono.

40. En los versos 13–14, "…si soy yo o es el otro, que concibe y labora por mí, porque…"se llama:

    (A) personificación

    (B) paradoja

    (C) anáfora

    (D) clímax

41. ¿Cómo se puede describir el tono de este poema?

    (A) Melancólico

    (B) Alegre

    (C) Trágico

    (D) Amoroso

GO ON TO THE NEXT PAGE.

Cabe distinguir, siguiendo a Ortega y Gasset, dos géneros fundamentales, casi contradictorios, en la novela. Comprende uno las infinitas variedades de
Línea relatos aventureros y narraciones situadas en ambiente
5 fantástico o idílico, todo cuanto interesa por los personajes mismos, extraordinarios y atrayentes, o por la complicación de las peripecias. A ésta, que podríamos llamar novela ilusionista, pertenecen desde los libros de caballerías que secaron el cerebro de Don Quijote, y las
10 ficciones pastoriles gratas a la gente del siglo XVI, hasta las novelas de aventuras, policíacas y folletinescas que hoy sugestionan, en ocasiones con tinte de realidad, a públicos infantiles o despreocupados del goce artístico. El otro género es la novela propiamente realista, que no
15 interesa tanto por las figuras presentadas y los hechos referidos, muchas veces semejantes a los que a cada paso nos ofrece la vida cotidiana, cuanto por la manera de pintarlos, por el veraz estudio de almas y ambientes. Sus dos variedades principales son la *novela psicológica*,
20 primordialmente atenta al análisis de los personajes, y *la novela de costumbres, que se concentra en la fiel* descripción de círculos sociales.

El ideal de la novela es que el autor proceda con objetividad absoluta, sin dividir a sus personajes en
25 buenos y malos, sino pintándolos con la compleja mezcla de virtudes y miserias que ofrece la mayor parte de la Humanidad…

42. Esta selección se trata de:
    (A) el género caballeresco
    (B) el género fantástico
    (C) el género de la novela
    (D) el género pastoril

43. ¿Qué son las dos clases distinguidas en la selección?
    (A) las pastoriles y las caballerescas
    (B) las ilusionistas y las policíacas
    (C) las aventureras y las folletinescas
    (D) las fantásticas y las realistas

44. La importancia de la novela realista, según la selección ested en:
    (A) la descripción de las figuras realistas
    (B) la descripción de las acciones realistas
    (C) la manera de describir las figuras y las acciones
    (D) el retrato de los temas realistas

45. La novela psicológica y la novela de costumbres pertenecen a:
    (A) la novela realista
    (B) la novela moderna
    (C) la novela fantástica
    (D) la novela aventurera

46. La novela psicológica se dedica a:
    (A) la ciencia de la humanidad
    (B) las personalidades de los personajes
    (C) los detalles de la vida cotidiana
    (D) el desarrollo de un argumento complicado

47. La novela de costumbres se dedica a:
    (A) la descripción de la vida social
    (B) la descripción de la vida cotidiana
    (C) la descripción histórica
    (D) la descripción exagerada de los personajes

48. El ideal de la novela realista es:
    (A) describir a los personajes de una forma objetiva
    (B) expresar la opinión personal
    (C) retratar caricaturas
    (D) retratar a los buenos y los malos

GO ON TO THE NEXT PAGE.

Al comenzar el Renacimiento, la atención por lo individual fomentó el desarrollo de la novela sentimental, con un primer análisis de afectos y pasiones. El punto
Línea de arranque fue la *Fiammetta*, de Boccaccio (1313–1375),
5 historia de amor desgraciado que termina con el suicidio de la protagonista. En el siglo XV español lo sentimental aparece frecuentemente asociado con elementos alegóricos y caballerescos, como en la *Cárcel de amor*, de Diego de San Pedro.

10 El mundo idealizado de la égloga, que tanta sugestión ejercía sobre los espíritus del Renacimiento, fue tratado por la novela pastoril, que tiene como tema casi exclusivo el amor: zagales y pastorcitas descubren lacrimosamente sus lacerados corazones; van entrelazándose historias,
15 y al final hay siempre una maga benéfica para dar a todos la felicidad. Por lo general son obras de clave, que con nombres pastoriles aluden a episodios realmente sucedidos.

49. Según la selección, la novela sentimental surgió a causa de:

(A) las novelas pastoriles anteriores

(B) la situación política

(C) las novelas caballerescas

(D) el interés en el individuo

50. En la España del siglo XV, la novela sentimental se asocia con:

(A) un desarrollo psicológico de los personajes

(B) un argumento complicado

(C) unos temas amorosos

(D) unos elementos alegóricos y caballerescos

51. ¿Qué es la égloga?

(A) Es un homenaje a una persona muerta.

(B) Es un poema pastoril.

(C) Es una novela caballeresca.

(D) Es un poema religioso.

52. ¿Qué es el tema principal de la novela pastoril, según la selección?

(A) La muerte

(B) El honor

(C) La historia política

(D) El amor

53. ¿Qué significa en la selección cuando se refiere a las novelas pastoriles como novelas de clave?

(A) Son novelas de alto nivel literario.

(B) Son novelas de fantasía.

(C) Son novelas de fórmula parecida.

(D) Son novelas divertidas.

GO ON TO THE NEXT PAGE.

Eran las cuatro de la tarde. Hacía el típico calor
insoportable de agosto en Andalucía. El sol aplastaba a
las hormigas en sus caminatas por la acera. Mi padre y
Línea yo llegamos jadeantes, medio muertos de sed. Habíamos
5 venido andando ocho kilómetros a pleno sol. No había
ni un coche en la carretera. Íbamos a la casa de mi abuela
cuando de repente, se nos estropeló algo en la rueda
izquierda trasera del coche. No sabíamos si era la llanta
o la rueda misma. Vimos el bar de lejos. No sabíamos
10 si había gente dentro o no, pero era uno de esos bares
donde los dueños vivían por encima del comercio.
Estábamos preparados para llamar a la puerta si hiciera
falta. Teníamos que llamar a un mecánico, pero también
nos habíamos quedado sin comer. Así que nos moríamos
15 de hambre y de sed, y teníamos la rueda estropeada
del coche. Por suerte, la puerta del bar estaba abierta.
Entramos, y vimos a los ancianos del pueblo jugando al
dominó. El dueño estaba sentado con ellos, pero cuando
nos vio se levantó en seguida y nos puso dos bebidas bien
20 frías en la barra. ¡Qué intuición tenía aquel hombre! ¿O
éramos como dos ánimas en pena pasando por la puerta
de su bar? Tomamos las bebidas con gusto y parecía que
recobramos un poco de vida. Llamamos a abuelita y al
mecánico, y por fin se solucionó todo. Llegamos a la casa
25 de abuelita a las once y media de la noche.

54. La acción descrita en este pasaje tiene lugar en:

    (A) un coche y una gasolinera

    (B) la casa de la abuela y el restaurante

    (C) la carretera y un bar

    (D) la calle y el garaje

55. ¿Qué hacía el narrador antes de suceder la acción principal?

    (A) Se iba de vacaciones.

    (B) Iba a visitar a su abuela.

    (C) Iba a trabajar en el garage.

    (D) Iba al bar.

56. ¿Qué tiempo hace?

    (A) Hace frío.

    (B) Hace viento.

    (C) Está nublado.

    (D) Hace mucho sol.

57. ¿Por qué caminan ocho kilómetros?

    (A) Porque quieren hacer ejercicio

    (B) Porque hace buen tiempo

    (C) Porque van a visitar a la abuela

    (D) Porque se estropeló algo en el coche

58. ¿Quiénes estaban dentro del comercio?

    (A) Los dueños

    (B) Los niños del pueblo

    (C) La gente mayor del pueblo

    (D) La abuela

59. ¿Qué hace el dueño del local cuando ve entrar a los dos?

    (A) Se levanta y les sirve dos refrescos.

    (B) Sigue jugando al dominó.

    (C) Los saluda.

    (D) Hace una llamada telefónica.

60. La frase, "¿O éramos como dos ánimas en pena..." (líneas 20–21) es un ejemplo de:

    (A) personificación

    (B) anáfora

    (C) apóstrofe

    (D) símil

61. ¿Cómo contribuye el punto de vista narrativo al significado de la selección?

    (A) Añade un elemento cómico.

    (B) Tiene más impacto para el lector.

    (C) Es más abstracto.

    (D) Es menos personal para el lector.

GO ON TO THE NEXT PAGE.

Todos esperaban ansiosamente la fiesta de disfraces. Empezaba a las siete y media en punto, pero todavía faltaba gente. El viento afuera chillaba cada vez con más
Línea fuerza. Caían relámpagos y truenos. Eran las ocho y
5 cuarto y el último invitado acababa de llegar. Todo estaba preparado para empezar el juego de misterio. Antonio entró corriendo, vestido de vampiro y quejándose de la lluvia tormentosa. El señor Gomez entró en la cocina vestido de vaquero y en ese momento, se apagaron
10 las luces. La señorita. Salas chirrió. Todos se quedaron callados, intentando averiguar si el apagón era parte del juego o no. Pero de repente, un mugido ronco rompió el silencio. El florero de cristal cayó al suelo, despedazado. Después se oyó un golpe fuerte en el suelo. Alguien
15 salió torpemente del salón y saltó por la ventana, quebrantando más vidrio. Por fin el señor Gomez encontró una vela, la encendió y entró en la sala. Allí encontró al pobre Don Gonzalo, el anciano rico caído en el suelo con una herida grave sobre el pecho. ¡Alguien lo
20 mató!

62. ¿Qué describe esta selección?

(A) Un asesinato

(B) Un juego misterioso

(C) Un cambio brusco en el tiempo

(D) Una fiesta de disfraces

63. La frase en la línea 3 "El viento afuera chillaba cada vez con más fuerza", es un ejemplo de:

(A) metáfora

(B) sinestesia

(C) personificación

(D) apóstrofe

64. ¿Por qué entra Antonio corriendo?

(A) Porque llovía

(B) Porque tenía prisa

(C) Porque hacía ejercicio

(D) Porque alguien lo perseguía

65. ¿Por qué se cayó el florero de cristal?

(A) El viento lo derribó al suelo.

(B) La señorita Salas lo tiró al suelo porque tenía miedo.

(C) Don Gonzalo chocó con el florero al caerse al suelo.

(D) El señor Gómez chocó con el florero al buscar la vela.

STOP
END OF SECTION I
IF YOU FINISH BEFORE TIME IS CALLED, YOU MAY CHECK YOUR WORK ON THIS SECTION.
DO NOT GO ON TO SECTION II UNTIL YOU ARE TOLD TO DO SO.

SPANISH LITERATURE

SECTION II

Total Time—1 hour and 50 minutes

Each question counts for 20 percent of the total exam grade.

Directions: Write a coherent and well-organized essay IN SPANISH on the topic that appears below.	*Instrucciones*: Escribe un ensayo coherente y bien organizado EN ESPAÑOL sobre el siguiente tema.

Análisis de poesía

(Suggested time—30 minutes)

1. Analiza la actitud poética hacia el arte de la poesía en el siguiente poema, tomando en cuenta los recursos técnicos y el lenguaje poético que emplea el poeta.

V

Vino, primero, pura
vestida de inocencia.
Y la amé como un niño.

Luego se fue vistiendo
de no sé qué ropajes.
Y la fui odiando, sin saberlo.

Llegó a ser reina,
fastuosa de tesoros…
¡Qué iracundia de yel y sin sentido!

…Mas se fue desnudando.
Y yo le sonreía.

Se quedó con la túnica
de su inocencia antigua.
Creí de nuevo en ella.

Y se quitó la túnica,
y apareció desnuda toda…
¡Oh pasión de mi vida, poesía
desnuda, mía para siempre!

Línea
5

10

15

GO ON TO THE NEXT PAGE.

Directions: Write coherent and well-organized essays IN SPANISH for each of the topics that appear below.

Instrucciones: Escribe ensayos coherentes y bien organizados EN ESPAÑOL sobre cada uno de los siguientes temas.

Análisis temático

(Suggested time—40 minutes)

2. La muerte es uno de los temas que más aparece en la literatura latinoamericana y española.

Escoge UNA de las obras siguientes. Escribe un ensayo que analice este tema en la obra. Tu ensayo debe incluir ejemplos del texto que apoyen tus ideas.

El sur, Jorge Luis Borges

La prodigiosa tarde de Baltazar, Gabriel García Márquez

(Suggested time—40 minutes)

3. Según Ana DiGiulio, crítica y autora de *Enlaces literarios*:

"...*La prodigiosa tarde de Baltazar* es una de las manifestaciones más prolíficas de la relación que enlaza la opulencia con la pobreza. Penetra tanto a los personajes como a cada faceta del cuento. Es a través de esta compleja relación que entendemos que lo rico es pobre y lo pobre es rico."

Refiere al cuento y escribe un ensayo que apoya la afirmación de Ana DiGiulio.

STOP
END OF SECTION II
IF YOU FINISH BEFORE TIME IS CALLED, YOU MAY CHECK YOUR WORK ON THIS SECTION.
DO NOT GO ON TO SECTION II UNTIL YOU ARE TOLD TO DO SO.

14

LITERATURE PRACTICE TEST: ANSWERS AND EXPLANATIONS

LITERATURE PRACTICE TEST
ANSWER KEY

Section I

1.	C	23.	A	45.	A
2.	B	24.	A	46.	B
3.	D	25.	A	47.	A
4.	D	26.	C	48.	A
5.	D	27.	C	49.	D
6.	C	28.	B	50.	D
7.	B	29.	A	51.	B
8.	D	30.	B	52.	D
9.	C	31.	D	53.	C
10.	A	32.	C	54.	C
11.	B	33.	D	55.	B
12.	A	34.	A	56.	D
13.	D	35.	A	57.	D
14.	D	36.	C	58.	C
15.	B	37.	D	59.	A
16.	B	38.	A	60.	D
17.	C	39.	B	61.	B
18.	C	40.	D	62.	A
19.	A	41.	A	63.	C
20.	B	42.	C	64.	A
21.	A	43.	D	65.	C
22.	D	44.	C		

Section II

See explanations beginning on page 258.

SECTION I

Translation of the Reading Comprehension Passage Found on Page 221

Explosion

If life is love, blessed be!
I want more life to love! Today I feel
That a thousand years of thought are worth
Less than one blue minute of feeling.

My heart was dying, sadly and slowly…
Today it opened like a fevered flower;
Life bursts out like a violent sea
Wheresoever the hand of love strikes!

Today I left the cold, sad night,
My melancholy wings broken;
Like an old stain of hurt
In a distant shadow dissolving…
My whole life sings, kisses, laughs!
My whole life is a flowering mouth!

1. Why did the author write this poem?

   (A) To contemplate an abstract idea

   (B) To describe a concrete problem

   (C) To celebrate a strong feeling

   (D) To articulate an absurd belief

The poem as a whole focuses on the effect of love on the poetic narrator. While some may consider love either an abstract idea (A) or an absurd belief (D), the language of the poem clearly indicates that the author considers it a strong feeling. The correct answer is (C).

2. What is the tone of the poem?

   (A) Capricious

   (B) Ecstatic

   (C) Regretful

   (D) Perturbed

The poem associates strong, overwhelming imagery with the emotion of love. The narrator is clearly in an ecstatic state. The correct answer is (B).

3. According to the poem, what is the value of thought?

   (A) Much greater than that of love

   (B) Much less than that of a flower

   (C) Immeasurable

   (D) Much less than that of feeling

Lines 3–4 clearly indicate that thought is valued far less than is feeling. The correct answer is (D).

4. "Life bursts out like a violent sea/ Wheresoever the hand of love strikes!" is called a(n):

(A) alliteration

(B) hyperbole

(C) metonymy

(D) simile

Alliteration is the repetition of the same initial consonant in several words. Hyperbole is an exaggeration of the quality of a being. Metonymy is when a part is used to represent a whole. Simile is when one thing is compared with another to bring an idea to life. These lines compare life with a violent sea, so the correct answer is (D).

5. The title of the poem refers to:

(A) death

(B) a bomb

(C) a heart attack

(D) passion

The explosion that occurs in the poem is an explosion of feeling and love. The best answer is therefore (D), passion.

Translation of the Reading Comprehension Passage Found on Page 222

My grandmother was also the one who took me to see the sea for the first time. One of her daughters had managed to find a reliable husband, and he worked in Gibara, the seaport closest to where we lived. I took a bus for the first time; I think it was also the first time my grandmother, seventy years old, had ever taken a bus. We went to Gibara. My grandmother and the rest of my family had never been to the sea, despite the fact that we lived only thirty or forty kilometers away. I remember the time my Aunt Coralina came in tears to my grandmother's house and said, "Do you know that I'm already forty years old and I've never seen the sea? Any time now I'm going to die, and I'm never going to see it." From that moment, I couldn't do anything but think of the sea.

"The sea swallows a man every day," my grandmother would say. And so I felt an irresistible urge to go to the sea.

What can I say about the first time I was next to the sea! It would be impossible to describe that instant; there's only one word: sea.

6. Why did Aunt Coralina cry?

(A) She was very ill, and was going to die soon.

(B) She had just gone to the sea, and was frightened.

(C) She thought she would never go to the sea.

(D) Grandmother refused to take her to the sea.

We can eliminate (A) because there's no indication she's ill; she's simply afraid she'll die before she can go to the sea. There's no indication that Grandmother refuses to take her, so eliminate (D). Choice (C) is the best answer.

7. What is the narrator's grandmother like?

(A) Happy

(B) Old

(C) Melancholy

(D) Astute

The only answer that's directly supported by the passage is (B).

8. Why does the narrator go to the sea?

(A) To visit his aunt and uncle

(B) Because his aunt's husband had died

(C) So he could take the bus

(D) Because he felt an irresistible pull

The end of the second paragraph provides support for answer choice (D).

9. What does the selection describe?

(A) The narrator's family

(B) A bus trip

(C) The narrator's first trip to the sea

(D) The wedding of the narrator's aunt

Although the passage discusses both (A) and (B), the main focus of the passage is (C).

10. What is the tone of the passage?

(A) Nostalgic

(B) Sad

(C) Sarcastic

(D) Bored

The narrator of the passage is looking back fondly at events from the past, so the best answer is (A).

Translation of the Reading Comprehension Passage Found on Page 223

Once upon a time, there was a man who lived in Buenos Aires. He was very happy because he was healthy and industrious. But one day, he got sick, and his doctors told him that only by going to the countryside could he recover. He didn't want to go because he had younger brothers he had to feed, and so he became sicker with each passing day. Finally, a friend of his, the director of the zoo, told him:

"You are my friend and are a good and industrious man. Because of this, I want you to go live on the mountain, to exercise in the clean air and get better. And since you are an excellent marksman with a rifle, you can hunt the beasts of the mountain and bring me their skins, and I'll pay you beforehand so you can make sure your little brothers eat well."

The sick man accepted, and went to live on the mountain, far away, farther even than Misiones. It was very hot there, and this did the man well.

He lived alone in the forest, and cooked for himself. He ate the birds and beasts of the mountain, which he hunted with his rifle, and he also ate fruit. He slept beneath the trees, and when the weather was bad, he would build a shelter from palm leaves, and pass time there sitting and smoking, very content in the middle of the forest that roared with wind and rain.

11. The action described in the second part of the passage takes place in:

(A) the zoo

(B) a forest on a mountain

(C) the house of the man's younger brothers

(D) Misiones

Eliminate (D) because the mountain is farther away than Misiones. The man never goes to (A) or (C) in the passage. The answer is (B).

---

12. In the beginning, the man refuses to go to the countryside because:

(A) he has to care for his brothers

(B) he still feels healthy

(C) he doesn't like fresh air

(D) he needs to recover before he goes

The man refuses to go because he needs to feed his brothers. The answer is (A). Eliminate (B) because it's clear that he's getting sicker and sicker. Eliminate (D) because going to the country is the only way he will recover.

---

13. How does the man react to bad weather?

(A) It frightens him.

(B) He hunts various beasts.

(C) He eats fruit.

(D) He relaxes.

We're told that when there's bad weather, he quickly builds a small shelter and sits under it, "very content." So the best answer is (D), he relaxes.

---

14. What does the man do for the director of the zoo?

(A) He captures exotic animals.

(B) He gives the director money to buy food for his brothers.

(C) He builds the director a shelter.

(D) He gives the director skins from mountain beasts.

The director asks him to give him the skins of mountain beasts. There's no indication that he captures the animals rather than kills them, so eliminate (A). It's the director who gives food to the man's brothers, so eliminate (B). The best answer is (D).

---

15. At the end of the passage, the man is:

(A) sicker

(B) healthier

(C) happier

(D) poorer

There are several indications that the time in the mountains is good for the man's health. While we're also told that he's happy in the mountains, we know he was happy in the city, so we don't know whether he's happier. The best answer is (B).

Translation of the Reading Comprehension Passage Found on Page 224

Poetry and Verse

Poetry is the highest expression of the literary art. It is characterized as having a primarily aesthetic objective; but this does not mean that the poetic work has to be completely devoid of other objectives: The author can glorify a hero, explain or defend an idea, serve a purpose, court a woman, etc., making use of the very works themselves. The important thing is that in the conception and elaboration of the ideas, the aesthetic objective rises above the ideological or essential motives.

The usual form of poetry is in verse; but the two are not forcefully wed. There is very elegant poetry at times in prose, and at times vulgar verses that do not deserve the name of poetry. This distinction became clearer around 1925 when the thesis of pure poetry surfaced. According to this doctrine, true poetry is not made up of ideas, images, rhymes, words, or sounds: It is something mysterious that from time to time allows itself to seize upon something that the poet says; then the words are infected with the poetic charm, they become electric, and they gain uncommon power. We discover the trace of poetry and we feel the effectiveness of its virtue, but we cannot define it because it is inexpressible and beyond reason. Years before the idea of pure poetry appeared in France, raising a memorable debate, our Bécquer had formulated it with complete clarity; in Rima V the poetry itself says:

> I, in the end, am that spirit
>
> Unknown essence,
>
> Mysterious perfume
>
> Of which the poet is the glass.

16. According to the selection, what general purpose does poetry have?

    (A) It has a didactic purpose.

    (B) It has an aesthetic purpose.

    (C) It has a purpose of social criticism.

    (D) It has a religious purpose.

The purpose of poetry is clearly stated in the beginning of the reading. A given poem may also have any one of the other answer choices stated as a purpose, but note the use of the word "general" in the question. That is, almost all poetry has this purpose, and that is expressed best by answer choice (B).

17. What is the habitual form of poetry?

    (A) Prose

    (B) Drama

    (C) Verse

    (D) Lines

This question is a bit tricky. Most students refer to the verse of a poem even in Spanish as *líneas* when in fact they should be called *versos*. Answer choice (C) is correct.

18. What is pure poetry, according to the passage?

    (A) A poetic secret

    (B) All that the poet says

    (C) Something difficult to define, inexpressible

    (D) A French modernist school of poetry

Remember that you need to answer the question according to what you see in the passage. Pure poetry is defined as something mysterious, ineffable, thus it is difficult to define. Choice (C) is correct.

19. What is suggested by the verses quoted above?

    (A) That poetry is like a mysterious liquor

    (B) That poetry is unknown by the majority of the people

    (C) That poetry is a science

    (D) That poetry is rational and logical

This question is similar to the one preceding it, except that the verses give us a poetic image of poetry, not a rational description of poetry. It is compared with a mysterious perfume, a spirit, and an unknown essence, which is best described by choice (A).

Translation of the Reading Comprehension Passage Found on Page 225

The nineteenth century is an era that has engendered an important production and development of the novel. It begins with the historical and folkloric antecedents seen in the works of Alarcón and Fernán Caballero. Later it continues to develop with the traditionalism and regionalism of Valera and Pereda. At the end of the century, Pardo Bazán initiates a movement toward naturalism, which develops some realistic aspects with greater liberty and fewer inhibitions. Also part of this realistic scheme, and perhaps more universal, is the work of Benito Pérez Galdós. Almost as a midpoint between two extremes, the fecund production of Galdós goes beyond the mere literary era. Specifically, we would like to examine in detail his novel *Miau* as a work reflective of this era but also as a universal novel.

To begin, let's consider the work of his era. As part of the preoccupation of the Spanish reality of that time period, Galdós establishes through his character Villaamil the theme of the individual in society. Related to this main theme are numerous and varied secondary themes; the establishment of the bureaucracy, money, religion, and even some fantastic aspects. We see the fight of Villaamil with the bureaucracy and at the end, his abandonment of the society dominated by it. It is a symbolic battle too, symbolic of Spain's battle to find itself. We see that the ideals of society do not coincide with those of Villaamil. Also notable is his inability to solve problems without using the mechanisms of the bureaucratic society. That is to say that Villaamil is a victim of society but also of his own values, which fit neatly inside the enemy society. His lack of control in government life is complemented by his lack of control in his personal life. His wife, Doña Pura, is always in charge. That is to say that he lacks freedom in his professional life and his personal life. It is understandable later at the end of the novel when he commits suicide and for the first time acts of his own accord, and for the first and last time exercises to the maximum point his precious liberty.

It is also interesting to examine the role of Luisito. Almost parallel to Villaamil, Luisito is also searching for his own role in this society. His juvenile point of view lends even more sensitivity to the violent battle of his grandfather in his attempt to gain another job in the government. More accentuated perhaps is the innocence of Luisito seen in contrast to the mediocrity and corruption of the bureaucratic society. The fantastical aspects seen in his dreams about God illustrate yet another type of innocence or purity that reflect his juvenile experience in a more adult society that is filled with corruption.

Most important, perhaps, is a more abstract or universal reading. Is Villaamil's situation not comparable to our own human experience? Do we not each one of us have to attain a position in the human community in some form or another? In more abstract terms, we can see the battle of Villaamil as the battle of man with his destiny. It is also important to note the role of free will presented in the novel. How tragic that Villaamil did not know how to make use of his free will until the moment of his death! Up to a certain point, therefore, Galdós goes deeper into the human reality and does not limit himself to the character of Villaamil. It is through the novelistic form that Galdós gives us a work that supercedes literary classification. Although part of the realistic work of the nineteenth century, *Miau* goes even further. Through this work Galdós speaks to us about profound issues relative to our human condition. These are the types of works that give us pause for thought about our own lives and makes the study of literature worthwhile.

20. How is Galdós's narrative characterized?

    (A) It is a naturalistic narrative.

    (B) It is a realistic narrative.

    (C) It is a folkloric narrative.

    (D) It is a surrealistic narrative.

In the opening paragraph of the reading, the work of Galdós is classified as part of the realistic scheme. Some of the other answer choices are mentioned, but after careful consideration of the reading, (B) is clearly the correct answer.

21. What is the general theme of *Miau*?

    (A) The role of the individual in society

    (B) Man in search of his own identity

    (C) War

    (D) Love

The correct answer, choice (A), becomes clear after careful consideration of the reading. Choices (C) and (D) can be fairly easily eliminated because they seem too general, and you may remember that they are not even mentioned in the reading.

22. According to the selection, all of these ideas are secondary themes EXCEPT:

    (A) religion

    (B) money

    (C) government

    (D) love

If you can see government as another way of stating bureaucracy, then your answer choice is clear; choice (D), love, is the only secondary theme not mentioned in the passage.

23. How is the life of the protagonist Villaamil characterized?

    (A) By a lack of freedom in his professional and personal life

    (B) By his religious and pious devotions

    (C) By his criminal behavior

    (D) By his lack of love

In this case the best looking answer is the first one, so go with it. The other choices are designed to confuse you or lead you astray. There is no reference to choices (B), (C), and (D) in the passage.

24. When does Villaamil exercise his free will for the first time?

    (A) When he kills himself

    (B) When he quits his job

    (C) When he abandons his family

    (D) When he kills his boss

Unfortunately for Villaamil, (A) is the correct choice. None of the other choices is mentioned in the passage, although (B) may seem like a logical choice. Remember to answer the question according to the information in the passage.

25. What role does Luisito have?

    (A) His innocence contrasts with the corrupt society.

    (B) He makes life difficult for his grandfather.

    (C) He symbolizes the future of the country.

    (D) He represents the decadence of youth.

The passage makes various references to the innocence of Luisito. In fact, it also states that his innocence is a sharp contrast to the corruption of society.

26. In universal terms, how are we to interpret the battle of Villaamil?

    (A) It is indicative of his personal problems.

    (B) It is an indication of the decadence in Spain.

    (C) It is analogous to the battle of man with his own destiny.

    (D) It is a symbol of innocence and simplicity.

Choices (A) and (B) may in fact be true but do not really answer the question given. Choice (D) would apply more aptly to Luisito. The correct answer is (C).

Translation of the Reading Comprehension Passage Found on Page 227

Lyric Poetry and Its Evolution

Lyric poetry is that which expresses the feelings, imagination, and thoughts of the author. It is the manifestation of his or her internal world and, therefore, the most subjective and personal poetic genre. There is lyricism confined to itself, almost completely isolated with respect to the exterior occurrences; but more frequently the poet takes inspiration from the emotions aroused in his soul by external objects or events; these, of course, fit into the lyrical works, if not as an essential element than as a stimulus of spiritual reactions. Thus, in the ode, "*Y dejas, Pastor Santo*," Fray Luis de León deals with the Ascension of the Lord, that enveloped in a cloud proceeds upward hiding itself from the gazes of men; but the depth of the poem is the feeling of helplessness that overtakes Fray Luis as he thinks of the end of the sensitive presence of Christ on Earth.

The subjective character of lyric poetry is not always equivalent to exclusive individualism: The poet, as an integral member of a human community—religious, national or whatever other type—can interpret collective feelings.

In relationship to the other poetic genres, lyric poetry is distinct because of its brevity, notable even in the longest compositions; it is also distinguished by its greater flexibility of its organization, which closely follows the imaginative or emotional beginnings without adapting itself to a rigorous plan; and lyric poetry is also distinguished by its great richness of varieties, much greater than that offered by the epic or the theater.

27. According to the selection, why is lyric poetry the most personal and subjective poetic genre?

    (A) Because it expresses only one point of view

    (B) Because it is limited by the laws of the genre

    (C) Because it expresses the interior world of the poet

    (D) Because it is the manifestation of the rules of lyric poetry

Choice (D) makes little sense in the context of the question and can be easily eliminated. Choice (B) doesn't make much more sense. Both (A) and (C) are plausible answers. If you closely examine the passage, however, you'll see that the *mundo interno* refers to the internal world of the poet.

28. How does the lyric poet get inspiration generally?

    (A) From study of the rules of the lyric genre

    (B) From the emotion felt in his soul as a result of external events

    (C) From the beauty of the natural world

    (D) From poetic history

Remember that this is a general question, which requires a general answer. Choice (A) is too specific and therefore is easily cancelled. Choices (C) and (D) are never mentioned in the reading, thus the correct answer is choice (B).

29. In the ode of Fray Luis de León, what emotion does the poet feel when he thinks of the end of the presence of Christ here on Earth?

   (A) Abandonment

   (B) Sadness

   (C) Happiness

   (D) Melancholy

Choice (C) can be quickly eliminated because it is very unlikely. Choices (A), (B), and (D) are all valid choices. After returning to the text, however, you would zero in on the word *desamparo*, which means "abandonment," so that makes (A) the correct answer.

30. Lyric poetry is distinct from other poetic genres because it has:

   (A) a rigid and rigorous form

   (B) a flexible form

   (C) a traditional form

   (D) an epic form

Choices (C) and (D) are similar enough to eliminate both. Lyric poetry would not be distinct from other poetry because it had a traditional or epic form. Choices (A) and (B) contradict one another, so one must be the correct answer. After returning to the text, you would see that (B) is the correct answer.

31. In general terms, lyric poetry is distinguishable because of its:

   (A) emotion

   (B) sensual images

   (C) musical cadence

   (D) brevity

This question is a bit tricky. Choices (A), (B), and (C) are all characteristics of most poetry. Choice (D) may seem like a wrong answer, but it really is the right one. After returning to the text, you would discover that easily.

Translation of the Reading Comprehension Passage Found on Page 228

The dramatic work is conceived and well-disposed for theatrical representation. The cases in which it does not occur in this manner are unusual; for the most part, they are poems or novels in dialogue like *Faust* by Goethe, or the *Celestina* or the *Dorotea* by Lope de Vega, which he didn't call tragicomedies but rather "action in prose," indicating its character that made it impossible to present. The scenic finality of the theatrical works imposes upon them determined conditions. Unity of subject matter, desirable in all literary creations, is needed here to avoid losing the attention of the spectators to the details of unconnected actions. The action needs to be dynamic: immobility that insists on one note is typical of the lyric genre because it accentuates the intense expression of the state of the soul; but in the theater one is witness to palpitating facts of life whose succession and fluctuations maintain interest. Verisimilitude is also needed, that is, deep, artistic truth is needed in the development of the action and of the characters: Each moment, each characteristic should have a harmonious motivation based on what preceded it. But this verisimilitude does not forcefully imply realism because the dramatic work is not a reproduction of reality but rather an interpretation of it. The author can count on the fantasy of the spectators, who are prepared to collaborate with him situating themselves on a convenient level, ideal or real, to admit the necessary suppositions.

32. According to the selection, for what purpose is the dramatic work created?

   (A) In order to be read by everyone

   (B) In order to be examined by the scholars of the universal theater

   (C) In order to be presented

   (D) In order to form part of a religious celebration

If you use your common sense, a dramatic work is created in order to be presented on stage, not to be read, which eliminates (A), nor to be studied, which cancels (B). In most cases it is not intended as a religious celebration, which eliminates (D). The correct answer choice is (C).

33. Why is the unity of subject matter important to the dramatic work?

(A) Because it is one of the laws of the dramatic genre

(B) Because it is a law of Aristotle

(C) Because it is related to the scenery limitations

(D) Because it is important to maintain the public's attention

This is a simple question really, though some of the answers give reason for second-guessing your first instincts. A play is written to be performed. To be successful, it must hold the attention of the audience. Although Aristotle is a heavyweight in the field of literary criticism, his opinions are not needed here, so (B) can be canceled. The scenery limitations will exist regardless of the subject matter, which eliminates (C). Choice (A) is easily canceled if you use common sense; choose the most logical answer. Sometimes your first instincts lead you directly to the correct answer, in this case, choice (D).

34. In what way is dynamism needed in the dramatic work?

(A) The action needs to be dynamic.

(B) The actors need to be dynamic.

(C) The rules of the genre need to be dynamic.

(D) The intense expression of a state of the soul needs to be dynamic.

This question also can be answered with a bit of common sense. Choice (D) is vague and therefore easily eliminated. Choice (C) is too general to be an appropriate answer, so it too can be canceled. Both (A) and (B) are really true statements, but according to the passage, (A) is the correct answer.

35. What is verisimilitude?

(A) Reality

(B) Creativity

(C) Artistic quality

(D) Dynamic action

This is a simple vocabulary question, if you know the meaning of verisimilitude. It is realism or reality.

36. In what way is it necessary for the dramatic work to be verisimilar?

(A) The actions must be a reproduction of reality.

(B) The actions must have artistic value.

(C) The actions must have a realistic and harmonious relationship.

(D) The actions must be dynamic.

Choice (A) is a direct contradiction to what is stated above in the passage and therefore should be eliminated. Choices (B), (C), and (D) may all be true, but only (C) is expressed in the passage above.

Translation of the Reading Comprehension Passage Found on Page 229

The Double

I no longer know if it is I or is it that man
who is there, in front of me, or in anyplace;
that one who disguises himself with a name
that is not mine, although my being he shares

That fearful and reverent being
that my friendship timidly implores,
who sometimes looks at me indifferently
and other times smiles, becomes desperate and cries

The being that accompanies me and follows me
fatally along the route where he follows
the doubt deepening in the uncertain future...
I don't know who I am nor who is writing this
if it is I or the other one, who conceives
and works for me because I have died.

37. Why was the poem written?

    (A) To illustrate a moral lesson
    (B) To paint a picture
    (C) To lament the passage of time
    (D) To express the duality of identity

These poetry questions are much easier than you may think. You don't need to come up with the literary analysis—just pick out the correct answers. They give you the questions as well, so don't be intimidated by these poetry passages. Remember to follow the tips in Chapter 10 on reading poetry: Read the poem as if it were prose, which means ignoring the poetic form while reading for content. Also pay very close attention to punctuation. You don't need to explicate the poems in this section of the test, but it helps if you know how to read them. In the question above, all of the answer choices are valid reasons for writing a poem, but only one applies to this particular poem.

38. According to the poem, what does the poetic voice do?

    (A) Meditates on his identity
    (B) Explains his aesthetic ideas on poetry
    (C) Expresses his self-love
    (D) Expresses his vision on life

Again, all of the above answer choices are valid answers, but only (A) refers to this particular poem. The various references to "I" versus "that man" make that answer choice clear.

39. What does the form contribute to the meaning of the poem?

(A) It is a happy form for a sad topic.

(B) It is a classical form directed to a classical topic.

(C) It is a modern form directed to the modern contemplation of the "I."

(D) The musicality of the form alleviates the seriousness of the tone.

If you can identify the form of the poem, this question becomes much easier. It is a sonnet, which is a classical form and appropriate for the meditation of identity, and has preoccupied mankind for centuries. The other answer choices may be tempting (although (A) should be easily eliminated), particularly the wording of choices (C) and (D), but notice that none actually identify the form. Without actually using the name, they are checking to see if you can identify the importance of the sonnet.

40. The poetic device in lines 7–8, "who sometimes looks at me indifferently and other times smiles, or becomes desperate and cries…" is called:

(A) personification

(B) paradox

(C) anaphora

(D) climax

This question is easy if you know your literary terms. This verse describes a progressing sentiment, which is best defined by choice (D), climax, which is a series or chain of thoughts that follow an ascending or a descending progression. Climax is sometimes called gradation. Of the other answer choices, (B) is the most appealing wrong answer, but there is more than paradox expressed in these verses. Choices (A) and (C) do not apply.

41. How can the tone of this poem be described best?

(A) Melancholic

(B) Happy

(C) Tragic

(D) Loving

Answer choices (B) and (D) can be easily eliminated because there really is nothing in the poem to suggest happiness or love. It then becomes a choice between (A), melancholy, and (C), tragic. You need to decide if the final verse ending with "I have died," and perhaps, in the second stanza, the verse that talks about becoming desperate and crying, justify a tragic tone. It is best to go with choice (A). The tone is more melancholic as he meditates on his own identity. Either way, you have greatly increased your chances of getting the correct answer by eliminating (B) and (D).

Translation of the Reading Comprehension Passage Found on Page 230

It is worth distinguishing, according to Ortega y Gasset, two fundamental genres almost contradictory in the novel. One is made up of the infinite varieties of adventure stories and narratives situated in a fantastic or idyllic atmosphere, all that is of interest to the very characters, extraordinary and attractive or by the complication of a change of fortune. This one, which we can call an illusionist novel, consists of chivalrous novels that dried up the brain of Don Quixote; the pastoral fictions so enjoyed by the people of the sixteenth century, even the adventure novels, police novels, and serial novels that today, occasionally with a tint of reality, influence the young public, who remain unconcerned with artistic pleasure. The other genre is the properly realistic novel, which isn't of interest because of the characters presented and the details described many times in similar fashion to that which may happen to us at any given time in daily life, but rather for the manner in which they are portrayed, for the truthful study of souls and atmospheres. The two main varieties are the psychological novel, primarily attentive to the analysis of the characters, and the folkloric novel, with accurate descriptions of the social circles.

The ideal of the novel is that the author proceeds with absolute objectivity, without dividing his characters into the good guys and the bad guys but rather painting them with the complex mix of virtues and misery that is offered to the majority of humanity.

42. This selection deals with:

   (A) the chivalrous genre

   (B) the fantastic genre

   (C) the genre of the novel

   (D) the pastoral genre

This is a general question so remember to look for the most general answer. Choice (C) is the correct answer.

43. What are the two distinct classes defined in this passage?

   (A) Pastoral and chivalrous stories

   (B) Illusionist and police stories

   (C) Adventure and serial stories

   (D) Fantastic and realistic stories

Though the passage has long and detailed sentences, the structure is clearly marked by "One" (genre) and "The other genre" so we know that they are talking about fantastic and realistic novels. Choices (A), (B), and (C) are all mentioned in the passage, but do not answer the question being asked.

44. The importance of the realistic novel, according to the selection is:

   (A) realistic figures

   (B) realistic action

   (C) the manner in which actions and figures are described

   (D) the themes

When you go back to the passage, the correct answer choice becomes clear: It is necessary for both the actions and the figures to be described in a realistic manner.

45. The psychological novel and the folkloric novel pertain to:

   (A) the realistic novel

   (B) the modern novel

   (C) the fantastic novel

   (D) the adventure novel

When introducing the second genre in the passage, the author immediately describes two types of realistic novels, so the correct answer is (A). The correct answer may be surprising to you; it may even contradict your gut reaction to the question, but be sure to base your answer on the information contained in the passage.

46. The psychological novel is devoted to:

(A) the science of humanity

(B) the personalities of the characters

(C) the details of daily life

(D) the development of a complicated plot

Answer choice (A) is clearly designed to lead you away from the passage. It would seem the logical choice, but according to the reading, (B) is the correct answer.

47. The folkloric novel is devoted to:

(A) the description of social life

(B) the description of daily life

(C) the historical life

(D) the exaggerated description of the characters

Again, remember to follow the passage; in this case it is quite simple to find the *novela de costumbres* and see the following definition of it, the "faithful description of social circles." (In Spanish the term *costumbres* is clearer in this context because it refers to customs, as in social customs.)

48. The ideal of the realistic novel is:

(A) to describe the characters in an objective manner

(B) to express a personal opinion

(C) to portray caricatures

(D) to portray the good and the bad

The key to this question of course is *sin* (without) in the passage above. Thus, the correct answer is (A), to portray characters in an objective manner.

Translation of the Reading Comprehension Passage Found on Page 231

At the beginning of the Renaissance, the interest in the individual sparked the development of the sentimental novel, with a primary analysis of emotions and passions. The starting point was the *Fiammetta* by Boccaccio (1313–1375), a story of unlucky love that ends with the suicide of the protagonist. In the fifteenth century in Spain, the sentimental novel appears frequently associated with allegorical and chivalrous elements, as in the *Cárcel de amor*, by Diego de San Pedro.

The idealized world of the eclogue, which so influenced the spirit of the Renaissance, was treated in the pastoral novel, which had love almost as its exclusive theme: Young lassies and shepherdesses uncover tearfully their lacerated hearts; they proceed intertwining stories, and at the end there is always a kind genie that makes everyone happy. In general they are formula works, with pastoral names that allude to events from reality.

49. According to the passage, the sentimental novel came about because of:

(A) the earlier pastoral novels

(B) the political situation

(C) the chivalrous novels

(D) the interest in the individual

Based on the passage above, the interest in the individual led to the development of the sentimental novel.

50. In the Spain of the fifteenth century, the sentimental novel is associated with:

    (A) a psychological development of the characters

    (B) a complicated plot

    (C) love themes

    (D) allegorical and chivalrous elements

If you return to the passage above, you will easily see the correct answer, choice (D).

51. What is the eclogue?

    (A) It is a tribute to a dead person.

    (B) It is a pastoral poem.

    (C) It is a chivalrous novel.

    (D) It is a religious poem.

Answer choice (A) is trying to confuse you with the word elegy in English. Don't be fooled! Look back at the passage, and you will see that *égloga* is a pastoral poem.

52. What is the main theme in the pastoral novel, according to the selection?

    (A) Death

    (B) Honor

    (C) Political history

    (D) Love

In fact, love is almost the exclusive theme of the pastoral novel, so choice (D) is the clear answer here.

53. What does it mean in the passage when it refers to pastoral novels as key novels?

    (A) They are novels of high literary value.

    (B) They are fantastic novels.

    (C) They are novels of similar formulas.

    (D) They are fun novels.

Pastoral novels are formula novels, which means they all have the same format, with a few different names here and there. They are not of very high literary value at all. They may be fun, but that is not what is meant by the word *clave* in Spanish.

Translation of the Reading Comprehension Passage Found on Page 232

It was four in the afternoon. It was typically hot with the unbearable heat of August in Andalucia. The sun was squashing the ants in their busy walks around the sidewalk. My father and I arrived panting, half-dead from thirst. We had walked eight kilometers in the full sun. There was not one car on the highway. We were going to Grandmother's house when suddenly something in the rear left wheel broke down. We couldn't tell if it was the tire or the wheel itself. We saw the bar from afar. We didn't know if there were people inside, but it was one of those bars where the owners live above the business. We were prepared to ring the outside bell if it were necessary. We had to call a mechanic, but we had also skipped lunch. So we were dying of thirst and hunger, and we had a broken wheel on the car. Fortunately, the door of the bar was open. We went in, and we saw the old folks from the village playing dominos. The owner was seated with them, but as soon as he saw us enter he got up right away and served us two cold drinks. What intuition that man had! Or was it that we looked like two souls in purgatory passing by the door of his bar? We drank the drinks with gusto, and it seemed that we were recovering a bit of life. We called Grandmother and the mechanic and finally solved everything. We got to Grandmother's house at eleven-thirty that night.

54. The action described in this passage takes place in:

   (A) a car and a gas station

   (B) Grandmother's house and the restaurant

   (C) the highway and a bar

   (D) the street and the garage

The two walk along the highway and finally find a bar, so (C) is the best answer choice.

55. What was the narrator doing before the main action occurred?

   (A) He was going on vacation.

   (B) He was going to visit his grandmother.

   (C) He was going to work in the garage.

   (D) He was going to the bar.

Both the narrator and his father are going to visit Grandmother.

56. What is the weather like?

   (A) It is cold.

   (B) It is windy.

   (C) It is cloudy.

   (D) It is very sunny.

The narrator complains of the hot sun, so (D) is the best choice.

57. Why do they walk eight kilometers?

    (A) Because they want to get some exercise

    (B) Because it is nice outside

    (C) Because they are going to visit grandmother

    (D) Because something broke down on the car

To be precise, the rear left wheel broke, so choice (D) is the best answer.

58. Who was inside the place of business?

    (A) The owners

    (B) The children of the village

    (C) The older people of the village

    (D) Grandmother

The word used in the passage is *ancianos*, which is actually a cognate, similar to the English word ancient. The old folks are in the bar. Yes, the owner is there too, but there is no reference to owners in the plural, and certainly there is reference to *ancianos*.

59. What does the owner do when he sees them enter?

    (A) He gets up and serves them two drinks.

    (B) He continues playing dominos.

    (C) He greets them.

    (D) He makes a phone call.

He was playing dominos, but *en seguida* means "right away," and implies an action, so (A) is the best choice.

60. The phrase, "Or was it that we looked like two souls in purgatory…" (line 22) is an example of:

    (A) personification

    (B) anaphora

    (C) apostrophe

    (D) simile

Of course you will know all of your literary terms before test day so this question would be easy; it is even without any studying for many of you. A simile is a comparison using "like" or "as," which is introduced by *como* in Spanish.

61. What does the narrative point of view contribute to the meaning of this passage?

    (A) It adds a comic element.

    (B) It has more impact for the reader.

    (C) It is more abstract.

    (D) It is less personal for the reader.

This is a favorite topic for the test writers. They love questions on point of view. The point of view in this passage is first person plural or "we," which personalizes the text for the reader, and therefore gives it more impact. Choice (B) is the best answer.

Translation of the Reading Comprehension Passage Found on Page 233

Everyone was waiting with anticipation for the costume party. It began at seven-thirty sharp, but many people had not yet arrived. The wind outside screamed each moment with greater force. There was thunder and lightning. It was eight-fifteen, and the last guest had just arrived. Everything was ready to begin the mystery game. Antonio entered on the run dressed as a vampire and complaining of the changeable weather. Mr. Gómez entered the kitchen dressed as a cowboy and at that moment, the lights went out. Miss Salas squealed. Everyone else was quiet, trying to determine if the power outage was part of the game or not. But suddenly, a hoarse bellow broke the silence. The crystal vase fell to the floor, shattering. Then a strong blow to the floor was heard. Someone left clumsily through the living room and jumped through the window. Finally Mr. Gómez found a candle, lit it, and entered the living room. There he found poor Don Gonzalo, the rich old man, fallen on the floor with a grave blow to the chest. Someone had murdered him!

62. What does this passage describe?

    (A) a murder

    (B) a mysterious game

    (C) an abrupt change in the weather

    (D) a costume party

All of these answers relate to the reading, but the one that best describes the content of the entire passage is choice (A).

63. The phrase in line 3 "the wind screamed each moment with greater force," is an example of:

    (A) metaphor

    (B) synesthesia

    (C) personification

    (D) apostrophe

This question, too, is testing for your knowledge of literary terminology. The wind does not normally scream, so choice (C), personification, is the best answer.

64. Why did Antonio enter on the run?

    (A) because it was raining

    (B) because he was in a hurry

    (C) because he was getting some exercise

    (D) because someone was chasing him

Choices (C) and (D) are not mentioned in the passage. Both (B) and (A) are valid answers, but if you examine the text closely, you will see that he complains about the rain, so we may infer that the rain caused him to run in the door, not his tardiness. Choice (A) is best.

65. Why did the crystal vase fall?

    (A) The wind knocked it down.

    (B) Miss Salas threw it on the floor in fright.

    (C) Don Gonzalo crashed into the vase when he fell to the floor.

    (D) Mr. Gómez crashed into the vase while looking for a candle.

Again, we are to infer that Don Gonzalo knocked into the vase because he fell down dead. The passage describes only the loud noises heard by the other characters. Choice (C) is the best answer.

SECTION II

THE POETRY ESSAY QUESTION

Translation of the Poetry Question Found on Page 234

1. Analyze the poetic attitude toward the art of poetry in the following poem, taking into consideration the poetic techniques and the poetic language employed by the poet.

V

She came, first, pure
dressed in innocence.
And I loved her like a child.

Later, she began dressing herself
with I don't know what clothing.
And I began hating her without knowing why.

She became a queen,
ostentatious with all of her treasures
What anger and wrath, all without meaning!

…But she began undressing.
And I smiled at her.

She remained clothed by the tunic
of her former innocence.
I believed in her again.

And she took off her tunic,
And appeared completely naked…
Oh, passion of my life, naked
poetry, mine always!

Sample Student Essay

El arte de la poesía es el ejercicio de escribir versos. En este poema vemos la emoción muy intensa del poeta hacia su arte, el de escribir versos. La relación pintada en el poema es muy íntima y amorosa, retratando la poesía como a una mujer amada. A través del poema, vemos la progresión de emoción del poeta empezando con un amor inocente y puro, pasando al odio y la desilusión, y terminando con un amor simple y pasional. El poeta claramente prefiere la poesía simple y pura, no le interesa la poesía ornamentada.

El poeta nos está dando su visión artística de lo que debe ser la poesía. Es un poema simple, sin rima que corresponde a la preferencia del poeta por los versos simples. Son seis estrofas simples y cortas, de tres a cuatro versos principalmente pero con una estrofa casi a mitad del poema de dos versos que marca un cambio en la progresión de emoción. Después de "…Más se fue desnudando…" la progresión de la emoción negativa cesa y se convierte en emoción amorosa de nuevo.

El lenguaje del poema es simple y corresponde con la noción de la poesía simple. Pero al mismo tiempo es un lenguaje con varios niveles de interpretación. Usa un lenguaje informal, pero muy emotivo. Los verbos amar y odiar y palabras como iracundia y "pasión de mi vida" expresan el nivel intenso de la emoción del poema. La mayoría de los verbos están en el pretérito para expresar la relación pasada negativa. Pero las palabras en el verso final del poema ("mía para siempre") ilustran la relación amorosa perdurable. El uso de los gerundios (vistiendo, odiando, desnudando) pone más énfasis en la progresión de emoción, sugiriendo que la relación entre el poeta y el arte poético estaba en cambio continuo hasta la resolución armoniosa al final.

El poeta habla principalmente de la poesía en tercera persona, pero al final emplea el apóstrofe para hacer más inmediata la relación entre el poeta y su amada poesía. Las palabras que se refieren a vestirse, o la forma de adornarse como "ropajes" y "tesoros" sugieren la técnica elaborada poética empleada por otros poetas. La "túnica", en contraste, es la ropa más simple, sin adorno y representa la forma preferida por el poeta aquí. Aún más fuerte es la imagen en la última estrofa, de la poesía desnuda y libre de toda técnica, que es la pasión más fuerte del poeta. Los puntos exclamativos al final marcan la intensidad de emoción del poeta, que culmina con la imagen de la mujer amada desnuda.

Así que hay dos conceptos principales en oposición en el poema. La primera parte del poema culmina con la imagen odiada de la poesía ornamental y complicada técnicamente. La segunda parte del poema pinta la imagen opuesta de la poesía más simple y pura. El tono del poema revela la progresión de emoción, ilustrando el cambio de tono y el correspondiente cambio de emoción. Es un poema simple pero muy bonito. Todo lo importante en la vida debe ser así de simple y puro.

Translation of the Sample Student Essay

The art of poetry is the exercise of writing verses. In this poem we see the very intense emotion of the poet towards his craft, that of writing verses. The relationship described in the poem is very intimate, very loving, portraying poetry as a woman who is deeply loved. Throughout the poem we see the progression of the poet's emotion starting with pure, innocent love, turning into hateful, angry disillusionment, and ending with simple passionate love. The poet clearly prefers simple and pure poetry, not ornamental poetry.

The poet is giving us his poetic vision on what poetry should be. It is a simple poem, without rhyme, which corresponds to the poet's preference for simple verses. There are six simple and short stanzas, of three to four verses each, though there is one stanza of two verses almost in the middle of the poem that marks a change in the progression of emotion. After, "…But she began undressing…" the progression of negative emotion halts and changes to a loving emotion once again.

The language of the poem is simple and corresponds to the notion of simple poetry. But at the same time it is language with various levels of interpretation. The language is informal, but very emotive. The verbs to love and to hate, and words like wrath and "passion of my life" express the intense level of emotion in the poem. The majority of the verbs are in the preterite to express the past negative relationship. But the words in the final verse of the poem ("mine always") illustrate the lasting loving relationship. The use of the gerunds (dressing, hating, undressing) puts more emphasis on the progression of emotion, suggesting that the relationship between the poet and his poetic art was in continuous flux until the harmonious resolution illustrated at the end of the poem.

The poet talks about poetry principally in the third person, but at the end uses apostrophe to make the relationship more immediate between the poet and his beloved poetry. The words that refer to dressing, or adornments such as clothing, and treasures suggest the elaborate technique employed perhaps by other poets. The tunic, in contrast, is the most simple form of attire, without adornment, and represents the poet's preferred form for the art of poetry. Even more powerful is the image in the last stanza of naked poetry, free from all technique, which is the great passion of the poet. The exclamation points at the end mark the intensity of emotion of the poet that culminates with the image of the beloved naked woman.

Thus, there are two main concepts in opposition in the poem. The first part of the poem culminates with the despised image of ornamental poetry, with complicated poetic techniques. The second part of the poem paints the opposing image of the most simple and pure poetry. The tone of the poem reveals the progression of emotion, illustrating the change of tone and the corresponding change of emotion. It is a simple, but very beautiful poem. All of the important things in life should be as simple and as pure.

Explanation

This is a high-scoring essay because it gets right to the heart of the question from the very first paragraph. Notice how he defines his terms, how he understands the poetic attitude toward the art of poetry. He talks about emotions right away and identifies the progression of emotion, which is an excellent way of demonstrating his understanding of the poem as a whole. The strong command of language suggests that this essay was written by a native speaking student, but that shouldn't intimidate you. The real strength of this essay is in its analysis of the poem. In the second paragraph he reiterates the poetic vision, which, after all, is the attitude of the poet toward the art of poetry. This essay is very clearly directed at the question being asked. There is also discussion of the tone and of the language used by the poet, particularly verb forms. The image of a naked woman and the unnecessary ornate clothing and adornments is also discussed fully. Notice too how he ends the essay with a summarized discussion of opposition, which is very pertinent to this poem. Although this may not be the best explication of a poem that you have ever read, it certainly does what is needed to score well on the AP exam!

THE ONE-AUTHOR ESSAY QUESTION

Translation of One-Author (Essay) Question Found on Page 235

Death is one of the themes that appears most in Latin American and Spanish literature. Choose ONE of the following works. Write an essay that analyzes this theme in the work. Be sure to use examples from the text that support your ideas.

Sample Student Essay

La muerte es una consecuencia impersonal de la vida de varios personajes de Borges. Es un resultado de unas circunstancias históricas, muchas veces hostiles a la victima. No es necesariamente un escape de un mundo horrible, como en otros autores. Tampoco es una experiencia religiosa, Incluso puede ser accidental o casual, particularmente durante momentos claves y difíciles en la vida de uno. Es la consecuencia simple de vivir en un universo impersonal y caótico. Al mismo tiempo, la muerte en sí es una forma de valor a una vida que no haya llegado a su cima. En "El sur" vemos varias presentaciones de la muerte que sugieren un universo impersonal y frecuentemente hostil al individuo, pero al mismo tiempo ayudan a dar valor a una vida terminada.

En "El sur" Juan Dahlmann elige la muerte romántica de su antepasado soldadesco. Quiere morir de manera romántica en vez de manera enfermiza o deshonrada. Esta muerte es una fabricación de su muerte perfecta que ocurre mientras se está muriendo en el hospital. Sale de la realidad y entra en un mundo irreal y fantástico. En una tienda cerca de su vieja casa, muere en una lucha de cuchillos. El orgullo, criollismo, y valor del ser gaucho lo hace sentir importante, valorado, y que su vida sirvió algún propósito en la Tierra. Esta muerte imaginada le permite morir con dignidad. La muerte de Dahlmann también sirve para definir más, y aún glorificar su vida. Como lectores sabemos que Dahlmann no podrá ganar la batalla a cuchilladas con los gauchos. Pero Dahlmann valerosamente acepta su destino en un esfuerzo para definir mejor su vida anteriormente poco heroica. Parece importarle poco que pague con su vida. Su muerte también resulta de unas circunstancias hostiles, de mala suerte para Dahlmann. Su presencia en aquel bar donde están también sentados aquellos guachos es completamente accidental. Como lectores, de nuevo sentimos la injusticia de una muerte sin sentido. Dahlmann tiene la mala suerte de encontrarse en una situación hostil y violenta. Su muerte es la consecuencia impersonal de un universo caótico sin sentido.

En la obras de Borges, y en particular en el cuento "El sur" la muerte es el paso final en un laberinto de la experiencia humana. En el caso de Dahlmann, la muerte le da la oportunidad de mejorar o perfeccionar su vida, a pesar de que sus esfuerzos son inútiles en un universo impersonal y caótico.

Translation of Sample Student Essay

Death is an impersonal consequence of life for various characters of Borges. It is a result of particular historical circumstances, in many cases, circumstances that are hostile to the victim. It is not necessarily an escape from a horrible world, as with other authors. Nor is it a religious experience. In fact, it can be accidental or casual, particularly during key and difficult moments in one's life. It is the simple consequence of living in an impersonal and chaotic universe. At the same time, death itself is a form of value to a life that has not reached its summit. In "El sur" we see various presentations of death that suggest an impersonal universe, frequently hostile to the individual, but at the same time they help to give value to a life that has ended.

In "El sur" Juan Dahlmann chooses the romantic death of his forebear, the soldier. He prefers to die romantically rather than a sickly or cowardly death. This death is a fabrication in his mind of the perfect death that occurs while he is dying in the hospital. He leaves reality and enters an unreal and fantastic world. In a store near his old home, he dies in a knife fight. The pride, local flavor, and the value of being a gaucho makes him feel important, valued, and that his life on Earth serves some purpose. This imagined death allows him to die with dignity. Dahlmann's death also serves to further define and glorify his life. As readers, we know that Dahlmann cannot win the knife battle with the gauchos. But he bravely accepts his destiny in an effort to glorify his previously unheroic life. It appears of little importance to him to pay with his life. His death also results from bad timing, hostile circumstances that Dahlmann walked into by complete chance. His presence in that bar where the gauchos are also seated is completely accidental. As readers, we again are struck by the injustice of another meaningless death. Dahlmann has the bad luck to find himself in a hostile and violent situation. His death is the impersonal consequence of a chaotic and meaningless universe.

In the works of Borges, in particular "El sur," death is the final step in the impersonal labyrinth of human experience. In the case of Dahlmann, death is a means by which he improves or perfects his life, futile as his efforts may be, in such an impersonal and chaotic universe.

Explanation

Remember that this is a classic one-author Spanish AP question. You need to be certain to define the topic and how it applies to the works you studied. This essay has a strong discussion of death in Borges. Notice again how well she defines her terms in the opening paragraph. There is a bit of plot summary, but notice how it all relates to the illustration of her ideas. The concluding paragraph does a good job of tying the main ideas together, although it is too bad that the idea of opposition or contrast is not more fully developed. Nonetheless, this too is a high scoring essay. She demonstrates a clear understanding of the readings. And she certainly addresses the question being asked. Remember: Your essays don't have to be perfect. Just follow The Princeton Review's condensed outline format—it won't let you down.

The Critical Excerpt Essay Question

Translation of the Critical Excerpt Essay Question Found on Page 235

According to Ana DiGiulio, critic and author of *Enlaces literarios*:

"…La prodigiosa tarde de Baltazar is one of the most prolific manifestations of the relation that links wealth with poverty. It penetrates not only the characters, but every facet of the story. It is through this complex relationships that we understand that rich is poor and poor is rich."

Refer to the story and write an essay that supports the critique of Ana DiGuilio.

Sample Student Essay

En el cuento "La prodigiosa tarde de Baltazar" vemos una glorificación de los pobres y una presentación negativa de los ricos. El lector llega a entender que el dinero no trae felicidad. Presenciamos esto en la tristeza del niño de Montiel. Tiene todo lo que necesita gracias a la posición elevada de su familia en la sociedad. Por el contrario, Baltazar vive simplemente, pero está contento con su vida ya que tiene su novia y no se aflige por su falta de riqueza material. En la familia Montiel, se ve que el dinero y la vida do privilegio no traen ni la paz ni ol rospeto. Es una familia pobre de espíritu y calor humano. En realidad, Márquez demuestra que las mejores cosas en la vida no cuestan nada.

La jaula es la clave al poder y es ahí donde se convierte el marginado en el rico y el privilegiado en el necesitado. Es un poco irónico que una jaula pueda representar una manera de ganarse la libertad, ya sea económica o personalmente. Con la venta de la jaula, Baltazar podrá escapar la monotonía y dureza de su vida. Y aunque él realmente necesita vender la jaula, por su bondad decide obsequiársela al niño. Sin embargo, se enriquece aun más al darle la jaula al niño, ya que éste puede escapar de la falta de felicidad que abarca su vida familiar. También recibe gran apoyo de sus compañeros, y quiere hacerles feliz, una vez más a costo propio. Baltazar nació pobre, pero por la creación de la jaula y su gran acto bondadoso, termina siendo un ser divino. Su manera de actuar es similar a los hombres sabios de la Biblia, y su generosidad y amistad sin esperar nada a cambio lo hace parecer a Jesús, quien también era carpintero.

En resumen, las posesiones y la riqueza jamás podrán reemplazar la sensación de libertad y poder que uno experimenta al estar libre de mente y espíritu. Ser libre es ser rico. El hecho de que un hombre pobre pueda tener la mayor felicidad posible con una vida sencilla afirma que la riqueza es algo relativo y personal para cada uno de nosotros. También, como afirma DiGuilio, Baltazar y el niño representan dos lados que hasta se completan y se complementan, aunque superficialmente sean ajenos y opuestos.

Translation of Sample Student Essay

In the short story "La prodigiosa tarde de Baltazar" we see a glorification of the poor and a negative presentation of the rich. The reader comes to understand that money does not bring happiness. We see this in the sadness of the Montiel boy. He has everything he needs, thanks to the high status of his family in society. Conversely, Baltazar lives simply, but is happy with his life as he has his girlfriend and is not depressed by his lack of material wealth. In the Montiel family, we see that money and a life of privilege do not yield peace or respect. It is a family poor in spirit and human warmth. In reality, Márquez shows that the best things in life don't cost anything.

The cage is the key to power and it is here where the outcast becomes rich and where the rich become needy. It is slightly ironic that a cage can represent a means through which one becomes free, either economically or personally. With the sale of his cage, Baltazar can escape the hardship and monotony of his life. And although he really needs to sell this cage, out of his kindness, he decides to give the cage to the boy. However, he becomes even richer upon giving the cage to the boy as he allows the youngster to escape the lack of happiness that penetrates his family life. He also receives great accolades from his peers, and looks to bring them happiness, once again at his own expense. Baltazar was born poor but through the creation of the cage and his kind act, he winds up becoming a divine being. His way of being is similar to that of the wise men of the Bible, and his generosity and friendship in exchange for nothing make him appear like Jesus, who was also a carpenter.

In summary, possessions and wealth could never replace the sensation of freedom and power that one experiences when one has a free mind and spirit. To be free is to be rich. The fact that a man can have the greatest joy possible from a simple lifestyle affirms that wealth is something relative and personal for each one of us. Also, as DiGuilio explains, Baltazar and the boy represent two sides that actually complete and compliment each other, even though superficially they may be complete opposites.

Explanation

This essay has a strong flow and some unique points that are sure to impress the readers. Notice that the writer kept summarizing to a minimum. The biblical references show great insight and originality, and deep analysis like this is probably not common in many student answers. Original, creative thought always impresses the readers. In order to help yourself develop this skill, you should also read outside critiques of the texts on the reading list. This will help you focus on interesting insights, symbolism, and comparisons when writing your essays.

ABOUT THE AUTHOR

Mary Leech has been teaching AP Spanish at Rye Country Day since 1989. She lives with her husband in Bedford, New York.

Completely darken bubbles with a No. 2 pencil. If you make a mistake, be sure to erase mark completely. Erase all stray marks.

1. YOUR NAME:
(Print) _____ Last _____ First _____ M.I. _____

SIGNATURE: _____ DATE: ___ / ___ / ___

HOME ADDRESS: _____
(Print) _____ Number and Street

_____ City _____ State _____ Zip Code

PHONE NO. : _____
(Print)

5. YOUR NAME

First 4 letters of last name				FIRST INIT	MID INIT
Ⓐ	Ⓐ	Ⓐ	Ⓐ	Ⓐ	Ⓐ
Ⓑ	Ⓑ	Ⓑ	Ⓑ	Ⓑ	Ⓑ
Ⓒ	Ⓒ	Ⓒ	Ⓒ	Ⓒ	Ⓒ
Ⓓ	Ⓓ	Ⓓ	Ⓓ	Ⓓ	Ⓓ
Ⓔ	Ⓔ	Ⓔ	Ⓔ	Ⓔ	Ⓔ
Ⓕ	Ⓕ	Ⓕ	Ⓕ	Ⓕ	Ⓕ
Ⓖ	Ⓖ	Ⓖ	Ⓖ	Ⓖ	Ⓖ
Ⓗ	Ⓗ	Ⓗ	Ⓗ	Ⓗ	Ⓗ
Ⓘ	Ⓘ	Ⓘ	Ⓘ	Ⓘ	Ⓘ
Ⓙ	Ⓙ	Ⓙ	Ⓙ	Ⓙ	Ⓙ
Ⓚ	Ⓚ	Ⓚ	Ⓚ	Ⓚ	Ⓚ
Ⓛ	Ⓛ	Ⓛ	Ⓛ	Ⓛ	Ⓛ
Ⓜ	Ⓜ	Ⓜ	Ⓜ	Ⓜ	Ⓜ
Ⓝ	Ⓝ	Ⓝ	Ⓝ	Ⓝ	Ⓝ
Ⓞ	Ⓞ	Ⓞ	Ⓞ	Ⓞ	Ⓞ
Ⓟ	Ⓟ	Ⓟ	Ⓟ	Ⓟ	Ⓟ
Ⓠ	Ⓠ	Ⓠ	Ⓠ	Ⓠ	Ⓠ
Ⓡ	Ⓡ	Ⓡ	Ⓡ	Ⓡ	Ⓡ
Ⓢ	Ⓢ	Ⓢ	Ⓢ	Ⓢ	Ⓢ
Ⓣ	Ⓣ	Ⓣ	Ⓣ	Ⓣ	Ⓣ
Ⓤ	Ⓤ	Ⓤ	Ⓤ	Ⓤ	Ⓤ
Ⓥ	Ⓥ	Ⓥ	Ⓥ	Ⓥ	Ⓥ
Ⓦ	Ⓦ	Ⓦ	Ⓦ	Ⓦ	Ⓦ
Ⓧ	Ⓧ	Ⓧ	Ⓧ	Ⓧ	Ⓧ
Ⓨ	Ⓨ	Ⓨ	Ⓨ	Ⓨ	Ⓨ
Ⓩ	Ⓩ	Ⓩ	Ⓩ	Ⓩ	Ⓩ

IMPORTANT: Please fill in these boxes exactly as shown on the back cover of your test book.

2. TEST FORM

3. TEST CODE

4. REGISTRATION NUMBER

0	Ⓐ	0	0	0	0	0	0	0	0	0
1	Ⓑ	1	1	1	1	1	1	1	1	1
2	Ⓒ	2	2	2	2	2	2	2	2	2
3	Ⓓ	3	3	3	3	3	3	3	3	3
4	Ⓔ	4	4	4	4	4	4	4	4	4
5	Ⓕ	5	5	5	5	5	5	5	5	5
6	Ⓖ	6	6	6	6	6	6	6	6	6
7		7	7	7	7	7	7	7	7	7
8		8	8	8	8	8	8	8	8	8
9		9	9	9	9	9	9	9	9	9

6. DATE OF BIRTH

Month		Day		Year	
◯ JAN					
◯ FEB					
◯ MAR	0	0	0	0	
◯ APR	1	1	1	1	
◯ MAY	2	2	2	2	
◯ JUN	3	3	3	3	
◯ JUL		4	4	4	
◯ AUG		5	5	5	
◯ SEP		7	7	7	
◯ OCT		8	8	8	
◯ NOV		9	9	9	
◯ DEC					

7. SEX
◯ MALE
◯ FEMALE

The Princeton Review
© The Princeton Review, Inc.
FORM NO. 00001-PR

Section ①

Start with number 1 for each new section.
If a section has fewer questions than answer spaces, leave the extra answer spaces blank.

1. Ⓐ Ⓑ Ⓒ Ⓓ
2. Ⓐ Ⓑ Ⓒ Ⓓ
3. Ⓐ Ⓑ Ⓒ Ⓓ
4. Ⓐ Ⓑ Ⓒ Ⓓ
5. Ⓐ Ⓑ Ⓒ Ⓓ
6. Ⓐ Ⓑ Ⓒ Ⓓ
7. Ⓐ Ⓑ Ⓒ Ⓓ
8. Ⓐ Ⓑ Ⓒ Ⓓ
9. Ⓐ Ⓑ Ⓒ Ⓓ
10. Ⓐ Ⓑ Ⓒ Ⓓ
11. Ⓐ Ⓑ Ⓒ Ⓓ
12. Ⓐ Ⓑ Ⓒ Ⓓ
13. Ⓐ Ⓑ Ⓒ Ⓓ
14. Ⓐ Ⓑ Ⓒ Ⓓ
15. Ⓐ Ⓑ Ⓒ Ⓓ
16. Ⓐ Ⓑ Ⓒ Ⓓ
17. Ⓐ Ⓑ Ⓒ Ⓓ
18. Ⓐ Ⓑ Ⓒ Ⓓ
19. Ⓐ Ⓑ Ⓒ Ⓓ
20. Ⓐ Ⓑ Ⓒ Ⓓ
21. Ⓐ Ⓑ Ⓒ Ⓓ
22. Ⓐ Ⓑ Ⓒ Ⓓ
23. Ⓐ Ⓑ Ⓒ Ⓓ
24. Ⓐ Ⓑ Ⓒ Ⓓ
25. Ⓐ Ⓑ Ⓒ Ⓓ
26. Ⓐ Ⓑ Ⓒ Ⓓ
27. Ⓐ Ⓑ Ⓒ Ⓓ
28. Ⓐ Ⓑ Ⓒ Ⓓ
29. Ⓐ Ⓑ Ⓒ Ⓓ
30. Ⓐ Ⓑ Ⓒ Ⓓ

31. Ⓐ Ⓑ Ⓒ Ⓓ
32. Ⓐ Ⓑ Ⓒ Ⓓ
33. Ⓐ Ⓑ Ⓒ Ⓓ
34. Ⓐ Ⓑ Ⓒ Ⓓ
35. Ⓐ Ⓑ Ⓒ Ⓓ
36. Ⓐ Ⓑ Ⓒ Ⓓ
37. Ⓐ Ⓑ Ⓒ Ⓓ
38. Ⓐ Ⓑ Ⓒ Ⓓ
39. Ⓐ Ⓑ Ⓒ Ⓓ
40. Ⓐ Ⓑ Ⓒ Ⓓ
41. Ⓐ Ⓑ Ⓒ Ⓓ
42. Ⓐ Ⓑ Ⓒ Ⓓ
43. Ⓐ Ⓑ Ⓒ Ⓓ
44. Ⓐ Ⓑ Ⓒ Ⓓ
45. Ⓐ Ⓑ Ⓒ Ⓓ
46. Ⓐ Ⓑ Ⓒ Ⓓ
47. Ⓐ Ⓑ Ⓒ Ⓓ
48. Ⓐ Ⓑ Ⓒ Ⓓ
49. Ⓐ Ⓑ Ⓒ Ⓓ
50. Ⓐ Ⓑ Ⓒ Ⓓ
51. Ⓐ Ⓑ Ⓒ Ⓓ
52. Ⓐ Ⓑ Ⓒ Ⓓ
53. Ⓐ Ⓑ Ⓒ Ⓓ
54. Ⓐ Ⓑ Ⓒ Ⓓ
55. Ⓐ Ⓑ Ⓒ Ⓓ
56. Ⓐ Ⓑ Ⓒ Ⓓ
57. Ⓐ Ⓑ Ⓒ Ⓓ
58. Ⓐ Ⓑ Ⓒ Ⓓ
59. Ⓐ Ⓑ Ⓒ Ⓓ
60. Ⓐ Ⓑ Ⓒ Ⓓ

61. Ⓐ Ⓑ Ⓒ Ⓓ
62. Ⓐ Ⓑ Ⓒ Ⓓ
63. Ⓐ Ⓑ Ⓒ Ⓓ
64. Ⓐ Ⓑ Ⓒ Ⓓ
65. Ⓐ Ⓑ Ⓒ Ⓓ
66. Ⓐ Ⓑ Ⓒ Ⓓ
67. Ⓐ Ⓑ Ⓒ Ⓓ
68. Ⓐ Ⓑ Ⓒ Ⓓ
69. Ⓐ Ⓑ Ⓒ Ⓓ
70. Ⓐ Ⓑ Ⓒ Ⓓ
71. Ⓐ Ⓑ Ⓒ Ⓓ
72. Ⓐ Ⓑ Ⓒ Ⓓ
73. Ⓐ Ⓑ Ⓒ Ⓓ
74. Ⓐ Ⓑ Ⓒ Ⓓ
75. Ⓐ Ⓑ Ⓒ Ⓓ
76. Ⓐ Ⓑ Ⓒ Ⓓ
77. Ⓐ Ⓑ Ⓒ Ⓓ
78. Ⓐ Ⓑ Ⓒ Ⓓ
79. Ⓐ Ⓑ Ⓒ Ⓓ
80. Ⓐ Ⓑ Ⓒ Ⓓ
81. Ⓐ Ⓑ Ⓒ Ⓓ
82. Ⓐ Ⓑ Ⓒ Ⓓ
83. Ⓐ Ⓑ Ⓒ Ⓓ
84. Ⓐ Ⓑ Ⓒ Ⓓ
85. Ⓐ Ⓑ Ⓒ Ⓓ
86. Ⓐ Ⓑ Ⓒ Ⓓ
87. Ⓐ Ⓑ Ⓒ Ⓓ
88. Ⓐ Ⓑ Ⓒ Ⓓ
89. Ⓐ Ⓑ Ⓒ Ⓓ
90. Ⓐ Ⓑ Ⓒ Ⓓ

91. Ⓐ Ⓑ Ⓒ Ⓓ
92. Ⓐ Ⓑ Ⓒ Ⓓ
93. Ⓐ Ⓑ Ⓒ Ⓓ
94. Ⓐ Ⓑ Ⓒ Ⓓ
95. Ⓐ Ⓑ Ⓒ Ⓓ
96. Ⓐ Ⓑ Ⓒ Ⓓ
97. Ⓐ Ⓑ Ⓒ Ⓓ
98. Ⓐ Ⓑ Ⓒ Ⓓ
99. Ⓐ Ⓑ Ⓒ Ⓓ
100. Ⓐ Ⓑ Ⓒ Ⓓ
101. Ⓐ Ⓑ Ⓒ Ⓓ
102. Ⓐ Ⓑ Ⓒ Ⓓ
103. Ⓐ Ⓑ Ⓒ Ⓓ
104. Ⓐ Ⓑ Ⓒ Ⓓ
105. Ⓐ Ⓑ Ⓒ Ⓓ
106. Ⓐ Ⓑ Ⓒ Ⓓ
107. Ⓐ Ⓑ Ⓒ Ⓓ
108. Ⓐ Ⓑ Ⓒ Ⓓ
109. Ⓐ Ⓑ Ⓒ Ⓓ
110. Ⓐ Ⓑ Ⓒ Ⓓ
111. Ⓐ Ⓑ Ⓒ Ⓓ
112. Ⓐ Ⓑ Ⓒ Ⓓ
113. Ⓐ Ⓑ Ⓒ Ⓓ
114. Ⓐ Ⓑ Ⓒ Ⓓ
115. Ⓐ Ⓑ Ⓒ Ⓓ
116. Ⓐ Ⓑ Ⓒ Ⓓ
117. Ⓐ Ⓑ Ⓒ Ⓓ
118. Ⓐ Ⓑ Ⓒ Ⓓ
119. Ⓐ Ⓑ Ⓒ Ⓓ
120. Ⓐ Ⓑ Ⓒ Ⓓ

The Princeton Review

Completely darken bubbles with a No. 2 pencil. If you make a mistake, be sure to erase mark completely. Erase all stray marks.

1. YOUR NAME:
(Print)
Last   First   M.I.

SIGNATURE: _____ DATE: ___/___/___

HOME ADDRESS: _____
(Print)
Number and Street

City   State   Zip Code

PHONE NO. : _____
(Print)

5. YOUR NAME

First 4 letters of last name				FIRST INIT	MID INIT
Ⓐ	Ⓐ	Ⓐ	Ⓐ	Ⓐ	Ⓐ
Ⓑ	Ⓑ	Ⓑ	Ⓑ	Ⓑ	Ⓑ
Ⓒ	Ⓒ	Ⓒ	Ⓒ	Ⓒ	Ⓒ
Ⓓ	Ⓓ	Ⓓ	Ⓓ	Ⓓ	Ⓓ
Ⓔ	Ⓔ	Ⓔ	Ⓔ	Ⓔ	Ⓔ
Ⓕ	Ⓕ	Ⓕ	Ⓕ	Ⓕ	Ⓕ
Ⓖ	Ⓖ	Ⓖ	Ⓖ	Ⓖ	Ⓖ
Ⓗ	Ⓗ	Ⓗ	Ⓗ	Ⓗ	Ⓗ
Ⓘ	Ⓘ	Ⓘ	Ⓘ	Ⓘ	Ⓘ
Ⓙ	Ⓙ	Ⓙ	Ⓙ	Ⓙ	Ⓙ
Ⓚ	Ⓚ	Ⓚ	Ⓚ	Ⓚ	Ⓚ
Ⓛ	Ⓛ	Ⓛ	Ⓛ	Ⓛ	Ⓛ
Ⓜ	Ⓜ	Ⓜ	Ⓜ	Ⓜ	Ⓜ
Ⓝ	Ⓝ	Ⓝ	Ⓝ	Ⓝ	Ⓝ
Ⓞ	Ⓞ	Ⓞ	Ⓞ	Ⓞ	Ⓞ
Ⓟ	Ⓟ	Ⓟ	Ⓟ	Ⓟ	Ⓟ
Ⓠ	Ⓠ	Ⓠ	Ⓠ	Ⓠ	Ⓠ
Ⓡ	Ⓡ	Ⓡ	Ⓡ	Ⓡ	Ⓡ
Ⓢ	Ⓢ	Ⓢ	Ⓢ	Ⓢ	Ⓢ
Ⓣ	Ⓣ	Ⓣ	Ⓣ	Ⓣ	Ⓣ
Ⓤ	Ⓤ	Ⓤ	Ⓤ	Ⓤ	Ⓤ
Ⓥ	Ⓥ	Ⓥ	Ⓥ	Ⓥ	Ⓥ
Ⓦ	Ⓦ	Ⓦ	Ⓦ	Ⓦ	Ⓦ
Ⓧ	Ⓧ	Ⓧ	Ⓧ	Ⓧ	Ⓧ
Ⓨ	Ⓨ	Ⓨ	Ⓨ	Ⓨ	Ⓨ
Ⓩ	Ⓩ	Ⓩ	Ⓩ	Ⓩ	Ⓩ

IMPORTANT: Please fill in these boxes exactly as shown on the back cover of your test book.

2. TEST FORM

3. TEST CODE

4. REGISTRATION NUMBER

⓪	Ⓐ	⓪	⓪	⓪	⓪	⓪	⓪	⓪	⓪	⓪	⓪
①	Ⓑ	①	①	①	①	①	①	①	①	①	①
②	Ⓒ	②	②	②	②	②	②	②	②	②	②
③	Ⓓ	③	③	③	③	③	③	③	③	③	③
④	Ⓔ	④	④	④	④	④	④	④	④	④	④
⑤	Ⓕ	⑤	⑤	⑤	⑤	⑤	⑤	⑤	⑤	⑤	⑤
⑦	Ⓖ	⑦	⑦	⑦	⑦	⑦	⑦	⑦	⑦	⑦	⑦
⑧		⑧	⑧	⑧	⑧	⑧	⑧	⑧	⑧	⑧	⑧
⑨		⑨	⑨	⑨	⑨	⑨	⑨	⑨	⑨	⑨	⑨

6. DATE OF BIRTH

Month		Day		Year	
◯ JAN					
◯ FEB					
◯ MAR	Ⓤ	Ⓤ	Ⓤ	Ⓤ	
◯ APR	①	①	①	①	
◯ MAY	②	②	②	②	
◯ JUN	③	③	③	③	
◯ JUL		④	④	④	
◯ AUG		⑤	⑤	⑤	
◯ SEP		⑦	⑦	⑦	
◯ OCT		⑧	⑧	⑧	
◯ NOV		⑨	⑨	⑨	
◯ DEC					

7. SEX
◯ MALE
◯ FEMALE

The Princeton Review
© The Princeton Review, Inc.
FORM NO. 00001-PR

Section 1
Start with number 1 for each new section.
If a section has fewer questions than answer spaces, leave the extra answer spaces blank.

1. Ⓐ Ⓑ Ⓒ Ⓓ   31. Ⓐ Ⓑ Ⓒ Ⓓ   61. Ⓐ Ⓑ Ⓒ Ⓓ   91. Ⓐ Ⓑ Ⓒ Ⓓ
2. Ⓐ Ⓑ Ⓒ Ⓓ   32. Ⓐ Ⓑ Ⓒ Ⓓ   62. Ⓐ Ⓑ Ⓒ Ⓓ   92. Ⓐ Ⓑ Ⓒ Ⓓ
3. Ⓐ Ⓑ Ⓒ Ⓓ   33. Ⓐ Ⓑ Ⓒ Ⓓ   63. Ⓐ Ⓑ Ⓒ Ⓓ   93. Ⓐ Ⓑ Ⓒ Ⓓ
4. Ⓐ Ⓑ Ⓒ Ⓓ   34. Ⓐ Ⓑ Ⓒ Ⓓ   64. Ⓐ Ⓑ Ⓒ Ⓓ   94. Ⓐ Ⓑ Ⓒ Ⓓ
5. Ⓐ Ⓑ Ⓒ Ⓓ   35. Ⓐ Ⓑ Ⓒ Ⓓ   65. Ⓐ Ⓑ Ⓒ Ⓓ   95. Ⓐ Ⓑ Ⓒ Ⓓ
6. Ⓐ Ⓑ Ⓒ Ⓓ   36. Ⓐ Ⓑ Ⓒ Ⓓ   66. Ⓐ Ⓑ Ⓒ Ⓓ   96. Ⓐ Ⓑ Ⓒ Ⓓ
7. Ⓐ Ⓑ Ⓒ Ⓓ   37. Ⓐ Ⓑ Ⓒ Ⓓ   67. Ⓐ Ⓑ Ⓒ Ⓓ   97. Ⓐ Ⓑ Ⓒ Ⓓ
8. Ⓐ Ⓑ Ⓒ Ⓓ   38. Ⓐ Ⓑ Ⓒ Ⓓ   68. Ⓐ Ⓑ Ⓒ Ⓓ   98. Ⓐ Ⓑ Ⓒ Ⓓ
9. Ⓐ Ⓑ Ⓒ Ⓓ   39. Ⓐ Ⓑ Ⓒ Ⓓ   69. Ⓐ Ⓑ Ⓒ Ⓓ   99. Ⓐ Ⓑ Ⓒ Ⓓ
10. Ⓐ Ⓑ Ⓒ Ⓓ   40. Ⓐ Ⓑ Ⓒ Ⓓ   70. Ⓐ Ⓑ Ⓒ Ⓓ   100. Ⓐ Ⓑ Ⓒ Ⓓ
11. Ⓐ Ⓑ Ⓒ Ⓓ   41. Ⓐ Ⓑ Ⓒ Ⓓ   71. Ⓐ Ⓑ Ⓒ Ⓓ   101. Ⓐ Ⓑ Ⓒ Ⓓ
12. Ⓐ Ⓑ Ⓒ Ⓓ   42. Ⓐ Ⓑ Ⓒ Ⓓ   72. Ⓐ Ⓑ Ⓒ Ⓓ   102. Ⓐ Ⓑ Ⓒ Ⓓ
13. Ⓐ Ⓑ Ⓒ Ⓓ   43. Ⓐ Ⓑ Ⓒ Ⓓ   73. Ⓐ Ⓑ Ⓒ Ⓓ   103. Ⓐ Ⓑ Ⓒ Ⓓ
14. Ⓐ Ⓑ Ⓒ Ⓓ   44. Ⓐ Ⓑ Ⓒ Ⓓ   74. Ⓐ Ⓑ Ⓒ Ⓓ   104. Ⓐ Ⓑ Ⓒ Ⓓ
15. Ⓐ Ⓑ Ⓒ Ⓓ   45. Ⓐ Ⓑ Ⓒ Ⓓ   75. Ⓐ Ⓑ Ⓒ Ⓓ   105. Ⓐ Ⓑ Ⓒ Ⓓ
16. Ⓐ Ⓑ Ⓒ Ⓓ   46. Ⓐ Ⓑ Ⓒ Ⓓ   76. Ⓐ Ⓑ Ⓒ Ⓓ   106. Ⓐ Ⓑ Ⓒ Ⓓ
17. Ⓐ Ⓑ Ⓒ Ⓓ   47. Ⓐ Ⓑ Ⓒ Ⓓ   77. Ⓐ Ⓑ Ⓒ Ⓓ   107. Ⓐ Ⓑ Ⓒ Ⓓ
18. Ⓐ Ⓑ Ⓒ Ⓓ   48. Ⓐ Ⓑ Ⓒ Ⓓ   78. Ⓐ Ⓑ Ⓒ Ⓓ   108. Ⓐ Ⓑ Ⓒ Ⓓ
19. Ⓐ Ⓑ Ⓒ Ⓓ   49. Ⓐ Ⓑ Ⓒ Ⓓ   79. Ⓐ Ⓑ Ⓒ Ⓓ   109. Ⓐ Ⓑ Ⓒ Ⓓ
20. Ⓐ Ⓑ Ⓒ Ⓓ   50. Ⓐ Ⓑ Ⓒ Ⓓ   80. Ⓐ Ⓑ Ⓒ Ⓓ   110. Ⓐ Ⓑ Ⓒ Ⓓ
21. Ⓐ Ⓑ Ⓒ Ⓓ   51. Ⓐ Ⓑ Ⓒ Ⓓ   81. Ⓐ Ⓑ Ⓒ Ⓓ   111. Ⓐ Ⓑ Ⓒ Ⓓ
22. Ⓐ Ⓑ Ⓒ Ⓓ   52. Ⓐ Ⓑ Ⓒ Ⓓ   82. Ⓐ Ⓑ Ⓒ Ⓓ   112. Ⓐ Ⓑ Ⓒ Ⓓ
23. Ⓐ Ⓑ Ⓒ Ⓓ   53. Ⓐ Ⓑ Ⓒ Ⓓ   83. Ⓐ Ⓑ Ⓒ Ⓓ   113. Ⓐ Ⓑ Ⓒ Ⓓ
24. Ⓐ Ⓑ Ⓒ Ⓓ   54. Ⓐ Ⓑ Ⓒ Ⓓ   84. Ⓐ Ⓑ Ⓒ Ⓓ   114. Ⓐ Ⓑ Ⓒ Ⓓ
25. Ⓐ Ⓑ Ⓒ Ⓓ   55. Ⓐ Ⓑ Ⓒ Ⓓ   85. Ⓐ Ⓑ Ⓒ Ⓓ   115. Ⓐ Ⓑ Ⓒ Ⓓ
26. Ⓐ Ⓑ Ⓒ Ⓓ   56. Ⓐ Ⓑ Ⓒ Ⓓ   86. Ⓐ Ⓑ Ⓒ Ⓓ   116. Ⓐ Ⓑ Ⓒ Ⓓ
27. Ⓐ Ⓑ Ⓒ Ⓓ   57. Ⓐ Ⓑ Ⓒ Ⓓ   87. Ⓐ Ⓑ Ⓒ Ⓓ   117. Ⓐ Ⓑ Ⓒ Ⓓ
28. Ⓐ Ⓑ Ⓒ Ⓓ   58. Ⓐ Ⓑ Ⓒ Ⓓ   88. Ⓐ Ⓑ Ⓒ Ⓓ   118. Ⓐ Ⓑ Ⓒ Ⓓ
29. Ⓐ Ⓑ Ⓒ Ⓓ   59. Ⓐ Ⓑ Ⓒ Ⓓ   89. Ⓐ Ⓑ Ⓒ Ⓓ   119. Ⓐ Ⓑ Ⓒ Ⓓ
30. Ⓐ Ⓑ Ⓒ Ⓓ   60. Ⓐ Ⓑ Ⓒ Ⓓ   90. Ⓐ Ⓑ Ⓒ Ⓓ   120. Ⓐ Ⓑ Ⓒ Ⓓ

NOTES

NOTES

NOTES

NOTES

NOTES

NOTES

NOTES

Navigate the admissions process with more guidance from the experts.

Ace the APs:

Cracking the AP Biology Exam, 2013 Edition
978-0-307-94508-2 • $18.99/$21.99 Can.
Ebook: 978-0-307-94580-8

Cracking the AP Calculus AB & BC Exams, 2013 Edition
978-0-307-94486-3 • $19.99/$23.99 Can.
Ebook: 978-0-307-94451-1

Cracking the AP Chemistry Exam, 2013 Edition
978-0-307-94488-7 • $18.99/$21.99 Can.
Ebook: 978-0-307-94452-8

Cracking the AP Economics Macro & Micro Exams, 2013 Edition
978-0-307-94509-9 • $18.00/$21.00 Can.
Ebook: 978-0-307-94581-5

Cracking the AP English Language & Composition Exam, 2013 Edition
978-0-307-94511-2 • $18.00/$21.00 Can.
Ebook: 978-0-307-94582-2

Cracking the AP English Literature & Composition Exam, 2013 Edition
978-0-307-94512-9 • $18.00/$21.00 Can.
Ebook: 978-0-307-94583-9

Cracking the AP Environmental Science Exam, 2013 Edition
978-0-307-94513-6 • $18.99/$21.99 Can.
Ebook: 978-0-307-94584-6

Cracking the AP European History Exam, 2013 Edition
978-0-307-94489-4 • $18.99/$21.99 Can.
Ebook: 978-0-307-94453-5

Cracking the AP Human Geography Exam, 2013 Edition
978-0-307-94514-3 • $18.00/$21.00 Can.

Cracking the AP Physics B Exam, 2013 Edition
978-0-307-94515-0 • $18.99/$21.99 Can.
Ebook: 978-0-307-94585-3

Cracking the AP Physics C Exam, 2013 Edition
978-0-307-94516-7 • $18.99/$21.99 Can.

Cracking the AP Psychology Exam, 2013 Edition
978-0-307-94517-4 • $18.00/$21.00 Can.
Ebook: 978-0-307-94586-0

Cracking the AP Spanish Exam with Audio CD, 2013 Edition
978-0-307-94518-1 • $24.99/$28.99 Can.

Cracking the AP Statistics Exam, 2013 Edition
978-0-307-94519-8 • $19.99/$23.99 Can.

Cracking the AP U.S. Government & Politics Exam, 2013 Edition
978-0-307-94520-4 • $18.99/$21.99 Can.
Ebook: 978-0-307-94587-7

Cracking the AP U.S. History Exam, 2013 Edition
978-0-307-94490-7 • $18.99/$21.99 Can.
Ebook: 978-0-307-94447-4

Cracking the AP World History Exam, 2013 Edition
978-0-307-94491-7 • $18.99/$21.99 Can.
Ebook: 978-0-307-94445-0

Essential AP Biology (flashcards)
978-0-375-42803-6 • $18.99/$20.99 Can.

Essential AP Psychology (flashcards)
978-0-375-42801-2 • $18.99/$20.99 Can.

Essential AP U.S. Government & Politics (flashcards)
978-0-375-42804-3 • $18.99/$20.99 Can.

Essential AP U.S. History (flashcards)
978-0-375-42800-5 • $18.99/$20.99 Can.

Essential AP World History (flashcards)
978-0-375-42802-9 • $18.99/$20.99 Can.